Politics and the European Commission

The European Commission, with its reputation as a 'bureaucrat's paradise', has come to both fascinate and repulse a wide range of politicians, journalists and social scientists. This book investigates the Commission's relationship to politics, arguing that, in contrast to prevailing opinion, the process of European integration constantly requires political choices and powering from its civil servants.

The authors collected here develop a variety of case studies – focusing on issues such as health, development aid, preparations for Eastern enlargement, the resignation of the Santer Commission and the euro – in order to study the relationships, networks and interdependencies which link commissioners and Commission officials to national politicians, civil servants and interest groups. The book also looks in detail at how the Commission publicizes its work, notably through producing public information and liaising with the media, thereby throwing fresh light upon the complex question of the organization's legitimacy.

Politics and the European Commission provides a framework for generating new information about, and interpretations of, the power struggles at the heart of the European Union. As such, it will interest all students and researchers of politics and the EU.

Andy Smith is Senior Research Fellow in Political Science at the CERVL, Institut d'Etudes Politiques de Bordeaux.

Routledge/ECPR studies in European political science
Edited by Thomas Poguntke,
Keele University, UK
and
Jan W. van Deth,
University of Mannheim, Germany on behalf of the European Consortium for Political Research

The Routledge/ECPR Studies in European Political Science series is published in association with the European Consortium for Political Research – the leading organization concerned with the growth and development of political science in Europe. The series presents high-quality edited volumes on topics at the leading edge of current interest in political science and related fields, with contributions from European scholars and others who have presented work at ECPR workshops or research groups.

Politics and the European Commission

Actors, interdependence, legitimacy

Edited by Andy Smith

Routledge
Taylor & Francis Group

LONDON AND NEW YORK

ecpr

First published 2004
by Routledge
2 Park Square, Milton Park, Abingdon, Oxon, OX14 4RN

Simultaneously published in the USA and Canada
by Routledge
270 Madison Ave, New York NY 10016

Routledge is an imprint of the Taylor & Francis Group

Transferred to Digital Printing 2006

Typeset in Baskerville by Wearset Ltd, Boldon, Tyne and Wear

British Library Cataloguing in Publication Data
A catalogue record for this book is available from the British Library

Library of Congress Cataloging in Publication Data
Politics and the European Commission : actors, interdependence,
legitimacy/edited by Andy Smith
    p. cm.
 Includes bibliographical references and index.
 1. European Commission. I. Smith, Andy, 1963 July 24–
JN33.5.P65 2004
 341.242'2—dc22

ISBN10: 0-415-32407-6 (hbk)
ISBN10: 0-415-42972-2 (pbk)

ISBN13: 978-0-415-32407-6 (hbk)
ISBN13: 978-0-415-42972-6 (pbk)

2003027986

For my Mum and her powers of listening

Contents

Contributors

Olivier Baisnée is a Lecturer in Political Science at the Centre de Recherches sur l'Action Politique en Europe (CRAPE), Institut d'Etudes Politiques de Rennes.

Véronique Dimier is Professor in Political Science at the Université Libre de Bruxelles.

Helen Drake is Senior Lecturer in French and European Studies at Loughborough University.

François Foret is Research Fellow at the Centre for Media Studies, University of Stirling.

Didier Georgakakis is Senior Lecturer in Political Science at the Groupe de sociologie politique européenne (GSPE), Institut d'Etudes Politiques de Strasbourg.

Sébastien Guigner is a doctoral student in Political Science at the Centre de Recherches sur l'Action Politique en Europe (CRAPE), Institut d'Etudes Politiques de Rennes.

Jean Joana is Senior Lecturer in Political Science at the Centre d'Etudes sur la Politique en Europe Latine (CEPEL), University of Montpellier.

Hussein Kassim is Senior Lecturer in Politics at the Birkbeck School of Politics and Sociology, University of London.

Jeannette Mak is Research Fellow at the Department of Political Science, University of Amsterdam and at the Amsterdam School for Social Science Research.

Cécile Robert is a Research Fellow in Political Science at the Centre d'études et de Recherches sur l'Administration Publique (CERAPS), University of Lille.

Andy Smith is Senior Research Fellow in Political Science at the CERVL (*Pouvoir-Action-Publique-Territoire*), Institut d'Etudes Politiques de Bordeaux.

Jarle Trondal is qualifying professor in Public Administration and European integration at the Centre for European Studies, Agder University College, Norway.

Series editor's preface

The complicated relationships between politics and technology, between politicians and bureaucrats, and between values and expertise have attracted the attention of many scholars at least since the late nineteenth century. A long time has passed since Frank Goodnow presented his seminal examination of the emerging problems of modern government in his *Politics and Administration* (1900). His general recommendation was that to secure both responsible government and administrative efficiency we have to start by 'frankly recognizing that new conditions need new measures'.

The process of European integration certainly presents 'new conditions' that, consequently, require 'new measures'. A huge bureaucratic apparatus has been erected in Brussels to deal with an incredibly detailed and complex system of European rules, instructions, interventions, programmes, guidelines, and subsidies. At the same time, new political decision-making processes developed with the European Commission as the main actor to perform executive functions and to initiate legislation. In this way, the Commission functions as the major political counterpart for national governments of the member states.

The growing complexity of European integration and the delicate balances of political power between member states and the Commission on the one hand, and among member states on the other, has attracted the attention of many observers in the last decades. A new science arose – *comitology* – especially designed to analyse the role and position of the Commission and the ways it deals with its bureaucratic apparatus and its political tasks. The contributors to the present volume prefer a different approach: instead of examining the role of the Commission they want to open the 'black box' and to study the internal dynamics of the Commission in terms of its resources and constraints.

In order to understand the tensions between the technocratic and political tasks of the Commission detailed knowledge about the interdependencies of national and European policy-making processes is required. The painstaking practice of collecting and interpreting information about such complex and complicated matters is but one of the aims of the contributions to this volume. They all aspire to examine the available theoretical approaches. Are existing approaches – which still rely heavily on anthropological and institutional ideas – useful for understanding decision-making processes by the Commission? The contributors to this volume clearly differ in their study designs, selected material, and the scope of their analyses. But they all start from the idea that the Commission occupies a unique position *vis-à-vis* the governments of member states and that this position can best be understood by focusing on the tensions between technocratic and political challenges.

The first set of contributions to this volume approaches these tensions from the perspective of *interdependencies* between various actors and institutions, whereas the second set addresses the question of the apparent weakness of the Commission's *legitimacy*. Before these two sets of contributions are presented, Andy Smith offers an overview of the main approaches and contested conclusions about the Commission in his introduction. The first part of the volume consists of six contributions mainly addressed to policy-making by the Commission and its chief bureaucratic branches. Cécile Robert examines policies to aid Eastern Europe and the 'camouflage politics' used by the Commission to solve some of the uneasy consequences following from its institutional position (Chapter 1). As Jean Joana and Andy Smith show, understanding the Commission's decisions has to be based on careful analyses of the way individual commissioners behave and use their voting right within the Commission (Chapter 2). Hussein Kassim pays attention to the crucial role of the Secretariat General of the Commission (Chapter 3), while Jarle Trondal focuses on the attempt by the Commission to transform the loyalties and identities of civil servants recruited from national bureaucracies (Chapter 4). The tensions between politics and administration are further illustrated by Véronique Dimier in her analyses of the rise of the Directorate General for development (Chapter 5). In the last contribution to this part, Sebastien Guigner investigates public health policies as a major area where expertise and expert advice can be used to make up for a lack of political legitimacy of the Commission (Chapter 6).

The second part of the volume addresses the opportunities to promote the Commission's legitimacy directly. In the first of the five contributions to this part, Didier Georgakakis carefully reconstructs the resignation of the Santer Commission (Chapter 7). Olivier Baisnée examines the ways in which the Commission deals with one of the biggest press corps in the world and its own political ambiguities (Chapter 8). Political ambiguities are also documented by François Foret in his study of the production of public information by the Commission – booklets, comics, brochures etc. (Chapter 9). Jeannette Mak shows that the Commission hardly used the introduction of the *euro* for political goals and so missed an exceptional opportunity to strengthen its legitimacy (Chapter 10). In the last contribution to this part Helen Drake discusses the crucial role of the President of the Commission on the basis of a detailed examination of the impact of Jacques Delors' presidency (Chapter 11). Finally, Andy Smith returns to the central questions of this volume – the tensions between technology and politics – in his concluding chapter.

Understanding decision-making by the Commission is not an easy task. The many policy areas are multifaceted, multileveled, and highly complicated. Institutional, historical, economical and political factors for different member states as well as for the EU have to be taken into account in order to understand the opportunities and problems of the Commission. The unique character of this volume is that it offers many new interpretations and explanations on the basis of careful empirical analyses of the role of the Commission in important decision-making processes. The volume evidently promotes our understanding of the EU and European integration by leaving the conventional territory of 'comitology'. Moreover, the contributions all challenge the idea of a simple dichotomy between politics and technology, between politicians and bureaucrats, and between values and expertise. The realisation of Goodnow's old idea of the successful combination of 'responsible government and administrative efficiency' by the Commission will be decisive for the further development of European integration.

Jan W. van Deth, *Series Editor*
Mannheim, November 2003

Abbreviations

A.C.E.	Archives de la communauté européenne
A.M.A.E.	Archives du ministère des affaires etrangères
API	Association de Presse Internationale
CAP	Common Agricultural Policy
CEC	Commission of the European Communities
CECA	Communauté européenne de charbon et de l'acier
CoE	Council of Europe
COREPER	Comité des représentants permanents (des Etats membres)
DG	Directorate General
EbS	European Broadcasting System
ECSC	European Coal and Steel Community
EFTA	European Free Trade Association
EU	European Union
GAP	Groupe des affaires parlementaires
HLCH	High Level Committee on Health
IGC	Intergovernmental Conference
IGH	Interservice Group on Health
JHA	Justice and Home Affairs
MEP	Member of the European Parliament
PHARE	Pologne, Hongrie: actions pour la reconstruction économique
PPP	Priority Publications Programme
SG	Secretariat General
SGCI	Secrétariat général du comité interministériel de la coopération
SEA	Single European Act
TEU	Treaty on European Union (The Maastricht Treaty)
WHO	World Health Organization
WTO	World Trade Organization

Introduction

Andy Smith

Over the last four decades, the European Commission has come to fascinate a range of politicians, journalists and social scientists. From the point of view of national actors and the media, this fascination stems largely from observations of an apparent contradiction: although its members are unelected, the Commission wields considerable influence within the European Union (EU). Also sparked by this contradiction, the interest expressed by a growing number of academics has given rise to a considerable quantity of research focused essentially upon the following questions: Who works in the Commission? How do they operate? With what resources and under what constraints?

The origin of this volume is a collective desire to focus specifically upon a major blind spot in existing knowledge about the Commission: its relationship to politics. More precisely, in nearly all the existing studies of this body, 'politics' is frequently alluded to but rarely defined and seldom used as an analytical device with which to open up a number of 'black boxes', such as the college of commissioners, the role of the Commission's press and communications service or 'inter-service' negotiations. More particularly, previous research and publications on the Commission have tended to over-eagerly adopt the language used by interviewees within the organization itself who frequently express the view that some issues, arenas and actors are 'political' whereas others are 'technical'. Practitioners can hardly be criticized for terminological imprecision, but academics can. Certainly in this case they should be because behind this methodological error lie two major problems of analysis.

1   Instead of studying the relationships, networks and interdependencies which link commissioners and Commission officials to national politicians, civil servants and interest groups, too much research on the European Union limits itself to ascertaining whether, in general terms, supranational or intergovernmental bodies dominate European integration. Indeed, it is simply assumed that the Commission, the European Parliament and the European Court of Justice are

supranational, whereas the Council of Ministers is a purely intergovernmental arena.

2   This first problem has generated a second that can be described as the incapacity of existing approaches to link empirical research on the salient characteristics of the Commission to the complex question of this body's legitimacy.

This book is founded on the premise that tackling the relationship between politics and technical expertise within the Commission provides a means of better understanding both how this organization functions and why its actions are so frequently contested by national actors, the media and the general public. 'Politics and the Commission' here is therefore not just a snappy title, but a catalyst for reframing analytical questions, research design and the interpretation of results. Before developing this contention and introducing the contributions to this volume, it is first necessary to set out its scientific context by briefly reviewing the existing literature upon which we have attempted to build.

Research on the Commission: the story so far

Genuine studies of the Commission largely tend to fall into one of three categories. They approach this organization from either the angle of European public policy-making, the anthropology of institutions or analysis of the Commission presidency. In briefly outlining the main lines of questioning and conclusions of these approaches, this section cannot possibly do justice to all the information and insights that each have generated. Instead our survey of these publications is centred upon how each research tradition tackles, or fails to tackle, the relationship between the Commission and politics.

Organizational and policy analysis

At least in terms of the quantity of their output, specialists of organizational theory and public policy-making clearly dominate the field of Commission studies. Dissatisfied with what they saw as the excessively general treatment of EC institutions developed by both intergovernmentalist and neofunctionalist authors, from the early 1970s onwards a stream of more detailed, case-study based, research steadily emerged (Coombes 1970; Wallace, Wallace and Webb 1983). After the adoption of the Single Market Act in 1987 and the expansion of EC law and policy that followed, this stream quickly became a flood. Indeed, since the late 1980s, the careful study of how Community policies are shaped, negotiated and implemented has provided a variety of 'microscopes' through which the Commission has indirectly been examined. The central hypothesis generally developed by such research is that through engaging itself in the definition of public problems at a European level, the Commission has been able to develop a degree of influence upon EU decision-making which greatly surpasses its formal role as laid down in the treaties. More precisely, acting as a 'purposeful opportunist' or a 'policy entrepreneur', this influence is the product of four structural characteristics of the organization.

The first of these is the way agents within the Commission use its formal duty to initiate proposals in order to shape and prioritize the EU's agenda. Numerous studies in sectors as varied as high technology (Peterson 1993) and environmental policy (Bomberg 1998) have shown that this resource has two particularly strong effects upon the work of the Commission. First, it authorizes and encourages Commission staff to consult widely with interest groups and thus build up networks of potential allies throughout the fifteen member states (Mazey and Richardson 1997). Second, the duty to initiate legislation means that any draft presented to the Council and the European Parliament (EP) is defended by Commission civil servants and European commissioners, thus giving them a specific place at the negotiating table. This is particularly so in the case of the Council where the Commission is clearly a sixteenth member with a difference: although not entitled to vote, its representatives are invariably listened to with considerable interest (Fouilleux, de Maillard and Smith 2002).

This special position enjoyed by Commission officials is also linked to the deep knowledge of policy sectors that many of them are able to build up over time. At least until very recently, most officials within this organization have spent relatively long periods of time (at least four years) in the same post. This is because career-making in the Commission is often slowed down by the 'need' to maintain a 'geographical balance' between personnel from the different member states (Stevens and Stevens 2001). More generally, compared to most national counterparts under pressure from electoral calendars, studies have shown that Commission officials have time on their side in order to progressively build up support and arguments for Community intervention, and then choose their moment for pressing such claims upon the Council and the EP (Pierson 1996).

The third characteristic of the Commission which has been shown to facilitate the policy-making task of its agents is the nature of Community law. More specifically, rather than depend upon large budget-hungry redistributive policies, much EU public intervention is of a 'regulatory' type (Majone 1996). As the 1985–1992 programme to complete the single market showed quite clearly, setting common standards and guidelines for the administration of competition and environmental protection provided Commission officials with a series of levers for influencing both the overall direction and the detail of EU policy. Although publicly identifiable collusion is usually avoided, tacit alliances between the Commission and the

European Court of Justice have clearly marked the history of European integration (Sandholtz and Stone 1998).

The fourth and final characteristic of the Commission identified by policy and organizational analysis is its internal fragmentation. Numerous studies pinpoint the 'administrative culture' of different Directorate Generals (DGs) and the strong inter-administrative rivalries which this both causes and reflects (Coombes 1970; Cram 1994; Cini 1996a). At least until the late 1990s, a running conflict between the DGs responsible respectively for competition and for industrial policy was often seen as the most glaring example of such competition. Today, a similar level of intensity seems to mark dealings between DG Enterprise and the DG responsible for the environment. More generally, some studies, for example of the invention of an EU rural development policy, have shown that the competitive nature of intra-Commission organization can paradoxically encourage policy innovation (Smith 1996). Most research on this question, however, rushes to conclude that 'bureaucratic politics' within the Commission slow down the production of policy proposals and dilute their content.

Through identifying and examining these four traits of the European Commission, policy and organizational analyses have certainly contributed a great deal to building up knowledge about the latent resources enjoyed by the personnel of this body. This said, comparatively little attention has been given to the 'political work' involved in translating these resources into actual influence. More precisely, this form of analysis has three 'blindspots' which have prevented it from tackling the relationship between the Commission and politics in a direct fashion.

The first of these neglected areas of research concerns the arenas for inter-sectoral negotiation within the Commission itself, in particular 'inter-service' meetings and the college of commissioners. More interested in retracing the history of particular policy decisions or organizational change, these arenas tend to be treated in anecdotal fashion. At best the different positions held by the various DGs or Commissioners are mapped in descriptive fashion (Radaelli 1999a). More generally, it is assumed that the DG or the commissioner who leads on a particular policy (*le chef de file*) invariably dominates internal Commission negotiations. In reality, decision-making within this body is much more competitive and therefore uncertain. First, inter-service meetings are not just about administrative turf wars and jealousies. Ideologically informed debate about the very goals of EU policy is often begun in earnest at this level. Second, such debate is regularly amplified when inter-sectoral issues are taken up by the range of inter-cabinet meetings which precede the weekly meeting of commissioners (Ross 1995). Attempts to politicize, or conversely technicize, issues mark this stage in the Commission's decision-making process, attempts which become more publicly visible if differences of opinion are left to settle by the commissioners themselves (Joana and Smith 2002).

Indeed, in the work of policy and organizational analysts, the neglect of inter-sectoral arenas within the Commission reflects the weak importance such studies give to the role of speech-making and other forms of political communication as a means of influencing both public problem-shaping and decision-taking.

If policy and organizational analysis understudies the role of inter-sectoral mediation in the Commission, it does little better on grasping how national governments seek to influence the work that goes on within this body. Occasional references are made in this literature to how a DG has been 'captured' by a particular member state (eg. agriculture by France) or how an individual commissioner acted like the delegate of his or her national government (eg. Edith Cresson over the Crédit Lyonnais state aids case). However, little attempt is made to show how national administrations constantly attempt to spread their influence within the Commission. They do this firstly by trying to orientate decisions upon recruitment and promotion within the DGs. The state of 'the geographical balance' is kept under constant surveillance by officials within each of the Permanent Representations (Page 1997). Vigilance on this point is even stronger in the case of the cabinets which are made up of varying mixtures of Commission civil servants and seconded officials from national capitals. In both cases, national governments attempt to use their fellow nationals as conduits for their policy preferences. It would certainly be erroneous to assume that this strategy is regularly successful. Commission officials and cabinet members also work under a range of countervailing pressures to remain independent which mean it is virtually impossible for them to act like national diplomats for any length of time. Nevertheless, studying the work carried out by national officials within the Commission provides a means of grasping an influence that is all too often treated as an amorphous 'context' for EU decision-making.

A second aspect of this so-called 'context' – rivalry with the Council and the EP – provides a third dimension of Commission activity which is largely neglected by policy and organizational studies. This rivalry is often downplayed using a term strongly favoured by Commission officials themselves: 'inter-institutional matters'. In reality, the work of Commission officials is strongly influenced by a desire to position their own organization's legitimacy as regards that of national delegations in the Council or of European parliamentarians. Opposing the right to be involved in decision-making of representatives of national or European 'electorates' is no easy task. Indeed, since the beginning of the 1990s and the rise of the narrative of the 'democratic deficit', the Commission's task has become much more difficult. But this constitutes a major reason why research should take the politics of rivalry between actors from the Commission, the Council and the EP much more seriously than it has to date.

Anthropologies of the Commission

How an actor represents their respective institution is one of the central questions of political anthropology, an academic discipline that has begun to be applied to the EU over the last ten years. More precisely, two sets of research targeting the Commission have been undertaken. Led by Marc Abélès, a French researcher who first began working on EU institutions through a major study of the EP (Abélès 1992), the first was actually financed as a report for the Commission itself (Abélès, Bellier and McDonald 1993). Based upon observations of officials' daily work practices within several DGs over a period of one year, this study and its sequels have subsequently become the empirical source for numerous publications (Abélès 1996, 1997; Abélès and Bellier 1996). Launched a little later in time, the second anthropologically-based take on the Commission has been developed by Cris Shore (2000). Despite their differences, through addressing a number of questions on the Commission that many political scientists fail to raise let alone answer, the grounding of these studies in anthropology has engendered at least three major findings.

The first concerns the role of national origins, cultures and stereotypes within the Commission's services. This work underlines that although nearly all the officials they observed clearly see themselves as working for a European entity which obliges them to transcend their national origins, they remain structured by the fact that they all come from one of the member states. As other approaches had already revealed but Shore shows more directly (2000: 132), national origin is important because it plays a determining role in the management of personnel. But national origin is also important because no matter how they work or behave, a Commission official is always perceived, both by outsiders and their colleagues, as British, French or Greek, etc. When national stereotypes are positive, this can work in their favour but, as many southern Europeans in the Commission experience daily, the obverse is also true. Jokes about 'the Club Med' countries can also be used as a stigma with which to delegitimize the point of view of ideological opponents (Abélès 1996).

Underlining that cultural differences do not necessarily have a benign or positive influence within the Commission is also behind a second major trait revealed by anthropologists working on this organization. This concerns the way in which Commission officials constantly have to find a synthesis between national political practices and traditions when putting together proposals for EU law and policy. More precisely, in anticipating cleavages within the Council, the staff of the Commission are adept in inventing policy concepts which are compromises between the ones used in different member states (Abélès and Bellier 1996). In this way 'universal service' has replaced 'public service' in sectors such as telecommunications, 'European citizenship' has been tacked onto national constitutions and 'subsidiarity' has been introduced to regulate powers between levels of government without setting up a central regulator. At one level, these 'compromise concepts' are the very tools that allow intergovernmental negotiation to continue and move forward. As such the inventivity of Commission officials in creating hybrid policy concepts can be seen as indispensable. However, the cost of such compromises is that they are often misunderstood or even rejected within the member states, thus further damaging the legitimacy of the EU in general and of the Commission in particular.

Indeed, the relationship between agents of the Commission and the general public is a third and final subject around which anthropological studies have uncovered some highly important findings. Driven by the concept of representation (Abélès 1997), this research begins to show how difficult those who speak in the name of the Commission find it not only to communicate information to a wider public, but also to convey meaning and emotion. The first problem here is the Commission's tendency to produce 'pasteurized' documents and symbols as a means of avoiding tensions with the member states over precise issues. More fundamentally, representatives of the Commission tend to 'represent with the handbrake on' because the legitimacy of their organization is so ambiguous.

In summary, anthropologically inspired studies of the Commission have undoubtedly contributed to providing a more rounded account of this organization's characteristics, practices and challenges. Indeed, many of the chapters in this book borrow the concepts and methods used in these studies in order to grasp the multidimensional nature of the relationship between politics and the Commission. However, they do so while attempting to go beyond two weaknesses of existing anthropological studies of this body. The first concerns the relationships which connect Commission officials to their national counterparts and representatives of interest groups. Centred upon the internal life of the Commission, neither Abélès nor Shore put themselves in a position from which to delve deeply into the linkages which constantly criss-cross national and EU organizations. The second problem with this research is that it tends to disconnect analysis of representational activities from that of decision-making. Perhaps because these studies pay so little attention to the role of hierarchy within the Commission, analysis of the relationship between representing and negotiating is left largely unexamined.

Leadership and the Commission presidency

In tackling the question of hierarchy head on, the third and final stream of research on the Commission provides some answers as to how this organization juggles with its responsibilities for shaping decisions and representing the EU. Three studies of the manner through which Jacques

Delors presided over the Commission provide the most thorough answers to this question. Targeted on a limited period (1991–1993) and based upon direct observation of the Delors cabinet, George Ross (1995) closely examines how this presidency identified and pursued opportunities for deepening European integration. Through a combination of precise and interlocking objectives set by Delors and the military-like organization and commitment of the cabinet driven by its director, Pascal Lamy, Ross explains how the Commission as a whole was able to make the most of a positive intergovernmental and geostrategic 'opportunity structure'. Ross also shows that once this structure of opportunities becomes less clear and more conflictual (after problems ratifying the Maastricht treaty, the onset of recessions etc.), the Commission presidency has had difficulty shaping its objectives and convincing many officials within the DGs to continue to follow them with sustained vigour.

Based also upon insider observation (through an internship in the Commission's 'Forward Studies Unit'), Ken Endo (1999) looks at the characteristics and effects of Delors' leadership more from the angle of officials in the DGs. Through a series of case studies of different Commission initiatives, the central hypothesis of this book is that the Commission is the product but also the victim of 'shared leadership'. From this perspective, Endo lists the resources and constraints of the Commission presidency in general, and that of Delors in particular. Ultimately the influence of the latter is attributed to his 'power to persuade' (1999: 24), but little attempt is made to unpack the relationship between the argumentative capacity of this political leader and the legitimacy of the Commission presidency as an institution. This question is treated more directly by a third book on Delors published by Helen Drake (2000). Driven by an underlying question regarding the role of individuals within institutions, Drake places Delors' leadership of the Commission firmly within the perspective of his career as a whole, his ideology and his (difficult) relationship with the world of party politics. Using detailed analysis of Delors' public speeches but also lengthy interviews with the man himself and his collaborators, emphasis is placed upon how Delors attempted to both dominate the college of commissioners and mobilize all Commission officials.

This research upon the Delors presidency has shed valuable light upon a number of characteristics of the Commission. In particular, it shows the need to understand the teams and networks which link the 'head' of the Commission to its 'body' of officials (Grant 1994). However, the focus upon one particular presidency means that comparative analysis is either impossible or tends to be tackled on the basis of uneven data sets (Peterson 1999).

More importantly still, little direct attempt is made to show how Commission presidents and commissioners deal with different facets of politics. Indeed, as with the anthropological and policy-making approaches mentioned earlier, politics is seen essentially as something representatives

Table I.1 Introduction

Approach	Vision of Commission	Vision of politics
Policy-making	A sectorialized policy entrepreneur	Intervention by national politicians
Anthropology	A multicultural institution	Intervention in the name of national traditions
Leadership	A centre with only latent resources	Intervention by national heads of government

of the Commission constantly seek to avoid. The first problem with such analysis is that one can find many empirical examples, such as the defence of 'cultural exceptionalism' in the audiovisual field, where agents of the Commission have very clearly adopted a political stance (Hooghe 2001). More fundamentally, as the above table underlines, there is a basic confusion in the literature between 'politics' and 'national influence'.

Studying politics and the Commission: concepts, questions and research design

Pressures placed upon the Commission by national actors are clearly a major part of the environment within which this organization functions. However, treating 'national influence' in an aggregative and actor-less fashion does not allow one to go very far in understanding how and when arguments which originate within the member states force Commission officials to limit, dilute or change their own objectives and ways of working. In short, both 'national influence' and 'politics' are concepts that need unpacking before one can develop research designs capable of generating new information on how they really shape what goes on within and without the European Commission.

Based upon original, empirical research, the texts brought together in this volume interpret the relationship between 'politics and the Commission' by analysing the polysemic nature of two adjectives frequently used to analyse the Commission: *technocratic* and *political*. More specifically, the different chapters look at the resources and constraints of this organization's personnel from two competing yet complementary angles.

The first uses ideal-type definitions from normative democratic theory to define, a priori, the technocratic and the political. They then seek, through empirical study, to ascertain to what degree the practices of Commission personnel fit these categories. Following the example set by Claudio Radaelli (1999a), three criteria in particular are put forward:

1   *Political competition*: Through examining the way actors are recruited, promoted or nominated to their posts, a number of important power

relations are highlighted which, contrary to some analyses (Page 1997), do not limit politics to what politicians do.

2   *Publicness:* The degree of publicity given to the activities of the Commission is investigated as a means of ascertaining how individuals and teams within this body perceive their own roles.

3   *Arguments for decision-making:* Proposals based upon values are taken to be political, whereas those based upon the opinion of 'experts' are seen as technocratic.

This first approach to the politics–technocracy divide reveals that Commission personnel often oscillate between behaviour that, in abstract terms, can be named political and technocratic. Used on its own, however, such an approach fails to grasp how the actors being studied consciously or unconsciously deploy the lexicons of politics and technocracy. As a broad strand of thought in social science brought together under the umbrella term of 'social constructivism' has underlined, 'politics' and 'technocracy' are not necessarily categories that have universal meaning (Dubois and Dulong 1999; Christiansen, Jørgensen and Wiener 2001). Rather, actors constantly construct, reshape and use these categories. This is often done unconsciously, thus revealing mechanisms of socialization at work within the Commission. But at other times actors strategically use terms such as 'political' or 'technical' in order to bolster their own (and/or their organization's) resources and reduce constraints upon their autonomy.

Constructivist premises are therefore built into the methodologies of a number of the authors in this book. However, their chapters all acknowledge that constructivism cannot be the sole building block for an overarching approach to the European Commission. Motivated more by understanding what determines actor behaviour, interdependencies and the distribution of power, social constructivism is therefore not used here as a synonym for post-modernist musing about the European Union. Instead, the fundamental postulate that 'reality' does not simply impose itself upon the world of action, but rather is defined in competitive contexts by identifiable actors, is employed to link empirical study to the two key questions addressed throughout the book:

1   what shapes and conditions interdependencies both within the Commission and between its agents and their opposite numbers in the member states?

2   how can one explain the relationship between the apparent strength of the EU's institutions and the evident weakness of their legitimacy?

The chapters in Part I of this book essentially address the first question as a means of shedding light upon question two. Cécile Robert's chapter begins this part by analysing how European civil servants relate to the political dimension of their action in the European Union. Based upon a study of Commission involvement in EU policy on Central and Eastern European countries, Robert's objective is to reveal how the Commission's relationship to politics drives and structures the daily practices of civil servants on the one hand and, on the other, leads the European Commission as a whole to select particular types of policy-making.

Examining European integration as the product of a multiplicity of national and transnational levels of action is the objective of the next three chapters. Centred upon the college of commissioners, Jean Joana and Andy Smith contest the generally accepted idea that commissioners differ because of their 'personality' or 'portfolio'. They claim instead that the key variable is how each commissioner interprets and represents their own role and that of the Commission. More precisely, this chapter focuses on how these actors approach the 'non-portfolio' dimension of their mandate as a means of understanding the technical, diplomatic and political aspects of this role. In setting out to discover the role of the Commission's General Secretariat, and of its Secretary Generals in particular, Hussein Kassim sheds light not only upon the inner functioning of the Commission itself, but also upon how the agents of this institution work with their counterparts in national administrations. Finally, in studying what he labels as the 'parallel administration' of the European Commission, Jarle Trondal attempts to answer the following question: does the European Commission manage to transform the loyalties and identities of Commission officials seconded on short-term contracts from national institutions? In this sense, the 'parallel administration' is treated as an important laboratory for studying integration across the EU/nation state interface.

Part I of the book closes with two chapters on the invention of individual Directorate Generals. Véronique Dimier analyses the strategies of legitimation used by the Directorate General development (DG VIII) during what she defines as the crucial period of its institutionalization (1958–1975). These strategies were based on deliberately organized 'dramatizations' which took the form of official tours in Africa and Europe. This research shows that the success of such strategies depended greatly upon the capacity of the DG's agents to adapt themselves to an audience that was both African and European. More precisely, the audience targeted was mainly made up of a specific elite through which the Commission hoped to build its legitimacy and appeal to a larger public. Much closer to us in time, the invention of a Directorate General for health and consumer affairs (DG SANCO) is unpacked by Sébastien Guignier as a means of showing the political importance of internal struggles within the Commission). Various food safety scares in the 1990s, in particular the BSE crisis, were clearly a major impetus for this change in Commission organization and practice. However, Guignier shows that the underlying causes of this change are more varied, and the consequences more important, than is often appreciated. By retracing the invention of this DG, this chapter underlines in particular how concern for public health at a European level has if anything been hindered rather than helped by this institutional invention.

Focused more specifically upon the relationship between the Commission and the media, chapters in Part II tackle the legitimacy question more directly and, in so doing, produce new knowledge about relationships and interdependencies that criss-cross the Commission and member state governments. Didier Georgakakis begins this part of the book by looking at the Santer Commission's resignation from an angle which revises the dominant interpretation of this episode as the result of 'poor communication'. Such a view is challenged by proposing instead that the key problem was more one of the legitimacy of the Commission as opposed to that of the Council and the Parliament, and of the college as regards the rest of the Commission's personnel. Indeed, the central hypothesis developed is that the external or inter-institutional dimension of the college's difficulties only became salient because internal conflict had laid the groundwork for the transformation of isolated issues into one single 'crisis'. Olivier Baisnée also looks at 'Santer's fall' but this time from the point of view of the Commission's relationship with the press before, during and after the event. Baisnée underlines that high-profile media criticisms led the new Commission to reflect upon its relationship with the accredited press in Brussels and provoked a reform of the communicational practices of the European executive. Having first characterized the milieu of community-level sources of information and their traditional dominance by the Commission, this chapter analyses this attempt at reform and its failure. These cases are used as a means of analysing an institution which, whilst seeking to highlight its role as a political actor by officializing its relationship with the press, has had great difficulty in being recognized as such by the journalists involved who are, above all, after more detailed information. In both chapters, analysing the Commission's relationship with the media is thus used as a means of observing the fundamental ambiguity of an institution where the technical and the political are inseparable and where problems of legitimacy are crucial causes of this relationship.

This ambiguity is tackled directly in Chapters 9 and 10 which are centred upon the production of public information within the Commission. François Foret shows that by publishing brochures on general questions designed to suit a wide-ranging audience, the Commission has sought to develop itself a position from which it can express its own views on Europe's behalf. However, research into the way this institution has actually played this potentially very political role reveals the Commission's tendency to take refuge in a more neutral and safe bureaucratic lexicon or register. In focusing more specifically upon the public information distributed about the euro, Jeannette Mak explores whether the Commission consciously and instrumentally used its information and communication activities on the EMU and the euro as an informal instrument to achieve three goals: policy acceptance, strengthen the legitimacy of the EU as a whole, improve the Commission's own status and position. The failure of the Commission, and more particularly the former DG X, to come up with a coherent and purposeful information strategy is explained as the result of a combination of internal and external limitations, as well as the persistence of the Commission's elitist approach to communication.

Finally, Helen Drake's chapter focuses upon how the influence of Commission President Delors has contributed, and continues to contribute, to the realization of visions and utopian dreams of the future of the European Union. The chapter argues that the primary political logic and rationale of the Commission presidency was to supranationalize power elites within and outside the Commission. This involved a transfer and legitimation of new ideas into national political cultures, a process which has characterized the vagaries of European integration from its beginnings and in which certain individuals, and Delors in particular, have played different, yet key, roles.

As the volume's conclusion underlines, in addition to a wealth of empirical information, each chapter includes theoretical arguments and conceptual developments, which are based upon a firm grounding in sociological approaches to politics. Indeed, in providing answers to its two key questions (transnational interdependence and institutional legitimacy), this book is an example of how political sociologies of 'real' actors and the cognitive and emotional frameworks that structure their behaviour, shed light upon the concrete difficulties faced by commissioners and Commission officials when attempting to deepen European integration. As such, this book shows not only that such actors 'matter', but that more sociological approaches to the study of politics are the way forward for research upon the European Union.

Acknowledgements

Initial versions of nearly all the chapters in this book first saw the light of day at one or more of three workshops. An initial seminar was organized by Helen Drake at the University of Loughborough in June 2000. The second took place during the European Consortium of Political Research (ECPR) 'Joint sessions' in Grenoble in March 2001 and the third during the inaugural conference of the ECPR's Standing Group on the EU held in Bordeaux in September 2002. I thank all those who participated in these seminars with such enthusiasm, perspicacity and good humour. Last, but certainly not least, a special vote of thanks is due to I. Bither for constant encouragement, laughter and hope.

Part I

Actors, institutions and interdependence

1 Doing politics and pretending not to

The Commission's role in distributing aid to Eastern Europe

Cécile Robert

Introduction

Academic research on the European Union (EU) has undergone a series
of evolutions, one of which is the increasing attention given to the European administration. This concern is twofold: on one hand, the growing
number of studies on EU policies has chiefly led to acknowledging the
decisive role played by the Commission in setting the agenda and formulating European public policies (Christiansen 1996; Cini 1997; Cram 1999;
Fouilleux 2003; Jourdain 1995; Nugent 1995; Peters 1992; Smith 1995); on
the other hand, observations made from a more anthropological perspective looking at the new meanings ascribed to notions of administration and
policy in Brussels, have revealed the specificity of EU institutions in comparison to existing administrative models (Abélès, Bellier and MacDonald
1993; Abélès and Bellier 1996; Bellier 1999).

Denying the political dimension of the Commission's work – observed
in the strategies it implements in order to enforce both its own understanding of issues to be considered and the solutions it propounds – is
thus out of the question. Yet few publications draw a parallel between this
political activity and the distinct position held by the European Commission in the European institutional system. The fact that it may simultaneously be deprived of democratic legitimacy while dependent upon
political circumstances for its work and the translation of intentions into
achievements, does not prevent the Commission from exerting a decisive
influence upon the European Union's decision-making process and the
definition of the broad orientations of European integration. In another
way, anthropological studies have also highlighted the constraints of the
Commission's institutional position, particularly its incapacity to claim
political legitimacy, and shown how these constraints are apprehended
within the organization itself. However, they have not systematically questioned the effects of these representations on the daily practices of Commission officials and the way they contribute to shaping public action.

Standing exactly at the crossroad of both approaches, I attempt to take
both sets of results and interpretations a stage further. Once it is admitted

that the classical opposition between administration and politics cannot account for the particular roles of the European Commission and its institutional partners (Parliament, Council), understanding the resilience of this opposition in the discourse and perceptions of real actors, as well as its consequences on the strategies and behaviours they adopt, is of considerable importance.[1]

From such a perspective, this paper analyses how the Commission relates to the political dimension of its action starting from two complementary hypotheses. First, the Commission constantly seeks to play a political role, without ever attaining the political legitimacy required to endorse such a role. It is therefore involved in acts seeking to legitimize the power it handles, and simultaneously to mask the political dimension of its activity. Second, this form of self-censorship is substantiated through several modes: modes of action and management within the Commission (through resorting to technicization and juridicization), or the officials' self perception of their role and function in the Commission, within which the operation of defining what politics, and what political officials should be, takes a central place. The Commission's relationship to the political dimension of its own action is thus used as a lens for examining the dynamics behind the production of European public policies.

These hypotheses are verified in the two parts of this chapter. The first observes and describes the different dimensions of the European Commission's relationship to politics as it manifests itself in the discourse the institution and its members produce about themselves and about their partners in the EU.[2] Centred upon EU policy towards Central and Eastern European countries (Robert 2001b), the second part endeavours to reveal to what extent the Commission's relationship to politics inspires and structures the daily practices of its civil servants and leads their organization as a whole to select particular types of policy-making.

The European Commission's relationship(s) to politics

The European Commission's relationship to politics is specific and manifold. More precisely, the hypothesis developed here considers the activity of the Commission to be political in nature, despite the fact that this institution and the actors who belong to it constantly strive to camouflage this reality. From this angle, two distinct and complementary aspects of the effort made to shrug off politics are examined: how civil servants construct their professional identity around specific characteristics which oppose those they attribute to their various opposite numbers – MEPs, Council personnel and members; the modes of legitimation favoured by the European administration in order to justify and account for its action within the European political system.

With regard to research carried out on the EU in the past two decades, the Commission's political role and ambition today appear unquestioned and unquestionable (Christiansen 1997). In particular, specialists on EU public policy-making have established that the European administration often plays a decisive role in the different steps surrounding reforms and new measures, from agenda setting to implementation, during which its work stretches much further than the mere execution of rules and decisions adopted by the Council (Eichener 1992). Moreover, numerous studies carried out on the Commission's personnel have shown the growing place and importance taken by political careers and resources (Donnelly and Ritchie 1994; Joana and Smith 2002; Page 1997; Smith 1996, 2002).

In this respect, the PHARE programme of technical assistance to the Eastern and Central European states represents a clear example. First of all, its genesis owes a great deal to Jacques Delors, President of the Commission from 1985 to 1995, who developed resources through a whole array of relations built during the course of his political career to convince and compel his partners outside and inside the EU to entrust the European administration with Western aid to Eastern Europe (Deloche-Gaudez and Lequesne 1996; Niemann 1998). Beside revealing this institution's ability to impose its own understanding of the key issues, such institutional activism as displayed by the Commission's representatives in creating PHARE shows that their organization, just like the Council or the Parliament, acts to further its own ends. These objectives more often than not amount to a willingness to expand its own institutional prerogatives (see Chapters 6 and 10). In short, obtaining the management of the PHARE programme was perceived by activists within the Commission as a means for the European administration to gain access to a domain of EU foreign policy that had previously been kept out of its reach.

Second, the room for manoeuvre left to the Commission by the successive and rather vague regulations adopted by the Council on PHARE,[3] emphasizes the creative dimension of the Commission's management of this programme. In fact, this legislation allowed the Commission to define for itself the priority sectors of Western aid, the nature of this assistance, the conditions of its implementation, as well as the personnel who would be in charge of it, i.e. companies and consultants entrusted with running projects in the field.

Finally, progressive institutionalization of the programme throughout the 1990s and the fact that it was clearly identified as one of the main instruments of European policy to applicant states, must be attributed to the Commission's capacity to hinge together technical and political patterns. In other words, the Commission's ability to enlist technical knowledge and aptitudes to produce solutions which also take into account political imperatives and constraints to which public choices are subjected (anticipatory management of conflict between member states, anticipation of the symbolic consequences of its activity on relationships with Eastern Europe, and/or their electoral impact (Robert 2001a).

If the fact that the activity of the European Commission is political in nature is now fully acknowledged, another characteristic of this institution is less frequently emphasized by researchers: the discourse the European administration produces about itself and its action tends to systematically lessen, even deny, the political dimension of its work. More generally, this dicourse institutes 'a-politicism' as the *raison d'être* of this institution and the very basis of its legitimacy.

On the one hand, 'a-politicism' is exhibited as a special disposition presented as a set of know-how and behaviour which belong exclusively to the Commission's civil servants. Interviews carried out with members of the Commission in the course of our research tended to show how, when referring to their professional identity, they make constant allusions to MEPs and Council members. This allows them to claim a whole pack of specific qualities – neutrality, independence, disinterestedness, scientific knowledge, technical competence, objectivity, ability to think in the long term – which are set against the 'defaults and weaknesses' of those involved in 'politics': national interest and selfishness, ignorance and remoteness from the field, pretence, inconsistency and incoherence, short term and electoral vision. As illustrated in the following citation, actors from the Commission draw upon this contrasted picture in order to apprehend and lend meaning to the daily tasks involved in implementing PHARE. They also use this classification to decipher their relationships with their institutional partners:

> When we worked together on the PHARE programme, Member States were always very careful about protecting [their own interest] (i.e. to offer European contracts to national consultants and enterprises). They played their part as a Member State, their role of defending a national interest, and we [the Commission] have represented the interest of the European Community, as usual, and the interests of applicant countries ... The European Parliament members were very enthusiastic about the PHARE programme but we have had to rationalize their mobilisation. For example, they wanted Romanian orphanages to become as modern as those of Western Europe overnight ... We [the Commission] were there to reason with them and take the actual needs of the Romanian people into account. To build luxury orphanages could have been a provocation for Romanian families. This story of the Romanian orphanages is a good example of our daily work with MEPs.[4]

Although perhaps more obvious among agents of the PHARE programme owing to its particular history, such dispositions are not, however, a particular specificity of DG IA. Instead they should be regarded as pervasive characteristics of the Commission's administrative culture:

Whatever their grade, European civil servants are supposed to act on a non-emotional basis and remain above influences, whilst listening to the demands of different representatives who make up part of their sources of information. In theory, they act rationally, which means they must use certain techniques for making choices, impartially, which is linked to concepts of independence and ethics. According to the insider viewpoint, even if the actions of the Commission and its agents are imperfect, they are founded upon quantifiable and evaluable criteria which are linked to established and controllable frameworks. According to the civil servants themselves, this is seen as being the opposite of how politicians behave because they are more open to the risks of elections which means they are not assured of permanency and are thus inclined to 'give in to emotions'.

(Bellier 1999: 47)

On the other hand, the claim to 'a-politicism' also translates into another discourse propagated by the Commission which describes its activity and supports the relevance of its proposals. What sets it apart from its institutional partners (Parliament, Councils, member states) is not so much its purely technical, juridical or administrative tasks, but the efforts it spends to present it as such, and appear as a mere tool with which to deal with social trends and fundamental principles. The Commission's effort to play down the political dimension of its work relates to the following two types of operation which, in reality, are frequently inter-twined:

- concealment of the creative dimension of its work through denying the extent of interpretative activity and the room for manoeuvre when implementing Council decisions and European rules;
- obliteration of the 'ideological' dimension – i.e. based upon a reference to values and involving making choices – of its positions and proposals, by presenting them as dictated by a certain rationale (juridical, technical) or as the obvious product of a European common interest.

Examples of EU policy towards Eastern European countries yet again help to illustrate this claim. First, when presenting the programming activity of the Commission in annual PHARE reports to Council, the Parliament and the general public, European civil servants are depicted as mere underlings while the Council's declarations and regulations are highlighted as guidelines that are precise enough to set the framework and content of their mission. Moreover, these reports never hint that certain choices may need to be made during implementation: programming is presented as a simple process that is both well controlled and objective because it is based upon seasoned techniques (particularly the so-called 'demand-driven' technique which consists in co-operating with aid beneficiaries) and relying upon a 'scientific' vision of the overall process of the transition to democracy. Thus identification of so-called priority sectors is presented as the twin outcome of preferences expressed by partner states, and as a practical exercise based upon unquestionable knowledge about the changes being experienced in the Eastern countries. This latter observation is similar to conclusions reached in studies carried out of other European policies, especially research (Jourdain 1996) or development aid for South American states (Le Naëlou 1995). These studies have all revealed a process whereby choices made during the implementation of these projects are naturalized, notably through constant reference to technical rationality as the ultimate and insurmountable justification for decisions made by the Commission.

This chapter is unable to address every explanation behind the Commission's relationship to politics. Suffice to say that camouflaging politics is a means for the European administration to solve some of the contradictions of its institutional position. Resorting to law and technical issues to make its positioning appear 'natural', allows the Commission to justify its prerogatives and proposals without calling upon a political argument, which it considers as prohibited anyway for want of democratic legitimacy. The qualities of independence, disinterestedness and expertise put forward by officials, attest to the capacity and legitimacy of these unelected and 'nation-less' men and women to define where Europe's general interest lies. Furthermore, European civil servants' relationship to politics and their conflicts of legitimacy with member states manifest common features with representations and behaviours typical of national administrative staff, already well studied by sociology and political science (Duran 1999; De Baecque and Quermonne 1982; Grémion 1979; Suleiman 1974). These similarities have a partial explanation in administrative history and, more precisely, in the types of legitimacy of each civil service. Nonetheless, such conflicts take on a particular aspect in the case of the European administration. Institutional rivalries first gain in acuteness, owing to the larger range of prerogatives handled by the European administration compared to national ones. At the same time, this administration faces more attacks and scepticism. Its legitimacy is therefore more demanding and more fragile. Moreover, the link made in Brussels between politics and the defence of national interests exacerbates such tensions between administration and politics, and allows European civil servants, rather than national ones, to claim a monopoly in handling 'European thinking' and in defining a common European interest.

The Commission exhibits 'a-politicism' to such an extent that it is at the root of its existence and autonomy as an institution and conditions both the affirmation and the practice of its authority. This, in turn, causes this institution to permanently produce evidence of its 'a-politicism', and leads its agents into perceiving themselves as such. If discourses and representations prevailing within the European administration on politics partly fulfil this function, the following part of this chapter suggests that these cannot be understood independently from the political practices which produce them. In other words, the Commission's privileged modes of legitimization determine, at least in part, the shape and content of its action in the European political system.

'A-politicism in action': resources and constraints for the Commission

Case studies analysed in the second part of this chapter are drawn from the history of the EU's preparation for Eastern enlargement during the 1990s. Returning to the role played by the Commission in elaborating and implementing European policy towards Eastern European countries, the following hypothesis will be discussed. At the beginning of the decade, the Commission's tendency to repress the political dimension of its action was activated as a resource which made possible the whole process of both institutionalizing such a policy and of achieving its leadership in the field of public policy-making. More recently though, on some issues relating to enlargement, the Commission's 'a-politicism' has seemed, on the contrary, to become a constraint from which the Commission has not been able to escape. Indeed, it has significantly limited the scope of potential positions and possible actions.

In the 1990s, the Commission managed particularly well to benefit from the perspective of enlargement in order re-negotiate its role and position within the European political system. Whereas in 1989 it successfully obtained responsibility for the PHARE programme, thanks to the close linkage made between the EU and Eastern Europe, over the next decade it went on to rely upon this initial position to secure growing autonomy and power, particularly with regards to conceiving and enacting European policy in the East (Robert 2001a). Careful examination of the strategies used by the Commission during this period shows that they relied heavily upon denying their political dimension.

First of all, by depicting itself as a neutral and independent expert, and never as a decision-maker, the European administration succeeded in presenting and pressing forth its understanding of issues pertaining to Eastern and Central European states. A chronological reconstruction of the Council's activities compared with reports submitted by the Commission clearly shows that the former has often simply re-used, sometimes literally, proposals put forward by the latter. However, the Commission never claimed this policy to be of its own making and the documents it publishes systematically present the Ostpolitik as the result of the efforts and commitment of the omnipotent European Council and its desire to integrate applicant countries. Besides keeping silent about its own contribution, the solutions the Commission put forward brush aside their arbitrary aspects, in other words the idea that they might have resulted from choices. In particular, the extremely strong juridical dimension given to the pre-adhesion strategy (based on the definition of the European *acquis*, and its inclusion in the law of candidate states), gave the Commission the opportunity to connect its actions directly to the EU Treaties and founding texts, i.e. solely based on respect for law and procedure. Such 'juridicization' was the key to the Commission's success with its partners because, in setting out a temporary and apparently legitimate response to the expectations of applicant countries, it also meant the Commission could bypass the member states, seen as incapable of reaching agreement on potentially conflict-prone issues. Hence the co-production of this policy came to repose upon a particular form of exchange between different European institutions. The Commission's autonomy in the making of this public intervention and the institutional gains derived from it were connected to its ability to provide member states with the possibility of endorsing the policy as a whole. To do so, it repressed the political dimension of its action: first by ascribing responsibility to member states, second by making the policy acceptable to the publics it was designed for (Roubieu 1999).

Second, the Commission's approach to politics seems to have partly determined the shape and the nature of relationships between those in charge of the implementation of the PHARE programme in DG IA, and their institutional partners: member state representatives in the PHARE management committee and MEPs in charge of controlling the expenditure of the assistance programme. These exchanges were marked by the technicization of issues and debates that surrounded the process of programming. For instance, this technicization took the form of systematically translating the objectives of assistance programmes and their mode of implementation into the technical terms of each highly specialized sector. This strategy reflected the Commission's concern to present its work as the rational implementation of competencies and 'scientific' unquestionable methods, whose respect is a guarantee of quality, neutrality and objectivity. In short, this was a means of institutionalizing the unchallengeable aspect of the projects it carried out in Eastern Europe. Yet technicization also allowed the Commission to limit its partners' ability to influence, control, and possibly sanction its activity in this domain. By compelling them to use technical language, in particular in the management committee, officials from PHARE made their counterparts work in a field of competencies they controlled and were at ease with. Technicization also made the programme's ground-level realities more difficult to understand for national representatives and Members of the European Parliament. Perceiving and comprehending political issues through the lens of the technical choices mentioned in official documents, requires a certain degree of experience in the debates and controversies which structure such domains of public policy-making (Eichener 1992; Grémion 1979; Institut für Europaïsche Politik 1989).

The Commission's efforts to repress the political dimension of its work thus operated not only through discourse but also through the practices of its agents, their choice of particular modes of action and relationships to their counterparts. Moreover, this 'embodied a-politicism' enabled the Commission to achieve a form of leadership in the policy designed for Eastern European states, and to preserve its autonomy in the making of this policy. Some aspects of this 'a-politicism', such as the officials' claim to neutrality or independence and their legitimate competence to define a European general interest, have been presented by some studies as strategic resources which offer an explanation for the Commission's success (Abélès 1994; Lequesne 1996; Nugent 1994). It should, however, be stressed that the Commission has not always benefited from its stance on politics and that this has not always turned out to be a means of expanding its prerogatives and range of competencies. More precisely, under certain conditions the Commission simply cannot escape from the necessity to silence the political dimension of its activity, despite the fact that keeping silent limits its room for manoeuvre and the choices available to its officials.

In this respect, a return to the debates that surrounded the Commission's definition of the *acquis communautaire* in the social domain are particularly significant. In the process of preparing for enlargement, a group principally made up of DG IA officials in charge of the PHARE programme, suggested that the *acquis communautaire* presented to the applicant states should not solely consist of European rules. Instead it should also take into account a number of political principles which were yet to obtain a juridical translation, such as the requirement for a high level of social security protection. This broad definition of the social *acquis communautaire* thus required officials to go beyond the domain of the law and take on board non-juridical arguments and legitimacy. DG V officials' negative reaction to this suggestion and the subsequent decision to 'bury the issue' by complying with a strictly and exclusively juridical definition, are precisely an outcome of the constraints upon the Commission which stem from its relationship to politics. Indeed, despite perceiving its benefits, DG V officials gave up on the defence of a more extensive understanding of the social *acquis* chiefly because such a stance would have led them to break with two unwritten rules governing the Commission within the European political system, both of which reflect the necessity to affirm its 'a-politicism' (Robert 2000).

First of all, DG V officials considered the defence of a wider social *acquis* as standing little chance of reaching broad support in the unpredictable and risky Council. Obliged to anticipate the reactions of its institutional partners (Cram 1994; Pierson 1996; Wendon 1998 and Chapter 10 of this book) in order to avoid conflict or failure over particular propositions, minimizing such risks is seen as the price to pay for the exclusive qualities the Commission wants to retain. These include its claim to be able to cope with every single demand that comes out of European society

– even when they are contradictory – as part of the process of building a common interest. Depicting themselves as little more than a simple mediating body deprived of any autonomous power, objectives and political projects, Commission officials rely upon their ability to stimulate consensus and produce compromise agreements (Abélès and Bellier 1996; Lamy 1991). As underlined by a French representative on the PHARE management committee, 'The Commission, who considers itself the repository of the Union's common interest, and rightly so, cannot stand being disavowed. So it does its utmost to ensure that this does not happen'.[5]

Moreover, the need felt by European civil servants to support the pertinence and relevance of their suggestions through reference to their intrinsic technical quality and rationality makes the very idea of conflict unacceptable. Whereas in the realm of national politics oppositions are accepted on the very basis that protagonists do not share the same values, the Commission appears to perceive opposition as a challenge not only to the technical qualities of its projects, but to the independence and neutrality of its designers, and even as a threat to its own ability to define and defend a European common interest. In cases where there is opposition from the Council, the Commission's biggest asset turns against itself: the strategy of arguing for its positions as 'rational' cannot cope with a failure to convince. To the extent that its argument links the validity of projects to the intrinsic qualities of the institution from which it originates, failure amounts to immediate disavowal of the Commission itself. Even though, within the administration, most officials are able to analyse situations in ways which distance themselves from the position approved by the Council, a negative vote by representatives of the member states is invariably seen as a form of individual and collective failure. Failure may have dire consequences, notably on professional careers, as noted by Mark Pollack: 'As one Commission official explained, having one's proposal referred from a committee to the Council can cast a long shadow over the career prospects of a young *fonctionnaire*' (Pollack 1997: 115).

In addition, the refusal of DG V officials to support the extra-juridical definition of the *acquis communautaire* is also attributable to the range of legitimizing tools available to the Commission. When discussing the creative dimension of its work, the Commission often presents its words and actions as the strict implementation of principles fixed elsewhere, be it law, science, or political statements approved by all of the member states. Deprived of democratic legitimacy, the European administration considers that on its own it cannot commit itself to an explicitly political argument based on the defence of values such as the need for high levels of social security. Indeed, in a general context characterized by the deafening silence of policy makers on the issue of the social dimension of Eastern enlargement, Commission officials ended up thinking they had no other choice than to stick to the letter of law, and this despite the fact that the *acquis* in social affairs is so limited that it justifies very little in terms of EU intervention (Pierson and Leibfried 1998). As a DGV civil servant put it:

> In a way, the Commission's administrative tradition is to focus on legal norms. We cannot tell an applicant country: you should do so and so, if there is no legal basis, because that would imply that the Commission suddenly gives orders to third countries on issues where it actually has no say within the Union. That would be somewhat schizophrenic and illogical, wouldn't it? So we have the Treaty, and all the secondary norms, these are the rules of the game, and the Eastern states have to accept them, as they stand today. They have to reply 'yes' or 'no'. Only if the answer is 'yes' can they become a member state.[6]

Conclusion

To conclude, two additional observations need to be made. The first deals with the status that can be granted to the Commission's relationship to politics in this analysis. Through several examples mentioned above, repression of the political dimension is enlisted as a resource, and as such makes up a powerful tool for the legitimation of the Commission itself and its activity. However, close study of the European Ostpolitik also indicates that, in certain political circumstances, the Commission is forced to erase the political nature of its work and of its role, and that such a constraint determines and limits the actions it can undertake. The Commission's 'a-politicism' cannot be apprehended simply as a choice which is transient and connected to the expectation of potential gains. If this constraint is often so powerful, the reason is that it is closely linked to the very position of the Commission in the European political system, and the modes of legitimation it has access to. Indeed, there is a cumulative logic at work here: when actors claim a set of qualities and dispositions relating to their 'a-politicism' in order to justify their existence and lend legitimacy to their projects, they are obviously coerced into behaving accordingly, or at least must pretend to. In short, Commission officials must adjust to the requirements of the role they are constrained into playing.

The second observation relates to the way the Commission communicates and strives to legitimize itself in the eye of national public opinion. One may indeed wonder if a good deal of obstacles met by the Commission in order to play a part in the daily reality of European citizens are not connected to the Commission's relationship to politics. The process of repression and self-censorship is in contradiction with the need to produce a discourse intended for European citizens which enables them to better understand the role played by the European administration and what it actually stands for. In turn this contradiction prevents the Commission from at least partly controlling the image it presents to member state nationals (see Chapter 8 in this book). In other words, one needs to reflect upon to what extent the games of inter-institutional legitimation are complementary to, and compatible with, the process of legitimation worked out by European institutions in relation to European citizens (Abélès 1996). These contradictions mirror fundamental tensions of the European integration process:

- between the control retained by member states and the direct responsibility of European institutions to EU citizens;
- between 'the political and legal nature of the European Union';
- between the requirement that the Commission be held responsible to the member states and European citizens, and its twin function as an executive body and a public administration (Christiansen 1997).

Notes

1 Our work is based upon the following hypothesis: the fact that EU institutional categories do not always describe the day-to-day reality of EU institutions does not imply that these categories have no effect on the perception and behaviour of EU agents and, thus, are of no interest to the social scientist. In this chapter, this hypothesis will be illustrated by the situation of the European administration, and more precisely by the Commission's constraints of legitimacy which stem from its institutional position in the EU political system. In this way, we agree with social constructivists (Christiansen, Jørgensen and Wiener 1999; Jørgensen 1999; Trondal 2001) in considering that the words 'administrative' or 'political' must be apprehended as social constructions: a job, a subject under negotiation, an issue are never 'naturally' political or technical; these categories are instead selected and used by EU actors to legitimize their respective strategies. Nevertheless, if an institution's outputs depend partly on how they are interpreted and operated by social actors, institutions also strongly determine their choices and behaviour by distributing resources and imposing a number of constraints and rules from which actors cannot escape.

2 Our hypothesis is that this relation to politics is a common feature of the entire staff of the European administration. However, this does not imply an understanding of the Commission as an homogenous and monolithic institution: the numerous conflicts and rivalries between services and DGs, each with their different administrative cultures, political goals and ways of working, have already been well researched (Cram 1994; Cini 1996a). This chapter does not treat the effects of internal fragmentation on the civil servant's relationship to politics. Suffice to say that this fragmentation can present a problem for the Commission: in endeavouring to appear as a neutral and technical expert in the service of the European common interest, it has to find ways of regulating internal tensions and masking them to external observers (Chapter 8 of this book; Robert 2001b: 440–465).

3 These regulations merely indicate that PHARE is designed for 'aiding Eastern states in their effort of economic restructuring'. Règlement (CEE) no. 3906/89 du Conseil du 18 décembre 1989 relatif à l'aide économique en faveur de la république de Hongrie et de la république populaire de Pologne, [JO L375, 23 décembre 1989: 11–12], modified in 1991, 1992, 1993, 1995, 1996, but only to add new beneficiary countries.

4 Interview with a former Director General of DG IA in charge of the PHARE programme. Paris, July 1999.
5 Interview with a civil servant from the French Ministry of Foreign Affairs, member of the PHARE management committee, Paris, November 1997.
6 Interview with a DG V official, Brussels, November 1996.

2 The politics of collegiality

The non-portfolio dimension

Jean Joana and Andy Smith

Introduction

Despite increased media attention and social science study of the European Commission as a whole, the college of commissioners is still very much a 'black box'. We all know that significant things shape this body and what goes on inside it, but we know little about the rules, practices and uncertainties that govern these processes. Similarly, European commissioners are deemed to vary in their approach to politics but little effort has been devoted to discovering why this is so. More precisely, there is an implicit assumption that variation can be ascribed either to the 'personality' of the incumbent or to the 'portfolio' of policy responsibilities they are given upon taking office. Although of some relevance to the study of commissioners and of the college, this chapter challenges and reassesses both these assumptions.

Instead of treating commissioners merely as individuals, we have set out to study them, their cabinets and other potential 'team members' as collective actors whose characteristics and working practices provide important insights into the workings of the Commission as a whole, and of the college in particular. Thus 'from a line of questioning on the practices of actors, we have set out to open up a reflection about institutional logics' (Guiraudon 2000: 5).

Such a perspective will also be used to question the implicit but direct link that is so often made between the portfolio of a commissioner and the nature of their behaviour in office. Here the doxa is that a commissioner who is delegated responsibility for policies that are already *communautaire* (agriculture, competition, external trade) will inevitably adopt a 'political' approach to their mandate, whereas their colleagues in charge of more inter-governmental policy-making (culture, research, education) will go about their work more 'technocratically'. Such an assertion is problematical not only because empirical evidence does not fit, but because the implicit definition of 'political' is that of the impact of commissioners upon Commission and EU decision-making. Although the question of impact is an important one, it actually tells us little about the type of logic adopted by a commissioner and their team, and therefore sheds no light on the political/techno-cratic cleavage. From a sociological perspective, it is more relevant to set up research on this question with the aim of understanding how each commissioner interprets and represents their own function and that of the Commission. From this angle, the portfolio certainly provides its respective holder with a set of latent resources, but their activation depends largely upon the relationship a commissioner develops with their 'role'.[1]

Based upon these twin theoretical pillars (collective actors and roles), our study of European commissioners in general, and eight from the periods 1989–1992 and 1995–1999 in particular,[2] has led us down a number of empirical paths. The one we set out to explore here concerns the involvement of these actors in issues which do not directly concern their respective portfolios ('non-portfolio' issues). Formally, the college has to approve each legislative proposal, decision or opinion that emanates from the Commission, a process that, at least in theory, gives each commissioner a right of influence in determining 'the European interest' in the face of inter-national and inter-sectoral struggles. Having examined in detail how a number of these actors have actually gone about trying to exercise this 'right', we first structure our analysis around the 'stance' on non-portfolio issues developed and expressed by the commissioners under study. In the second part of the chapter, this analysis is taken a stage further by looking more closely at the type of resources that different holders of this post have attempted to develop in order to enhance their chances of success in the college. More generally, if reassessing the political or technocratic nature of commissioner behaviour is our central goal, in shedding light on the nature of collegiality under the Delors and Santer presidencies, we also set out to provide data and interpretations which could structure comparisons of this phenomena over time (Smith 2003).

Developing a non-portfolio stance

Existing studies of the Commission have rightly stressed that commissioners adopt different postures to non-portfolio issues and to the college in general. George Ross (1995), for example, recounts that within the Delors team, Bruce Millan earned himself the nickname of 'the accountant' because he concentrated chiefly on his own portfolio of regional development whereas many of his colleagues held wider definitions of their tasks. As regards our panel of commissioners, four types of approach to this question broadly summarize our findings:

- 'accountants' who concentrated upon defending or changing the sector covered by their portfolio (MacSharry and Fishler);
- 'ideologists' who sought to influence a wide range of EU policy on the basis of their respective value systems (Brittan and Cresson);

- 'pragmatic' defenders of national interests (de Silguy and Dondelinger);
- 'European idealists' who were more (Oreja) or less (Scrivener) independent of their national governments.

As with any typology, this presentation is over-general and does not actually explain anything. Nonetheless it provides a useful starting point from which one can identify a problem with a major implicit assumption in existing literature on the Commission: examining a commissioner's 'political' or 'technocratic' past explains why different holders of this office interpreted their role as they did (Page 1997). This hypothesis holds good for actors such as Leon Brittan and Edith Cresson whose national careers were clearly formative factors, but why did Ray MacSharry (an ex-finance minister) restrict his activities essentially to reforming the Common Agricultural Policy (CAP)? Similarly, why did Christiane Scrivener (an ex-minister and MEP) concentrate essentially upon her tax and customs duties portfolio?

An alternative way of approaching this question is to trace the interpretation of what a commissioner should be and do, as held by each commissioner when they took up their post in Brussels. Where possible, we have asked the individuals concerned this very question. Notwithstanding some illuminating replies, such a method runs the risk of selective memories and a posteriori rationalizations. Instead our analysis is based more upon cross-checked information gleaned from interviews with members of the cabinets of each commissioner, in particular on the way these were set up and then put to work in the arenas that prepare the work of the college.

Cabinets as indicators of a commissioner's stance

Often written by practitioners, some publications on the European Commission as a whole provide useful descriptions of why cabinets were originally set up and of what they do (Donnelly and Ritchie 1994). In looking more closely at who is nominated to these bodies and what tasks they are given, cabinets can also be studied as concrete expressions of a commissioner's approach to their role in general and to its non-portfolio dimension in particular. A functionalist explanation (often favoured by ex-cabinet members) is that involvement in non-portfolio issues is only possible when the portfolio workload is not too great. According to such accounts, Yves de Silguy (monetary union) and the two commissioners responsible for agriculture (MacSharry and Fishler) 'simply did not have time to get involved in non-portfolio issues'. But this explanation is unconvincing if one looks at the size of the portfolios of other commissioners, such as Brittan and Cresson, and the emphasis they placed upon non-portfolio tasks when managing their respective teams. Our study suggests that regardless of the portfolio given to them, most commissioners begin their new jobs by forming themselves a team with which to put into practice their vision of what a holder of this post should be. From this perspective, they all make three series of choices.

The first choice concerns the balance they wish to strike between national and Commission civil servants. Because of the high number of applicants compiled and put forward both by national administrations and by the Commission, selection can take a considerable amount of time and energy. Leon Brittan, for example, recalls this process laconically:

> as I was yet to know my portfolio, the world and his wife came to see me. I've never been so busy! . . . However, I wasn't too happy with the people the Cabinet Office sent me so I contacted Chris Tugendhat, an ex UK and Conservative commissioner, who put me in touch with someone in the Secretariat General of the Commission – which is how I found Jim Currie, my first chef.
>
> (Interview, January 2001)

More generally, this recruitment process is marked by a number of strong unwritten rules and a good deal of leeway with which to interpret them. At least until the beginning of the Prodi presidency, the informal rules were that about half of each cabinet had to be Commission officials and that at least one member had to be of a different nationality to that of the commissioner. In practice 'the foreigner' was most often a Commission official specialized in portfolio issues, the *chef de cabinet* was a national civil servant whereas their deputy would be from the Commission. If these rules had significance, it is also important to underline that commissioners do not always find it easy to select cabinet members and thus often revert to personal recommendations in order to reach their judgements. As a member of Yves de Silguy's cabinet recounts:

> the head of cabinet found himself with a dilemma: he had to choose the members of his cabinet from a pile of 150 CVs. It was really difficult. He didn't know where to start . . . in the end, he decided to offer me the job because he knew me a little and that I was a specialist in monetary affairs.
>
> (Interview, October 2000)

More importantly, this point helps underline a criterion that, perhaps curiously, is rarely used to select a cabinet member: their political beliefs. With the exception of the Cresson team where, at least after summer 1997, socialist credentials became important, the criteria that dominate this process are 'competence' and 'loyalty'. The case that best illustrates this point is that of the Brittan cabinets. Although no one can doubt the commitment to the Conservative Party and to neo-liberal values of this commissioner, our interviews with members of his cabinets all confirm that party membership or commitment was not an issue. One cabinet official later became a Liberal Democrat MEP and underlined to us that:

> clearly I was not from the same party as Leon and he knew that. In fact, by 1997 probably only one member of Brittan's cabinet would have voted Conservative. But for cabinets, commissioners don't pick people on the basis of who they vote for – or at least they shouldn't, though I know many commissioners do.
>
> (Interview, November 2000)

The criterion of 'competence' naturally brings us to the second aspect of setting up a cabinet: prioritizing and assigning tasks. Formally, as Tables 2.1 to 2.3 illustrate, all cabinet members are assigned a number of portfolio and non-portfolio 'dossiers'. In practice, the latter can be followed with varying degrees of intensity. This point will be developed more fully in the next section, but the importance of a commissioner's stance on non-portfolio issues can be evaluated in part by the general brief given to cabinet members on such issues. Leon Brittan's instructions were particularly clear-cut: 'we had to cover the whole waterfront. Leon Brittan himself would and could do this, he was always capable of intervening on anything' (Interview with former cabinet member, April 2001); 'he wanted us to be everywhere and on every trip with him, briefings done on everything, press releases etc. In fact he wanted us active on three fronts: the portfolio, Commission affairs in general and Britain in Europe' (Interview with former cabinet member, February 2000).

Having been in charge of non-portfolio issues within ex-President of the Commission Ortoli's cabinet, Yves de Silguy also pushed his cabinet to seek omnipresence in inter-cabinet meetings. In practice, most of his team

Table 2.1 Leon Brittan's cabinet in 1995

	Career path	*Portfolio dossiers*	*Non-portfolio dossiers*
Colin Budd (*chef*)	Foreign Office	–	Staffing
Catherine Day	Commission	Trade (Eastern Europe)	–
Robert Madelin	Foreign Office, UKREP	Trade (Asia, Latin America)	State aids
David Wright	Commission	Trade	–
Anna Barnett	Ministry of Agriculture	Trade (agriculture)	Agriculture, fisheries
David Cogne	Commission	–	European Parliament, social affairs, Britain in Europe

Table 2.2 Yves de Silguy's cabinet in 1995

	Career path	*Portfolio dossiers*	*Non-portfolio dossiers*
Xavier Larnaudie-Eiffel (*chef*)	Budget ministry (ENA)	Monetary Union	Staffing
Jean-Claude Thébault (deputy)	Commission	–	Agriculture, budget
Jurgen Kreuger	Commission	Money (macro-economy)	–
Jacques Lafitte	Trésor	Monetary policy	Internal market, fiscality
Olivier Costes	French civil service	–	State aids
Benoît Woringer	European Parliament staff	–	European Parliament, audiovisual

worked principally on monetary affairs issues, leaving many non-portfolio tasks to be dealt with by the deputy head of cabinet, an experienced French Commission official. On state aid questions, however, a specialist from the French civil service was recruited with a particular brief to follow such matters.

In contrast, Ray MacSharry appears to have downplayed the importance of non-portfolio issues in favour of work concentrated upon agriculture and rural development policy where his cabinet acted as a filter and a relay between the commissioner and the vast majority of DG VI officials. Indeed, responsibility for following other matters was delegated to the least experienced member of the team.

A final indicator on a commissioner's interpretation of his or her role that can be gleaned from looking closely at their team is the type of spokesperson nominated. Although formally employed in the *Service de porte parole* (SPP), each spokesperson has responsibility for the dealings

Table 2.3 Ray MacSharry's cabinet in 1989

	Career path	*Portfolio dossiers*	*Non-portfolio dossiers*
Colm Larkin (*chef*)	Commission	Rural development	–
Patrick Hennessy	Ministry of Agriculture	Markets in general	Internal market issues
Herman Veisteiglen	Commission	Markets	–
Mary Minch	Commission	Trade	External relations
Eileen Magner	Personal assistant	–	European Parliament, social policy, culture, info., research

with the media of one particular commissioner. In practice, the role developed by each spokesperson is highly dependent upon a commissioner's perception of his or her own relationship to the media and to politics. In our panel, three approaches to this question have been identified. The first, employed by Leon Brittan and Yves de Silguy, involves developing a high profile in the media by personalizing communication strategies and associating the spokesperson with the policy-making work of the cabinet. Indeed, in such cases the spokesperson becomes a quasi-cabinet member. A second approach to the role of the spokesperson, favoured for instance by Ray MacSharry, is to consider them essentially as mouthpieces for policy statements prepared by the DGs and the cabinet. A third and final approach is to neglect the spokesperson as a means of communicating about what a commissioner does. As practised by Edith Cresson, this characteristic of her approach to communication fitted with an implicit division of her 'public' into two parts: portfolio interlocutors (researchers, industrialists, entrepreneurs etc.) and 'the French'. Her concentration upon the latter is borne out by both the book she published whilst in office (Cresson 1998) and her discourse during interviews to publicize it (for example on the television programme *7 sur 7*). In both instances, the fact that she was a commissioner was hardly mentioned and the European dimension to her opinions was only put forward as the logical 'horizon' for 'France'. If the Cresson approach to communication in general is undoubtedly an exception amongst commissioners, it does serve to highlight that on non-portfolio issues relations with the media are often considered more 'delicate' than on the portfolio. Second, it underlines that commissioners can choose whether or not to play the role of ambassador for European integration.

In summary, we have seen that a commissioner's interpretation of his or her role can, in part, be deduced from the manner in which they have gone about setting up their teams and setting them to work.

Cabinets as actors

Of course, the posture adopted by each cabinet on non-portfolio issues must also be evaluated by looking at how its members actually get down to doing this work. This question can be answered by looking in some detail at the way cabinet members prepared for the inter-cabinet meetings that in turn prepare the agenda of the weekly college meeting and, more generally, attempt to co-ordinate policy-making within the Commission. When intervening at this level on portfolio issues, a cabinet member relies considerably upon 'their' Directorate General for information and negotiating arguments. When intervening on non-portfolio issues, this source is no longer available. Instead, information and arguments have to be found elsewhere and be based either upon the (implicit) defence of a national or sectoral interest or couched in terms of general principles. We will deal with the question of information and the defence of particularist interests later in the chapter. What interests us more here is how each cabinet worked with their commissioner to prepare for inter-cabinet meetings as yet another indicator of the latter's conception of their role. From this perspective, the cabinet members studied worked in three different ways.

The first of these is based upon the idea that to have any credibility in inter-cabinet meetings, cabinet members must be able to speak 'in the name of the commissioner'. In concrete terms this meant frequent, if not daily, meetings between the commissioner and their cabinet, a practice developed in particular by the Brittan and de Silguy teams. A member of the former sums up the importance attached to this form of consultation in the following way:

> credibility in the college is based upon people needing to know you are speaking for your commissioner. We could do this because every day we spent an hour with our's. As a result we could speak for him with little fear of being caught out. The worst cabinets are those that are left to make up positions for themselves; either they just give their opinions on the basis of poor information (which is a waste of taxpayer's money) or they spread confusion and become known for their unreliability. For example, in inter-cabinet meetings if you say 'there's a reserve on that' and want it discussed at that level, and then your commissioner doesn't follow up in college, then you lose credibility. So you must not oversell your commissioner. You must not make it up.
>
> (Interview, July 2000)

A second approach to inter-cabinet negotiation can indeed come close to 'making it up'. When commissioners and their cabinet meet infrequently, or when such contact is often filtered through the *chef de cabinet*, such as in the case of Edith Cresson, the officials concerned have more autonomy to express their own interpretation of an issue. This view may reflect a general political line adopted by their commissioner, but it would seem that, in the politics of collegiality, having a general line is rarely the best means of winning arguments and influencing policy decisions.

A third and final approach to inter-cabinet 'pre-neogotiations' is simply not to speak at all in such fora. In some cases (MacSharry, Fishler), this may be due to a portfolio-centred view on the role of a commissioner. In others (Dondelinger, Oreja), such silence may reflect instead a conception of this role as that of a transnational diplomat working in the interests of 'Europe' through simultaneously representing the Commission and the nation state.

More generally, two differences in the approach to collegiality between the Delors and Santer presidencies may also provide some clues to the variations observed. The first of these concerns the manner through which inter-cabinet meetings are chaired. Given that a member of the President's cabinet always chairs these encounters, during the Delors period this institutionalized practice very quickly became a major resource with which to drive through potentially conflictual issues before reaching the college floor (Ross 1995). Members of the Santer cabinet, however, tended to adopt a much less directive stance to the chairing of meetings and thus allowed more issues to go up to the college for debate and decision-making. This characteristic brings us to a second difference concerning the role of the vote in college. A member of Brittan's cabinet who worked under both presidencies sums up a change in approach in the following way:

> Before 1995, you really had to vote in the college; given the context of 1992, there were objective reasons why this peaked in the early 1990s. But under Santer the college became a cosy club where it became commonplace to say 'we don't want to push things to a vote. It's not collegial to vote'. My foot it isn't! I think it's very dangerous to build up a mood where commissioners think they can't vote; you have to be able to vote, put it behind you and support a policy as a unit.
>
> (Interview, May 2000)

Other testimonies from members of other cabinets bear out the importance of this change in approach, some going so far as to underline that after mid-1997 hardly any votes were actually taken in the college at all. Without wishing to go down the treacherous path of quantitative analysis of voting in a context where anticipation of a vote is probably more important, this point helps underline the basic tension at the heart of a college of commissioners between pressures to specialize in a policy area (the portfolio) and the fact that all commissioners have the same power if issues are taken to a vote.

In summary, we have begun to see that politicization is considered to be an acceptable strategy of legitimation for commissioners, but that this comes with at least two strong caveats: not using one's national origin or party-political affiliation as vectors for breaking with more technical discourse and practice.

Resources for multi and bilateral bargaining

In order to take such analysis further, it is necessary to look more closely at the resources commissioners can mobilize in order to have influence in the college. Unlike national cabinets or councils of ministers, commissioners are rarely able to build up alliances amongst themselves based upon infra- or inter-party allegiances. Cross-cutting national, sectoral and partisan issues renders the emergence of stable coalitions within the Commission extremely unlikely. According to Leon Brittan, for example:

In my time there weren't really alliances between commissioners; there were attempts to do that but they were rarely successful. Personal and national differences make this difficult. After all, a college is a group of people from very different backgrounds who have been thrown together. It's very different from a British government where you're all from the same party – where at least at the outset you agree on a certain number of things.

(Interview, January 2001)

Rather than being a by-product of stable inter-commissioner alliances, in practice sources of information and support which are external but also internal to the Commission provide a key both to understanding how colleges work and how commissioners from large member states tend to tackle their mandate with a considerable headstart.

In general terms, this section confirms the implicit assumption made by intergovernmentalists (Moravscik 1998) that commissioners from Germany, France and the United Kingdom have more influence at the level of the college than their colleagues from smaller member states. However, this conclusion is not reached for the same reasons. For intergovernmentalists, commissioners from big countries count because they indirectly represent more powerful economic interests and can back up their positions with the threat of national resistance in the Council of Ministers and/or the European Council. This hypothesis both overstates the influence national governments tend to have over 'their' commissioner(s) and underestimates the impact of collegial rules upon the way national interests can be spoken for at this level. Instead, we argue that commissioners from large countries are most often in a position of comparative advantage because they and their cabinets are able to call upon networks of national actors when preparing arguments and objections on non-portfolio issues.

Sources of external support

Formal government position statements provide an initial source of information which tend to arrive in a commissioner's office whether they want it or not. Sent both by co-ordinating bodies in national capitals (the SGCI in France, the European Secretariat of the Cabinet office in the UK, etc.) and by the Brussels-based Permanent Representations, these documents provide commissioners and their staff with the official line. If such information usually sets out the initial negotiating positions of a government, according to many of our interviewees this information is at best difficult to use within the Commission, and at worst woefully out of tune with their needs when the college's focus is on medium and long term issues. According to one ex-cabinet member, if one were to use these documents as a brief for inter-cabinet or college meetings, one would immediately lose credibility with other colleagues for adopting 'COREPER-like behaviour'. Relying upon such documents is also problematical for officials in a cabinet because it presupposes that a government has a position on each and every draft piece of legislation or communication that goes through the college. In reality, sometimes cabinets are a conduit for demands for policy: 'on issues such as hunting licences, for example, a proposal would circulate on a Thursday and I would have to ring up London and tell them to get a policy by next Tuesday!' (Interview with former cabinet member, December 2000).

For these reasons, some commissioners and their cabinets place great emphasis on retaining or building up networks within national civil services in order to better anticipate national reactions to a Commission proposal, but also to encourage national officials to begin to anticipate and prepare their respective ministers for this eventuality. To quote one of Leon Brittan's *chefs de cabinet*: 'I looked after the Whitehall end of things. This means feeding messages back about the Brussels view of the world on policy issues' (Interview, December 2000). This concrete example of the existence and activation of networks external to the Commission is of course one of the reasons why commissioners have traditionally nominated around half of their cabinets from national administrations. To take another example from our interviews, this explains why French cabinets invariably feature an official from the Ministry of Agriculture. In the case of Christiane Scrivener, her agricultural specialist described his approach to the annual price round in the following manner:

> On the annual agricultural price package, you had to wait for the agricultural commissioner to make his propositions. If you want to intervene, though, you need to know what's in the price package before it gets to you. Things work better here if people know you are likely to oppose the proposition. So I sorted out a system for myself and made sure I knew what was going to be in the package. You need to talk to people in advance, go and see the people who are likely to support you etc. In certain cases I worked with people from Delors' cabinet because they would test me out to see what the best compromise solution would be.
>
> (Interview, January 2000)

The external networking practised by most cabinet members does not stop at the level of national administrations. In many instances this also entails establishing direct links with interest groups such as large companies or farmers' unions. On this point, however, the commissioners and cabinets we have studied tended to adopt widely differing behaviour. Some, such as Ray MacSharry, preferred not to meet interest groups at all, other than those working in the field of their portfolios. A second category of commissioners would meet interest groups from their respective countries more (de Silguy) or less (Brittan) often, but not commit themselves to doing anything other than listen. A third and final type of commissioner made no bones about seeking out the opinions of business leaders and other such actors. By this method, Edith Cresson was able to obtain support and information on both her research and education portfolios as well as wider industrial policy issues. Having set out this typology, it must be stressed that information on this particular point is difficult to compile and cross-check. Not meeting organized interests can of course be a strategy with which to foster an image of independence that does not prevent a commissioner and their staff from exchanging views more discretely by telephone, fax or e-mail. Nevertheless, from the point of view of analysing how a commissioner interprets their role, how they and their cabinet present this aspect of their work remains an important line of questioning.

More generally, studying the external networking carried out by a commissioner and their staff allows one to get an initial grasp upon the ambiguous link between these actors and interlocutors in their country of origin. In some cases, the direct result of these contacts may well be that a commissioner attempts to defend a national interest line on non-portfolio issues, prefacing what they say in college by the phrase 'in the country I know best'. These cases may be more common when a commissioner owes their nomination to particular members of a national government. However, the rules of collegiality tend strongly to discount the possibility that a commissioner will act consistently as a 'national delegate' who needs the support of their respective government in order to have any influence in the college. Indeed, this hypothesis is invalidated by the lack of difference, for the big member states, between the information received by 'the government commissioner' and their counterpart from a party in opposition. For example, after the election of a Labour government in Britain in 1997, Leon Brittan did not appear to lose either access to Whitehall networks or influence in the college. Instead, he just received fewer invitations to attend official functions (Interviews, several cabinet members).

Internal Commission networking

If external support alone can be counter-productive for a commissioner, sources of information within the Commission are vital to the positioning of commissioners in the college. More precisely, being able to seek support from informal networks of officials within the Commission can be an important resource. Journalists have already drawn attention to the importance of this question for understanding the Commission in general, and the way the presidency of Jacques Delors functioned in particular (Grant 1994: Chapter 6). In order to push such analysis further, and encompass the role played by commissioners in this process, it is important to study how these networks are built, how they can be maintained and a number of their effects.

Building a network within the Commission can be attempted by attracting the support of existing officials and that of new officials from one's own country from the moment they enter this organization. In both cases, commissioners can activate the resource offered them by the Commission's clientelistic model of staffing and promotion. Ostensibly meritocratic and transnational, recruitment to the Commission is in fact deeply influenced by who one knows and where one comes from. Passing an exam ('*le concours*') is one thing but once upon the '*liste de reserve*', an individual has to find themselves a job by identifying a forthcoming vacancy and mobilizing support for their candidature. In some instances, this may indeed depend upon merit, in others the support of a commissioner is highly sought after. This is particularly so because nominations have to respect a 'geographical balance' between different nationals. As Table 2.4 sets out, this balance is never actually achieved and thus provides a constant source of internal negotiation and tension. Indeed, 'respecting geographical balance' is undoubtedly even more of an issue when it comes to deciding who should be promoted to more senior positions within the Commission (unit heads, directors, director generals). On this question, the *chefs de cabinets* are constantly contacted by their fellow nationals for support and spend considerable amounts of time pressing the case of different individuals with the Secretary General and with other *chefs de cabinet*. One of Leon Brittan's *chefs* bemoaned the fact that staffing issues:

> probably took up about 10 per cent of my time – 6 hours in a 60 hour working week – which is absurd. It is absurd that there is so much

Table 2.4 'The geographical balance' of Commission A-grade officials

	1974	1980	1989	1994	1999
Austria	–	–	–	–	2.4
Belgium	13.1	13.5	12.1	12.0	10.7
Denmark	3.8	3.0	2.4	2.9	2.8
Finland	–	–	–	–	2.4
France	18.5	20.2	16.5	16.5	15.0
Germany	18.7	19.0	14.9	13.8	12.0
Greece	–	–	4.7	5.4	5.3
Ireland	3.9	2.9	3.3	3.4	3.0
Italy	18.2	17.4	13.4	13.1	12.3
Luxembourg	3.1	2.9	1.6	1.0	0.7
Netherlands	6.3	6.0	5.4	5.5	5.0
Portugal	–	–	3.9	4.1	3.9
Spain	–	–	10.1	10.5	10.5
Sweden	–	–	–	–	3.0
United Kingdom	14.9	14.5	11.7	11.4	10.8

Source: adapted from Shore (2000: 184) using European Commission data.

pressure from national capitals and that this is mediated through just one or two people. In the Commission there is no serious staff management system, no sensible system of promotion ... I spent a great deal of time mopping up after angry and bitter rejected officials, trying to convince the Secretary General of the need to find them 'slots'. There was a general idea that we had to make a comparable effort to what Delors had been doing. You are condemned to doing it, you cannot not do it.

(Interview, December 2001)

If this mode of personnel management can, perhaps rightly, be criticized from a normative point of view (Shore 2000), we are more interested in how the clientelistic practices it encourages influence commissioner behaviour and reveal another aspect of the way they see their role. Four types of stance on this question were identified by our research:

- consistent and unconditional support for nationals (de Silguy);
- frequent but conditional support (Brittan);
- conditional and not necessarily national support (Delors);
- largely ineffectual support given by commissioners from small countries such as Ireland and Luxembourg who have a relatively small 'quota' of posts to redistribute and who are often already 'over quota'.

If it is relatively easy to discover the general approach of a commissioner to the question of staffing, and implicitly to the distribution of favours that they hope to get returned in the shape of information, ideas and arguments, it is more difficult to understand how they go about mobilizing a network. Anecdotal evidence suggests that some commissioners and their cabinets throw regular cocktail parties to which their fellow nationals are invited. More importantly, the significance of this practice needs to be traced through the role of networks in precise case studies. In this respect, our research into how Ray MacSharry set out to reform the CAP in 1990, provides an example of the Delors network in action. Rather than use his cabinet and the hierarchy of DG VI to produce a proposition for reform, MacSharry set up a small group of officials comprised of just one cabinet member, one or two key heads of unit, the agricultural specialist from Delors' cabinet and his French Director General of DG VI, Guy Le Gras. By avoiding the official channels of inter-service and inter-cabinet consultation, MacSharry (and implicitly Delors) also reduced the chance of information on the new plan leaking to other commissioners and to national governments. At least in the short term, this 'anti-collegial' tactic paid off because it enabled MacSharry to force his proposal through the college and transform it into a formal Commission proposal to Council.

It is more difficult to compile information as to how commissioners and their staff activate their respective networks in order to have influence in the college over non-portfolio issues. Nevertheless, the largely effective opposition of commissioners such as de Silguy and Cresson to the outlawing of French state aids to industry (eg. over state aid to Crédit Lyonnais. Van Miert 2000), strongly suggests that an efficient network can be a powerful resource for certain commissioners.

On this point, an implicit hypothesis in the existing literature concerns the likelihood that Commission practices favour commissioners from national polities which feature clientelistic approaches to the personnel management of bureaucracies. The argument runs as follows: in political systems marked by clientelism, finding jobs for one's allies is part and parcel of everyday life for both top civil servants and ministers. In contrast, commissioners arriving in Brussels from polities where patronage is less easy to manipulate as a political resource, frequently have problems adapting to the needs and pressures of internal networking and thus often give the impression of being naïve. Certain individual cases may appear to substantiate such a claim. However, there is a very real danger here of falling back on culturalist explanations of patronage in government and simply transposing these to the way the European Commission functions. Our own analysis of the importance of internal networking has generated two more precise hypotheses, both of which need further research.

First, one logically assumes that because small member states have less Commission officials, their resource base is intrinsically weaker than that of larger countries. In this respect the fact that Jacques Santer came from Luxembourg (a member state which in the late 1990s provided only 0.7 per cent of Commission A-grade officials) was a handicap to his presidency less because he had weaker external support from his national government (Peterson 1999), and more because he and his staff had less 'natural supporters' to call upon within the Commission's services (Smith 2003). Nevertheless, it is important to avoid statistic-driven thinking about network building and activation. On this point, anecdotal evidence on the positions held by Spaniards within the Commission is particularly interesting. Although formally a 'big country' with a large quota of officials, the view of members of the Spanish permanent representation is that they are under-represented in senior positions:

> To be well-positioned, to fit into the Community, you need to have a friendly Commission, by which I mean find officials of your own nationality. But Spain is largely absent in this regard. For example, in the cultural sector, the director is French as is the head of unit for the MEDIA programme; in the audiovisual sector, the director is French and the head of unit is Greek; in education, the director is French and his assistant is British; in professional training, the Germans dominate.
>
> (Interview, official from Spanish Permanent Representation,
> January 2001)

In contrast, further anecdotal evidence suggests that officials from small countries such as Ireland manage to network effectively within the Commission and thereby 'punch above their weight'.

Second, it can also by hypothesized that the length of time a commissioner remains in this post also influences their capacity to build and mobilize a network. Delors and Brittan spent a decade at this level and were able to call in more favours as a consequence. Indeed, a number of our interviewees consider that Pascal Lamy the commissioner is still using and making the most of a network that he himself largely created in his days as *chef de cabinet* to Delors.

Conclusion

To conclude, we shall make two clarifications and underline two of the arguments made earlier. The first point that needs clarifying concerns the link between the way a commissioner approaches their portfolio and the non-portfolio aspects of their behaviour. Our research as a whole highlights the importance of this link as a means of understanding differences between the roles played by each commissioner. Our focus upon non-portfolio issues in this chapter means that this linkage has been downplayed, but a more even balance is restored in the remainder of our book.

The second clarification concerns the 'historical' nature of our subject matter. Some of the reforms introduced by Romano Prodi since 1999 may have modified commissioner approaches to non-portfolio issues and thus to their mandate as a whole. Only empirical research, however, can update analysis of this question and verify that genuine change has indeed taken place.

Notwithstanding these provisos, our analysis provides a number of keys with which to unlock the 'black box' that the college still remains for political science. Two arguments in particular have been made which revise much of the accepted wisdom about this body.

First, we have argued strongly that the college of commissioners is both a vital arena within the Commission and a major cause of this organization's working practices. Understanding the dynamics of the college provides a means of going beyond orthodox analyses of the Commission's 'fragmentation' so as to grasp the rules, norms and practices which, despite many centrifugal forces, have shaped this body over time, continue to influence the actions of its agents and, in so doing, render the college a vital arena for inter-sectoral and inter-national mediation. Studying these dynamics is best approached by conceptualizing commissioners and their cabinets as collective actors operating through teams and networks which constantly criss-cross the national/supra-national divide. More empirical research is needed which focuses specifically upon the composition and behaviour of these teams and networks.

Second, we have shown that the political/technocratic dichotomy is too simplistic a way of attempting to understand who commissioners are and what they do. Not only does one need to add the figure of the diplomat in order to grasp the different ways commissioners relate to their own mandates. More fundamentally, it is important to underline how 'political' and 'technocratic' labels are often used during European decision-making to legitimate or disqualify commissioners and the Commission (Dubois and Dulong 1999; Radaelli 1999a). Consequently, the impact of a commissioner's stance on non-portfolio issues upon Commission and EU decision-making is particularly difficult to trace. In most cases, commissioners use technocratic, political or diplomatic methods and strategies depending upon their interpretation of the interaction context within which each decision is made. Studying the sources and effects of these interpretations provides a means of grasping how agents within the Commission work within a highly competitive inter- and intra-institutional environment.

Notes

1 Contrary to the purely metaphorical use of this term so frequent in much of political science, the role will be used here as a concept that not only differentiates what an actor actually does from what their post allows them to do, but highlights how roles define what is *expected* from them by members of their respective societies (Lagroye 1997: 8).

2 This chapter is based upon research used to prepare a recent book on European commissioners (Joana and Smith 2002). Although part of our study looked at commissioners in general, the bulk of the empirical work was centred upon eight ex-holders of this office: five from the period 1989–1992 (Leon Brittan, Jean Dondelinger, Ray MacSharry, Christiane Scrivener) and four from the Santer college (1995–1999: Leon Brittan, Edith Cresson, Yves de Silguy, Franz Fishler, Marcelino Oreja). This panel reflects an attempt to test some implicit assumptions about what structures commissioner behaviour (nationality, big versus small country, portfolio, political or technocratic past, sex, etc.). Our methodology had three dimensions: 70 interviews with commissioners, their cabinets, and officials from different DGs; sociographic analysis of the careers of commissioners and their cabinets; quantitative and qualitative analysis of each commissioner's approach to public-speaking and the media.

3 The Secretariat General of the European Commission, 1958–2003

A singular institution

Hussein Kassim[1]

Research on the European Union has been largely preoccupied with the institutional behaviour and interaction of EU institutions, neglecting their internal dynamics, operation and culture, and focusing instead on their constitutional powers (Cassese and della Cananea 1992). This effort has contributed greatly to our understanding of the EU as *un objet politique non identifié*, enabling us to answer with some confidence important questions, such as 'who governs?' and 'where does power lie?' However, formal powers are only part of the story. Detailed investigation of the Community administration and of individual administrative units in particular may add further insight (see, for example, Wilks 1992; Cini 1996a; Ross 1995), revealing what happens in the 'black box' and the possibility of leading us to a deeper understanding of the processes, culture and thinking that underlie action on the part of the organization. Yet the internal workings of key parts of the machinery, including even such crucial bodies as the Secretariat General (SG) of the Commission, remain curiously unexplored. The pivotal position of the SG is routinely acknowledged (see, for example, Stevens and Stevens 2001), as is the influence of its first Secretary General, Emile Noël,[2] but there has as yet been no systematic investigation of its development, responsibilities and operation – a serious shortcoming given its centrality to the work of the Commission and the Community system more generally.

This chapter takes a first step towards remedying this neglect. It examines the development of the SG from its origins in 1958 until the early years of the Prodi Commission. It aims to answer five questions: What is the SG, and what does it do? Why was it created? How has it changed over time, and why? What has it contributed to the Commission and to the EU more broadly? How effective is it in carrying out its responsibilities? The main contention of the chapter is that the SG has not only performed key administrative functions inside the Commission, but also that it has contributed significantly to the Union as a collective system of governance in managing the Commission's interaction with other EU institutions. From its inception the SG has carried out tasks of both a routine and non-routine character, many of which are little known and about which the organigramme gives not even the merest suggestion. A second argument is that, although the core responsibilities of the Secretary General have remained fairly constant, the expansion of Community competencies and the increased institutional complexity of the Union, as well as the retirement of Emile Noël in 1987, have brought about significant changes in each decade of its existence. A further contention is that the SG has generally, for reasons to do with the structure of the Commission, been more effective in managing external relations between the Commission and other institutions than in the internal co-ordination of the Commission itself. Finally, the chapter argues that the SG, and particularly the first Secretary General, played a crucial role in institutionalizing the Commission: establishing and regularizing its procedures, shaping an independent administration, and creating an institutional identity.

The chapter is organized in four parts. The first looks at the origins of the SG, discusses the rationale for its creation, and explains how the SG differed from its counterpart in the High Authority of the European Coal and Steel Community. The second part looks at the SG under Emile Noël, its principal architect, who served as Secretary General for three decades. It discusses the conception that Noël had of the body, looks at how he shaped its responsibilities, functions and style of operation, and considers how he was able to exert such a strong influence on the organization. The changes introduced following Noël's departure are examined in the third section. They were prompted partly by the extension of Community responsibilities with the 1992 project and institutional developments – particularly, the strengthening of the European Parliament successively by the SEA and the TEU. However, the differing conceptions of the role of the SG harboured by Noël's three successors – David Williamson, Carlo Trojan and David O'Sullivan – and their attempts to remould it were also of considerable importance. The concluding section attempts an evaluation, looking at the capacities and powers of the SG in the unique institutional environment that it occupies, but also drawing comparisons with co-ordinating bodies in other political systems.

Origins: the creation of the Executive Secretariat

The decision to create an Executive Secretariat to support the work of the College was one of many taken in the early months of 1958, when the basic organizational structure of the Commission was put in place. Walter Hallstein, the first Commission President, with overall responsibility for administrative and personnel affairs (von der Groeben 1998: 104–105), emphasized the need to create 'une grande administration' (Noël 1992: 152; Narjes 1998: 110) in order to carry out the responsibilities entrusted to the Commission under the Treaty. Only a Commission that was expert and organized would allow it to emerge as 'a new factor in European and international politics' (Noël 1998: 132) with the credibility and authority to stand up to the member states and other parties.[3] At the same time, there was no obvious model on which to base the design of new organization. The High Authority of the ECSC, which had embodied Monnet's preference for a light and flexible administration, had run into difficulties, and the remit of the EEC was far broader than that of the Coal and Steel Community, calling for a more complex organization at its centre.

Nor was it obvious from the treaty how the Commission should be organized. It was clear only that it should operate as a corporate association (Noël, cited in Poullet and Deprez 1977: 160). Collegiality was, therefore, enshrined as the Commission's central organizing principle (see CEC 1958: 21–22; Noël 1992; Berlin 1987: 35). The breadth of the Community's remit made it necessary to allocate portfolios to individual members of the Commission. In order to preserve collective decision-making, however, it was decided that technical work would be undertaken by designated groups of commissioners, presided over by the commissioner holding the relevant portfolio and that an entire day each week would be devoted to a meeting of the college, during which – and only during which – decisions would be taken. Unlike governments at the state level, where ministers enjoyed considerable autonomy within their field of responsibility and cabinet discussion was reserved for a small number of serious or urgent issues, all Commission business would be discussed by all members of the college at a weekly meeting. It was also agreed that, while the functional departments (Directorates General) would receive instructions from individual commissioners, the services as a whole would constitute 'a single administration'. Thus, the opinions of all interested departments would need to be heard and reconciled before the college took the definitive decision.

Discussions about the internal organization of the Commission lasted until the end of March 1958. During the first few months, the Commission operated under straitened circumstances with only a handful of officials and with commissioners and cabinets running the administration from the centre. For several weeks, for example, the minutes of the college were taken not by an official, but by Hallstein's *chef de cabinet*, Swidbert Schnippenkötter (Noël 1992: 146). However, within ten weeks after its first formal meeting (on 15 January 1958) the Commission had decided on the allocation of portfolios, reached agreement on the departmental organization of the administration – there were to be eight functional departments, covering external relations, economic and financial affairs, internal market, competition, social affairs, agriculture, transport, and overseas development, an Executive Secretariat, a Legal Service and a department responsible for administration and personnel – and made appointments to senior positions in the administration.

As the central decision-making body within the Commission, the college would require considerable administrative support. The Executive

Secretariat was entrusted with this function. It was charged with responsibility for:[4]

- preparing and holding meetings of the Commission;
- transmitting the decisions of the college and overseeing their execution;
- liaising with other Community institutions and with the other Communities;
- maintaining links at the administrative level with the Assembly of the Communities and with other European Assemblies.

The Commission's internal Rules of Procedure, drafted in late February 1958, detailed its responsibilities (European Commission 1963). Under Article 16, the Executive Secretariat would be responsible for assisting the President of the Commission in preparing meetings of the college, conducting the written procedure, and in ensuring that the decisions of the Commission are followed up, as well as for the publication of the Official Journal (Coombes 1970: 249–250). The Executive Secretary or deputy Executive Secretary would attend all meetings of the college, unless the members of the Commission decided otherwise (Article 9), countersign the minutes (Article 10) and authenticate the decisions adopted by the Commission (Article 12).

Thus, the Executive Secretariat was to occupy a privileged place in the Commission administration. Indispensable to the work of the college, close to the President and 'the only body (other than the Commission itself) ... responsible for taking a view of the organization as a whole' (Coombes 1970: 250), it would also represent the Commission externally. Positioned at the interstices between EEC institutions, moreover, it would contribute to the overall coherence of Community processes and action. The Executive Secretary at its head would inevitably be an influential figure as the most senior official in the administration.

By the end of July, the organization of the Executive Secretariat had taken shape. The Executive Secretary was to be assisted by a deputy, also with general competence, so that the continuity of the Commission's work could be maintained, when the college met outside Brussels. Routine work was carried out by three divisions. The Registry – la *Greffe* – was responsible for preparing the work of the college, including organizing its agenda and taking minutes. A second unit was charged with ensuring that Commission decisions were circulated and implemented by the services and with liaising with the departments and keeping commissioners informed about Community business. The third division was to maintain contact with Community institutions, including the Council, the Assembly and the Court, the Commission's counterparts in the ECSC and Euratom (the High Authority and the Euratom Commission), and other European assemblies. A further unit provided the three divisions with administrative support.

As with the Commission administration more broadly (see Stevens and Stevens 2001), the Executive Secretariat was not modelled on an existing body at national level or elsewhere. It was created to perform a set of tasks that arose from the Commission's collegial nature and from the complex institutional environment in which the Commission operated, as one of three executive bodies in three multi-institutional Communities – the ECSC, the EEC and Euratom. Unlike the French Secrétariat Général du Gouvernement (SGG) in Paris, for example, to which it has often been compared (see Cassese and della Cananea 1992: 1; see also Berlin 1987: 67–69), or the Cabinet Secretariat in London (see Coombes 1970: 249) – it is worth noting that no similar body exists in the German system – the Executive Secretariat has since the very beginning represented the administration in its external relations with other institutions, a function that is as time-consuming as it is prestigious. In comparison with these other bodies, the Executive Secretariat was also very small, numbering no more than 20 officials (9 A-grade officials, 3 Bs and 8 Cs) in 1958. The body to which it bore greatest similarity was the SG of the ECSC's High Authority.[5] However, fundamental differences in responsibilities and structure of the two Communities, and the contrasting visions of Monnet and Hallstein, produced quite distinct bodies. The differences were further reinforced by the different pattern of involvement on the part of national governments in the decision-making processes of the respective Communities. Whereas in the ECSC COCOR, the committee composed of senior national officials in the ECSC met only very occasionally, COREPER brought together permanent representatives of the member states, creating a quite different and more intense Commission-Council dynamic. The SG's steady accumulation of functions further distinguished the Executive Secretariat from comparable organs elsewhere.

The Secretariat General under Emile Noël, 1958–1987

Emile Noël has, without doubt, been the most important figure in the history of the SG. As Executive Secretary of the Commission of the EEC from 1958 until 1967, and Secretary General of the Commission of the EC that resulted from the 1967 merger until 1987, Noël occupied the top administrative position in the Commission for thirty years, exerting an unparalleled influence on the Secretariat, and indeed on the Commission more broadly. Noël's personal qualities and individual standing (see below) were important factors in establishing the authority and identity of the Secretariat. However, the changing historical contexts in which he operated are also crucial to understanding both how the Secretariat evolved and how the nature of his influence changed. Three periods are distinguished below: the early years under Hallstein, 1958–1967 during which the Executive Secretariat was established and became institutionalized; the period from 1967 until 1984, when Noël's influence was perhaps at its greatest; and the three years, 1985–1987, that Noël served under Delors, which saw a clash between new and old methods and styles. However, Noël's background is considered first.

Background and appointment

Noël was appointed Executive Secretary in February 1958 at the age of 35.[6] A graduate of l'Ecole normale supérieure and with a degree in mathematics and physics from the University of Paris, Noël was a high-flying civil servant with strong connections within French and European elites, as well as Socialist circles. As Secretary of the General Affairs Committee (later the Political Committee) at the Council of Europe early in his career, he had worked closely with the French Socialist, Guy Mollet. From there, he moved on to become director of the Secretariat of the Constitutional Committee of the ad hoc Assembly, responsible for producing a draft treaty for the European Political Community that was linked to the ill-fated European Defence Community. Between 1955 and 1956, Noël headed Mollet's cabinet, while the latter was President of the Consultative Assembly of the Council of Europe. When Mollet became French Prime Minister, Noël returned to France initially to serve as his *chef de cabinet* and later his deputy Director. In this latter capacity, Noël was a member of the French delegation to the Conference on the Common Market and Euratom, and participated actively in the drafting of the Treaties of Rome.

Noël's experience in the European public service and the French administration, his high-level contacts in both worlds – including, for example, Jean Monnet, in whose Action Committee for Europe he was involved (Spence 1997: 110) and with whom Noël remained in regular touch (Duchêne 1994) – and the fact that he had participated in the negotiation of the treaties with many figures who occupied senior positions in the Communities in the early years,[7] gave him not only a privileged insight into government and politics at national and European level, but a personal authority that went beyond his formal status. As well as the personal qualities – extreme intelligence and subtlety of mind, excellent memory, skilled draughtsmanship, and a formidable capacity for work – he took to the job of Executive Secretary, Noël also brought standing to the Executive Secretariat and to the Commission.

The Executive Secretariat under Hallstein, 1958–1967

The Executive Secretariat played a significant part in realising Hallstein's ambition to build an administration to rival those of the member states, contributing in several ways to the building and operation of the Commission, and to the creation of its identity as an institution. Through the greffier function – collecting and circulating documents, preparing the college agenda, keeping the minutes of meetings – the Secretariat established, and at the same time became keeper of, the Commission's institutional memory, whilst by assuring compliance with internal rules, it contributed to the regularization of internal procedures. Moreover, by providing the main channel – performing what one commentator calls 'le role charnière' (Berlin 1987: 80) – between the college and the services, the Secretariat assisted in ensuring continuity between the political and administrative echelons of the Commission and thereby contributing to the overall cohesion of the organization. Important in this respect, and also to ensure that decisions taken by the college were transformed into action by the departments, was Noël's decision to meet weekly with the Directors General and with the assistants of the Directors General. The Executive Secretary also chaired the meetings of *chefs de cabinets* that began to meet weekly from early 1959 in advance of the college to prepare and co-ordinate its work. Finally, Noël, as Executive Secretary, represented the Commission formally at administrative level in meetings with other institutions, most notably in the weekly meeting of COREPER, which began in 1959.[8] Noël also played the role of informal ambassador for the Commission, and indeed the Community, to notables visiting Brussels. His diaries record a regular stream of meetings with politicians, diplomats and other dignitaries, particularly from Europe and the US.

Although Hallstein, as Commission President, bore ultimate responsibility for the Commission as an administration, he was happy to delegate organizational matters to Noël (Narjes 1998: 110). A senior member of Hallstein's cabinet, and later a deputy Secretary General of the Commission, illustrates this point as follows:

> One Thursday in February 1958, shortly before he was formally appointed Executive Secretary of the EEC Commission, Emile Noël took up his duties in Brussels. The first task he was given by President Hallstein was to draft the EC Commission's rules of procedure. The very next Monday the future Executive Secretary laid his draft before the Commission President. A few days later it was adopted with no significant amendments by the Commission, and from then on regulated its daily life.
>
> (Meyer 1994: 263–264)

Similarly, Noël played an important role in drafting the Staff Regulations, which set out in detail the rules that govern the conduct, rights and obligations of officials, and the procedures relating to their career, working conditions, salaries and disciplinary measures. He was also a central figure in the long process that culminated in the merger of the executives of the three Communities. Noël participated in the lengthy talks and negotiations, in which he represented the Commission, that led eventually to the 1965 Merger Treaty agreement, as well as in the extensive planning and organization of the fused executive created when the agreement entered into force in July 1967 (Interview with former member of the Commission).

The responsibilities of the Executive Secretariat expanded as the scope of the Commission and the Community grew and they became complex organizations. The Commission's engagement across a growing range of activities led to an increase in the number of divisions or specialized services from 100 in 1958 to 124 in 1967 (pre-merger) and officials from 1,108 to 2,924 (Poullet and Deprez 1977: 149, 144). Meanwhile, the institutional development of the Council changed the original institutional balance between Council and Commission, and, by creating a more complex environment, imposed demanding co-ordination requirements on the Commission and therefore the Executive Secretariat. The proliferation of Council formations, and COREPER's split into two parts, COREPER I and COREPER II, in 1962 were the most significant.[9] Interdependence between Commission and the Council in the decision-making process, moreover, necessitated close and intense relations between the Executive Secretariat of the Commission and the Council Secretariat. Structures and procedures were developed by both secretariats for this purpose. As well as the work generated by the need for the management of the Commission's external relations, the Executive Secretariat was entrusted with new responsibilities concerning the internal operation of the 'house' as the Commission became established and expanded. The Executive Secretary was involved personally in appointments and promotions processes.

More staff were recruited to the Executive Secretariat to deal with its increased responsibilities. The number of officials employed in the Secretariat rose from 36 (13 A-grade officials) in 1958 to 68 (16) in 1963 and 77 (17) in 1965. However, it remained small enough for an official working in it to know all his or her colleagues – a point made repeatedly in interviews conducted by the author with officials who worked there – and for its staff to be hand-picked by the Executive Secretary. It was also characterized by an unusually flat hierarchy with one less sub-division than was standard in other departments. Whereas other DGs were divided into directorates, which in turn were divided into divisions, the SG had three administrative units that were headed by chefs d'unités. The streamlined organization – there were no directors – was designed to deliver maximum flexibility. It also created a sense on the part of the SG's staff of working directly for and to the Executive Secretary himself (Interview, 19 April 2001).

Noël did not see the Executive Secretariat as a body whose functions were exclusively administrative. He considered it the appropriate home for activities aimed at promoting the European idea. Accordingly, the Secretariat set aside a small budget for this purpose. In a similar vein, Noël took very seriously the need to explain the nature of the European Community and the role of the Commission. He himself wrote a widely circulated pamphlet, *Comment fonctionnent les institutions des Communautés européennes*, translated into English as *Working Together*, that was intended to serve as a brief and accessible introduction to the Community and its procedures.[10] In addition, in several academic articles, Noël addressed issues that were of topical concern to students of the Community. Among the subjects tackled were the Luxembourg Compromise, the merger of the Communities, the development of COREPER, and the relationship between Commission and Council. Noël also communicated regularly with academics and gave presentations on Community-related subjects at universities inside and outside Europe.

By the end of the Hallstein era, the ambition of the President to create an administration that would be capable of carrying out the functions vested in the Commission had largely been met. The evidence was to be found not only in the institutional structures and procedures of the Commission, in the creation and support of which the Executive Secretariat had played an important part, but also in the range of policy achievements that it had recorded, the challenges successfully met by the organization, and the recognition it achieved among governments and other actors inside and outside the Community. The Executive Secretariat's contribution to these accomplishments was significant.

From Rey to Thorn, 1967–1985

The challenges facing the Rey Commission, and indeed his successors until the mid-1980s,[11] were very different from those that had confronted Hallstein. The autonomy and authority of the Commission had been firmly established by the time that Hallstein left office. However, Commission attempts to expand Community competencies were only partially successful and, with the Luxembourg Compromise and a greater assertiveness on the part of the member states, it faced a very difficult environment. Two waves of enlargement, the first of which brought three hesitant states (Denmark, Ireland and the UK) into the Community, serious economic crises, and a bitter budgetary row, added to the challenge.

The arrival of the new Commission in 1967 coincided with the entry into force of the Merger Treaty. As part of the latter, a single SG was formed out of the secretariats of the executives of the three Communities and Noël was appointed as the first Secretary General of the unified Commission. The new body was larger, reflecting the broader remit of the merged Commission, and divided into seven administrative units: Greffe; Secretariat of group meetings and meetings of the assistants to the Directors Generals; relations with the Council (I); relations with the Council (II); liaison with the European Parliament; and General Report and other periodical reports (CEC 1968: 9). In its operation and structure, however, the SG remained much the same as the Executive Secretariat.

In terms of status and centrality, the importance of the Secretariat increased. The commissioners who had served under Hallstein were technical experts and many had been long involved in European affairs. This was not true of the Rey College or of later Commissions. The presence of generalists rather than specialists and the diminishing number of veterans of the immediate post-war era had the effect of enhancing the SG's importance as an authoritative source of expertise and institutional memory. Within this vacuum, 'Noël supplied the institutions with some of the political vision which the commissioners often lacked' (Grant 1994: 102).

Other developments from the late 1960s onwards also reaffirmed the centrality of the SG. First, the Community became more active. The legislative activity of the Commission and Council, measured in legal events as recorded by CELEX, increased significantly from 1968 (*c.*120) and even more dramatically between 1972 (*c.*250) and 1986 (*c.*2,500) (Maurer 2003: 44). The Commission's output alone began to rise in 1976 and rose steeply between 1978 (*c.*50) and 1986 (*c.*2,000) (ibid.). As well as higher levels of activity, the Community became involved in new policy areas, most notably, foreign and economic affairs, which subjected it to new and different demands. Second, Community institutions met more frequently. The number of days spent in meetings in the Council rose significantly. In 1967, 1,233 days were spent in working groups, increasing to 1,403 in 1970 and stabilizing at around 2,000 from 1974, while the number of Council meetings grew steadily from 75.5 in 1967 to over 100 from 1983. Third, the Community became more institutionally differentiated and complex. The European Parliament became an increasingly important body. Summits became a regular feature from the late 1960s with the European Council bringing together heads of state and government three times a year during the mid-1970s. At the institutional level, the number of Council formations increased in the early 1980s from nine in 1974 to 17 in 1982. Finally, the Commission became a larger and more complex organization. After the merger, it had 5,149 officials, compared with a pre-merger figure for the EC Commission of 2,924. This figure rose to close to 7,000 following the first enlargement (Poullet and Deprez 1977: 144) and to more than 15,000 by 1987 (Page 1997: 23). As its competencies expanded, the number of DGs rose from nine in 1967 to 20 in 1970 before falling to 19 in 1973, where it stabilized, and of commissioners from nine (1967–1970, 1970–1973) to thirteen (1973–1977, 1977–1981) and fourteen (1981–1985).

The increased activity of EEC institutions, the broadening front across which the Community became active and the growth in the complexity of Community institutions increased pressure on the Commission and made greater demands of the SG as the body responsible for supporting the work of the college and its sub-systems, managing relations with external bodies and keeping 'the house' in good order. Under these changed circumstances – a far cry from the early days of the Commission with its small size and relatively simple organization – the coordinating functions of the

SG assumed even greater importance. Noël's long service and experience – Gaston Thorn referred to him as 'Europe's prime witness' (cited in Sutherland 1996)[12] – led Commission Presidents and commissioners – sometimes in the College – and senior officials alike to ask his opinion. As one former Commission President noted, a visit to the Secretary General's office before taking up one's responsibilities became part of the routine for incoming Commission Presidents and commissioners (Delors 1996).

The SG adapted to the new environment in several ways. It changed the way that it handled some existing responsibilities. With respect to Commission relations with Parliament, the SG devoted greater resources to ensuring that the Commission complied with its various obligations and instituted mechanisms to co-ordinate action on the part of the Commission. The most notable was, perhaps, the Groupe des Affaires Parlementaires (GAP), which brought together the member responsible for Parliament from each cabinet (Westlake 1994: 12). A closer relationship was also forged with the Parliament's Secretariat. In addition, the SG was entrusted with new tasks. The Secretariat General assumed responsibility for European Political Cooperation (EPC), launched in the 1970s, and remained responsible for external political relations until the early 1990s, when DG IA was created. This was the first instance of what became a trend: the SG would be used to incubate new responsibilities where no DG existed or where entrusted responsibility to an existing DG was regarded as problematic for some reason. On the external front, when the Commission finally won the right to be represented among the Community's heads of state and government (see Jenkins 1989), the Secretary General was granted the privilege of being the only official permitted to attend meetings.

In terms of its size and structure, the SG also changed. While staff numbers increased, additional divisions were created to reflect new demands and new priorities, and to manage new competencies. The number of units grew from seven in 1968 to nine in 1975, 11 in 1978, 12 in 1982 and 13 in 1983. New divisions included a secretariat of the ECSC Consultative Committee (1975), intergovernmental co-operation between member states (responsible for EPC) (1977), an industrial relations office (1977), which became the social partners office in 1978 and social partners office and youth forum in 1982, in-house information and in-service traineeships (1982), cultural questions (1982) and inspection, planning and organization (1983). A Central Advisory Group was also set up in the SG in 1977, which was briefly counted as a division (1982–1983). There were also changes in its hierarchical structure. The post of director was created for the first time in 1968.

In addition, as part of the exercise where positions were created for officials from the acceding states, a second deputy Secretary General post was created in 1973. One of the main tasks of the UK civil servant appointed to the position was to codify the internal rules of 'the house', which to incoming officials from the new member states seemed opaque. The outcome was the *Manual of Operating Procedures*, the definitive guide to the rules and internal processes of the Commission, covering the operation of the Commission and its departments, including its working methods, budget and financial control, relations with other EEC institutions and bodies, and external relations.

The centrality of the SG during this period has been affirmed by several observers. A description, written in the 1980s when the SG's influence was perhaps at its zenith, is worth recalling:

> This is not a service, like the Legal Service, that has official power over other DGs. However, because of its central position, the authority of its leader, and the fact that nothing happens within the Commission without him intervening in one way or another, the SG has become the memory of the institution, its principal advisor, its mediator and its overall guardian. Over the years, in this way it has acquired a dominant position within the services, and this to such an extent that virtually nothing can be done against the wishes of the Secretariat General.
>
> (Berlin 1987: 69)

Delors, 1985–1987

The arrival of Jacques Delors as Commission President in January 1985 brought a period of activism to the European Communities and a new style of leadership to the Commission (Ross 1995). Although Delors and the members of his cabinet had considerable respect for Noël, their far-reaching ambitions, their determination to get things done quickly, and their leadership style brought them into conflict (Endo 1999: 117). Delors, moreover, unlike his predecessors, had no need for Noël's services as an adviser or fixer, since these roles were played by the Commission President's *chef de cabinet*, Pascal Lamy. Delors and his cabinet were in a hurry, and grew increasingly irritated 'by the same old ways in which Noël conducted the in-house business, in particular his conciliatory run of the chefs de cabinet meetings' (Endo 1999: 117). There were constant clashes at the beginning of the Delors' Commission between the Commission President's cabinet, which sought to establish itself as the nerve centre of the Commission, and the Secretary General (Endo 1999: 43). These subsided somewhat when Noël was included in a small high-level Commission group to work on the Single European Act (Ross 1995: 32; Endo 1999: 42) and indeed represented the Commission at the IGC, but shortly after – in 1987 – he retired from the Commission.

Noël left behind a body that occupied a central position in the Commission, responsible for the flow of paper, the keeper of its rules and procedures, and the guardian of its institutional memory, and in the

Community system as a whole. It also bore his personal imprint. The SG was shaped by Noël, who was 'not a methodical manager' (Grant 1994: 102), but a 'man of the corridors' (Interview, 9 April 2001), the 'quintessential eminence grise' (Interview 2001), who exercised influence discreetly through a network of contacts throughout the Commission (Endo 1999: 42) and whose style was to resolve difficulties behind the scenes. However, this should not be taken to imply that Noël had self-interested objectives or sought power for himself. As a former colleague, Max Kohnstamm observed: 'He was like a monk from the Middle Ages, with a total devotion to a cause. He had one object in mind: European integration, or, as Jean Monnet described it, "Yesterday force, today law"' (cited in Turner 1996; see also the *Economist* 1996: 96).

The Secretariat General after Noël

The three individuals who have held the top position since Noël's retirement – David Williamson (1987–1997), Carlo Trojan (1997–2000), David O'Sullivan (2000–) have each sought to manoeuvre the Secretary General in slightly different directions. Each tenure has been marked by a distinct personal style and a different conception of the SG's role. Each, moreover, has faced particular challenges. What they share, however, is a preference for the SG as a less extraordinary and more normal administrative body than it was prior to 1987.

The SG under David Williamson, 1987–1997: towards normalization

David (since, Lord) Williamson acceded to the post of Secretary General with experience of both the British civil service and the European administration. He served in the UK Cabinet Office, as Head of the European Secretariat under Margaret Thatcher, and in the Commission, as a deputy Director General in DG VI (responsible for agriculture). His appointment led to a dramatic change in the style of the SG. The SG adopted a lower profile than under Noël and became more like a traditional bureaucracy. A number of important reforms were also introduced following the entry into force of the SEA and later the TEU.

Noël was a singular figure, and one of the first tasks that Williamson undertook was to 'de-singularise' (Interview, 19 April 2001) the SG. In organizational terms, this took the form of a re-structuring, which saw the SG become more like other DGs. By late 1988, an overhaul had resulted in the creation of eight directorates:

A – the Greffe;
B – internal coordination and data processing;
C – planning of Commission working and inspection of and information for delegations;

D – relations with the Council;

E – relations with the Parliament and the Economic and Social Committee;

F – intergovernmental cooperation between member states, including political co-operation, civil protection and human rights;

G – the Central Advisory Group;

H – co-ordination of fraud protection (CEC 1988).

As part of the re-organization, several new functions were added and some existing responsibilities extended. A unit in Directorate B, for example, assumed responsibility for monitoring the 1992 deadline and the implementation of Community laws, including state aids. This reflected a belief within the Commission that progress towards the internal market and ensuring compliance with Community rules should be monitored centrally. The creation of a Directorate to co-ordinate fraud protection, by contrast, was a response to concerns expressed by the European Parliament that the Commission was doing too little to combat fraud.

In the same spirit of normalization, Williamson sought to improve inter-departmental co-ordination, and thereby to correct what was widely acknowledged as a serious problem in an organization that was pre-occupied by 'building Europe' and had tended to neglect administrative issues (Stevens and Stevens 2001). A serious attempt was made to address the unwillingness of the services to share information and co-operate with other departments. Noël's strategy had been to use personal networks, but this was by definition an unsystematic approach. Williamson sought to encourage the setting up of ad hoc inter-services working groups, as a way of overcoming departmentalism. Given the formidable structural and cultural obstacles, it is unsurprising that he was only partly successful (Endo 1999: 118–119; see also Spence 1997: 111). If improving routine co-ordination proved problematic, Williamson did succeed in easing the flow of information within the Commission, as well as making the processes by which the Commission put together and monitored implementation of its annual programme more efficient (Ludlow 1991) – both considerable achievements, the latter involving the drafting of a meticulous set of rules incorporated in the Manual of Operating Procedures. Drawing up the Commission's work programme no longer involved 'an annual opening up of filing cabinets' (Ross 1995: 267–268), but became a top-down process.

Elsewhere, Williamson scored some notable successes. At the Brussels European Council in February 1988, for example, he was instrumental in achieving a settlement of the budgetary dispute, involving the UK's contribution (Spence 1997: 111). Moreover, Williamson adapted the SG to the growing power of the Parliament within the Community system. With the co-operation procedures introduced by SEA, the Parliament became an important legislative actor for the first time. Williamson established systems designed to ensure that events in Parliament were reported to the relevant DGs and commissioners on the same day, that briefings were supplied to Commission officials involved in meetings in the Parliament, and that the right officials appeared at the right meetings in the Parliament. These functions were performed by a Directorate within the SG. (This latter body also supported the work of the GAP). Similarly, following the TEU, Williamson introduced mechanisms to enable the Commission to manage the new (and complex) co-decision procedure effectively. A specialist unit was also created to handle relations with the new Committee of the Regions.

The implications of first the SEA, then the TEU, were not limited only to institutional matters. The expansion of Community competencies into new areas of activities also threw up challenges. For example, after the cohesion fund was increased as a result of the budgetary package that followed Maastricht, the Commission President asked the SG to take responsibility for its management on the grounds that the budget was too large to be handled by the relevant DG (Interview, Secretariat General, 20 June 1997). In 1993, Directorate H took charge of the cohesion funds. At the same time, a Task Force for Justice and Home Affairs was created in the SG as an embryonic Directorate General to handle matters relating to the third pillar created by the TEU.

The SG also handled difficult one-off issues that became more numerous in a period of intensive Community activism. It took over responsibility for the BSE crisis and the associated concerns relating to consumer health and the scientific committees. It also took charge of biotechnology – an area that had proved extremely controversial. Most dramatically, perhaps, the Community's policy towards German unification was co-ordinated from within the SG (Spence 1992).

Unlike his predecessor, Williamson enjoyed a good working relationship with Delors. This was evident not only in the routine work of the Commission, but also at the level of historic decision-making, such as in the Maastricht IGCs (see, for example, Ross 1995: 189) – for which purpose a Task Force had been set up in the SG under Michel Petite – and in the preparation of the Delors' 1993 White Paper on Growth, which was in the words of one official 'confectioné' in the SG (Interview, Secretariat General, 20 June 1997; see also Endo 1999: 199). However, Williamson's loyalty to Delors attracted criticism from the camps of other commissioners – notably, Leon Brittan's – which felt marginalized (Grant 1994: 102–103; Ross 1995). The difficulty encountered by members of the Commission in trying to put issues on the weekly agenda of the Commission, which the Commission President rigidly controlled (Interview, 20 September 2000), was cited as a particular grievance, as was the restriction to a limited few of involvement in planning major policy initiatives.

Although he did not enjoy the same personal influence as his predecessor – 'Noël's voice was', as Middlemas (1995: 221–222) observes, 'often decisive in meetings of the college, and always important where internal promotions were concerned'[13] – Williamson was highly respected. He contributed significantly to turning the SG into an efficient and more normal bureaucratic entity, and to enabling the Commission to confront its new challenges. Given the changed circumstances of the Commission and the increased demands on the SG, moreover, it was no longer possible for a single official, even a very talented one, to achieve the dominance that Noël had exercised.

The Secretariat General under Carlo Trojan, 1997–2000. Leaner and meaner?

Carlo Trojan was the first Secretary General to have previously worked in the Secretariat. He had been deputy Secretary General for ten years, working alongside David Williamson, and also had cabinet experience. Trojan took office with a clear idea of the changes that he wanted to make in the organization of the SG and the role that he wanted it to play. He envisaged a smaller body, stripped of extraneous responsibilities, that would concentrate on core functions – intra- and inter-institutional co-ordination, and serving the college – or, in his own words, 'a service that caters to other services'. He also wanted to 'lower the walls' between divisions dealing with related questions inside the Commission (Interview, 24 September 1998) – and to increase staff mobility. Trojan was supported in these aims by recommendations made in two reports, the first submitted by the Inspectorate General – a body created to provide in-house advice on management issues – and the second, resulting from the Commission of Tomorrow ('DECODE') exercise carried out in 1998.

Trojan's second ambition was for the SG to play a far more interventionist role in internal co-ordination. In terms of its formal status, the SG was on par with other Commission departments. This imposed significant limitations on its co-ordination strategy. Although it could insist that departments within the Commission observe certain formal procedures, such as those requiring the submission of documents on or before certain deadlines, it lacked the authority to intervene with respect to the substance of a topic under discussion and still less, in the style of the UK European Secretariat, to impose a solution where departments could not agree. Trojan sought a more powerful role that would enable the SG to give a steer to issues and sometimes more.

Trojan was only partially successful and then only in respect of his first ambition. The JHA Task Force, for example, the Fraud Office (UCLAF) became a free-standing entity, and the bureau de stage was transferred to DG IX (personnel and administration). The drugs coordination unit and the unit responsible for co-ordinating structural funds were also found new homes. The creation of a more powerful SG, however, was not something that the members of the Santer Commission were prepared to countenance. Meanwhile, the SG continued to perform its traditional functions. It notably took responsibility for co-ordination of the Agenda 2000 package, the multi-disciplinary set of proposals designed to prepare the Union for Eastern enlargement.

The Secretariat General under David O'Sullivan, 2000–: at the heart of a reforming Commission

David O'Sullivan became Secretary General after Trojan's resignation in the wake of the downfall of the Santer Commission. Appointed at the age of 48 – much younger at the time of his appointment than his two immediate predecessors – he had been a member of two cabinets, had held senior positions in the services and briefly was the *chef de cabinet* of Romano Prodi, who became Commission President in September 1999. O'Sullivan's aims for the SG have been influenced by two factors. The first is the strengthening of the Commission presidency by the Amsterdam Treaty. The upgrading of the office led Prodi famously to compare the Commission to a government. Since 1999, he has sought to develop an administrative machine capable of supporting the new prime ministerial function. The second is the commitment of the Prodi Commission to administrative reform (see Kassim 2004). The modernization programme foresees a key role for the SG in a reformed Commission.

Several steps have been taken to fulfil these ambitions. First, as part of the attempt to connect resource allocation with the setting of political priorities – a major theme of the reform – the SG became responsible for Strategic Planning and Programming (SPP). An annual policy cycle was established, whereby, following a discussion in the college, the President decides the Commission's programme for the coming year. Available resources are then allocated to the priority areas – programming became synchronized with the budgetary procedure. The resulting Commission work programme is broken down into action plans for the services, setting out clear objectives for a fixed time period, so that progress can be monitored and evaluated from the centre. The SG provides administrative support to the President, who is formally responsible for the process. Second, the SG is to play a far more active role in internal co-ordination, intervening at an early stage in the policy process, ideally, before drafts have been circulated. The idea is that it can 'add value', not by becoming involved in the substance of policy, but by encouraging dialogue before departments begin to engage in trench warfare, offering a bird's eye view of the issues, and providing arbitration where necessary. A further initiative concerns the simplification of procedures. A second deputy Secretary General was appointed and charged with the task of reducing and eliminating unnecessary bureaucratic procedures in the organization.

The Secretariat General has once again been restructured in order to implement these changes. In 2003, it was organized into six entities, as follows:

Directorate A – registry and Commission decision-making process;
Directorate B – relations with civil society;
Directorate C – programming and Commission policy co-ordination;
Directorate D – relations with the Council;
Directorate E – relations with the European Parliament, the European Ombudsman, the European Economic and Social Committee and the Committee of the Regions;
Directorate F – resources and general matters; and Task Force on the Future of the Union and institutional matters.

Other changes include the creation of a new unit in the Directorate responsible for relations with the Council to co-ordinate Commission participation in co-decision. More broadly, the Secretary General has been one of the leading figures in the reform process and has used the SG to introduce modern management techniques and instruments, such as policy evaluation and impact studies.

The Secretariat General: a concluding assessment

The SG has been a key body in the development and operation of the Commission. It contributed importantly to the Commission's institutionalization, through the drafting and enforcing of internal rules, and regularizing the procedures of the nascent organization. It has performed a series of core functions at the Commission's heart – supporting the work of the college, guarding the organization's institutional memory, and ensuring a vertical flow of information between the political Commission and the services. It has also acted as the Commission's ambassador, representing the institution in and to external bodies, managing relations between the Commission and other institutions, and ensuring that the institution meets its obligations by informing, advising and co-ordinating officials in respect of the demands made, for example, by the Council and the Parliament.

From a comparative perspective, two points are striking. The first is the combination of responsibilities attached to the SG. Whereas comparable institutions at the national level are essentially concerned with the internal functioning of the bureaucracies, in which they play a central role, the management of inter-institutional relationships is less of a concern. Interestingly, with respect to the SG, it has been its performance with respect to the latter that has been more impressive. Moreover, in its external representation of the Commission, the SG has not only performed a vital service to the Commission, but it has also contributed towards the promotion of coherence in an institutional system that is characterized by differentiation and fragmentation. Second, in relation to the Cabinet Office and the SGG with which it is most often compared, the SG is small in size and, until the Prodi Commission at least, has lacked an important resource. Whereas the Cabinet Office and the SGG derive much of their authority from their proximity to the Prime Minister, there has historically been no concentration of power at the centre of the Commission – a serious absence, given the tendency towards departmentalism and introspection on the part of Directorates General. The SG has, in internal coordination, therefore, had to rely upon persuasion and an ability to demonstrate its value in terms of information, knowledge and experience in its dealing with other Commission departments. Personality has also been important, both in terms of the figure that heads the SG and the Commission President.

Notes

1 I should like to express my gratitude to the former commissioner and the Commission officials, including a former Secretary General and a former deputy SG, who very kindly granted non-attributable interviews between September 1998 and May 2003 as part of the research for this chapter. Without the benefit of their experience, this chapter could not have been written. Thanks are also due to participants in the panel, 'Building the European Commission: the creation and early development of a supranational actor', inaugural conference of the ECPR standing group, Bordeaux, 26–28 September 2002, especially Andy Smith, as well as to Martin Westlake and David Spence, for their comments on earlier drafts, to 'fellow travellers' Véronique Dimier, Piers Ludlow, and Dionyssis Dimitrakopoulos for helpful suggestions and constant encouragement, and in particular to the librarians and archivists of the Historical Archives of the European Union in Florence and Brussels for invaluable assistance in tracking down documents and sources. Fieldwork in Brussels, Paris and Florence was made possible by small research grants from the Nuffield Foundation and the British Academy.
2 For practitioners' assessments, see Lemaignen 1964: 69–70; Marjolin 1986; Meyer 1994: 263–267; Narjes 1998: 110; Davignon cited in Turner 1996; Sutherland 1996; Delors 1996; for evaluations by scholars, see Coombes 1970: 250. Interestingly, Noël was not the first candidate for the post.
3 For this reason, he courteously disregarded the recommendations that had been prepared by the (intergovernmental) Interim Committee between the signing of the Treaty and its coming into effect. He did accept the High Authority's offer of financial support, which made it possible for the Commission to set up an administration before the budgetary law became effective in 1959–1960 and thus to present national governments with a fait accompli. Although individual officials were recruited to the new Commission from the ECSC executive, Hallstein chose not to allow the latter to take charge of any services or to recruit its senior officials to high office in the new administration (Noël 1992: 145).
4 Doc. 40/58, cited in COM (58) 159, 21 July 1958.
5 The Executive Secretariat of the High Authority of the ECSC was responsible for supporting the work of the College, ensuring that members of the High Authority were kept up to date with discussion in the working groups, linking the various divisions of the High Authority, and managing external relations.

6 It had been agreed that, since the Commission President was German, the Executive Secretary should be French (Interview with former member of the Commission, 29 May 2001).

7 Among the negotiators of the Treaties of Rome that were based in Brussels after 1958 were Hallstein (German, Commission President), von der Groeben (German, commissioner for Competition), and Marjolin (French, Commission Vice-President), Baron Snoy (Belgian, Permanent Representative) and Ophüls (German, Permanent Representative). See Noël 1992: 156.

8 Noël notes that Hallstein saw protocol as an important part of asserting the Commission's independent status. Thus, although commissioners received Permanent Representatives individually or as a group, commissioners did not attend meetings of COREPER, but were represented in that body by senior officials (Noël 1998: 132).

9 The Executive Secretary attends the first, his deputy the second.

10 The first edition was published in 1963, but has been revised subsequently.

11 They were: Franco Malfatti (1970–1972), Sicco Mansholt (1972), Francois-Xavier Ortoli (1973–1977), Roy Jenkins (1977–1981) and Gaston Thorn (1981–1985).

12 Or, in the words of George Ross (1995: 35), Noël, 'the Commission's eternal secretary general . . . held all the strings and knew all the secrets'.

13 By contrast, 'Delors allowed Williamson much less say on promotions, so that the role concentrated more on harmonizing the transaction of business as if he were a British cabinet secretary' (Middlemas 1995: 221–222).

4 Political dynamics of the parallel administration of the European Commission

Jarle Trondal

Introduction[1]

Despite much effort uncovering the wheels and cogs of European integration, the scholarly debate has largely been trapped in a neo-functionalist versus intergovernmentalist dichotomy. The 1990s, however, witnessed a theoretical turn in the study of European integration towards less focus on either/or 'unifying story-lines' and more in the direction of both/and middle-range theories (Geyer 2003). This theoretical move partially reflects a more general 'institutionalist turn' in the study of public administration and European integration (Jupille and Caporaso 1999; March and Olsen 1998). This chapter suggests an institutional middle-range approach that makes conditional assessments of the transformative potential of the parallel administration of the European Commission. The goal is to outline a research agenda for future empirical studies of the political dynamics of system transformation in Europe.

More specifically, this chapter challenges the political-technocratic dichotomy by studying political dynamics at the micro-level of civil servants of the European Commission (Smith 2003: 150). This, however, is not a reductionist move because I conceptualize the roles and identities evoked by civil servants as institutionally constituted and constrained (March and Olsen 1989: 4). The main argument of this chapter is that political institutions are transformational institutions, and that transformational institutions are supranational institutions. To substantiate this claim, the chapter poses the following question: Does the Commission manage to transform the loyalties and identities of national civil servants seconded on short term contracts to the European Commission? Arguably, identity transformation among seconded Commission civil servants serves as a yardstick of the political dynamics within the parallel administration of the Commission. I basically argue that the 'political' aspect of the European Commission primarily has a non-territorial and supranational component. Hence, it is the supranational dynamics which ultimately distinguish the European Commission as a political institution (Trondal 2004).

Secondment refers to national civil servants hired on temporary con-
tracts within the European Commission. Studying the mix of national and
supranational loyalties amongst Commission officials is important in order
to assess the transformative power of the European Commission writ large.
Supranational loyalties denote Commission officials identifying with the
EU as a whole, with the European Commission, with the Directorate
General (DG) in which they are employed, or with particular task roles.
Hence, supranational loyalty means simply identifying with EU institutions
at different levels. Despite the existence of several partially competing
organizational logics within the Commission (Christiansen 1997), it is
important to uncover the relative primacy of supranational dynamics. This
chapter highlights one under-researched 'Cinderella' of the European
Commission where territorial dynamics may have ample chance of survival
and viability: the parallel administration of seconded national civil servants (Cini 1996a; Shore 2000; Wessels 1985). Hence, a 'least likely'
research design underpins the study.

One rationale for studying national civil servants seconded to the European Commission is to assess the extent to which individual officials come
to construct new additional supranational loyalties, identities and role perceptions. By controlling for a self-selection dynamic, this represents a critical examination of the socializing and re-socializing power of the
European Commission. Arguably, the emergence of supranational identities and roles amongst seconded Commission officials is indicative of
system transformation as perceived at the level of individual civil servants.
According to the White Paper on European Governance issued by the
Commission in 2001, 'exchange of staff and joint training between administrations at various levels would contribute to a better knowledge of each
other's policy objectives, working methods and instruments' (European
Commission 2001d: 13). Couched in more analytical terms, 'the future
organization of Europe involves a struggle for people's minds, their identities and normative and causal beliefs' (Olsen 2003: 58).

The European Commission is the core executive body at the heart of
the EU (Nugent 1997) and a catalyst of European integration and transformation of national government systems. However, few studies have penetrated the internal life of the European Commission (e.g. Cram 1994;
Edwards and Spence 1997; Shore 2000; Smith 2003). Not surprisingly, the
parallel administration of the Commission has been subjected to even less
scholarly attention. I argue, however, that seconded Commission personnel represent an adequate testing-ground for institutional approaches on
the political dynamics of system transformation. Seconded national civil
servants are heavily 'pre-packed' and pre-socialized prior to entering the
Commission. Their stay at the Commission is relatively short and the
majority return to prior positions in national ministries or agencies when
their temporary contracts come to an end. Hence, one should expect
these officials to be fairly reluctant Europeans. However, the *prospective*

emergence of supranational allegiances amongst seconded personnel in the short, medium or long term is indicative of the supranational character of the Commission. Moreover, the enactment of supranational allegiances amongst seconded national civil servants is indicative of the transformative power and thus the political dynamics of the European Commission writ large.

The chapter is sequenced as follows: the next section provides a short review of the parallel administration of the European Commission, succeeded by two concepts of system integration across levels of governance: a weak and a strong. Finally, a middle-range institutionalist perspective to system integration is outlined that suggests conditions under which supranational allegiances are likely to precede national and sectoral allegiances amongst seconded civil servants. Suggestively, supranational allegiances are likely to be evoked under the following conditions:

H1   if the officials have the European Commission as their primary institutional affiliation;

H2   if the European Commission is organized according to principles that challenge the governance dynamics of domestic government systems;

H3   if the seconded personnel are employed in the European Commission for long periods of time and participate intensively in the day-to-day decision-making processes of the Union;

H4   if the seconded personnel are weakly pre-socialized at the national level and/or strongly pre-socialized at the international level before entering the Commission;

H5   if the seconded personnel are strongly integrated into the social life of the Commission.

Based on these conditional hypotheses, this study outlines a middle-range research agenda for future empirical analyses on the political dynamics of the European Commission.

The parallel administration of the European Commission

There is a surprising dearth of in-depth empirical studies of the European Commission (Christiansen 1997: 83; Egeberg 1996; Shore 2000: 127). Most studies that do exist of the Commission are focused on the President, the commissioners, the formal organization, the permanent bureaucratic staff and the historical evolution of the Commission. Thus, it should come as no surprise that the parallel administration of the Commission is severely under-researched (Christiansen 1997: 84).

Organizations often consist of two parallel procedures for recruitment and two sets of personnel: permanent and temporary officials recruited respectively on the basis of merit and quotas, or *parachutage*. The construction of new organizations often warrants hiring external officials on a temporary basis. This was also the case when constructing the High Authority in the 1950s. However, envisaging an independent European bureaucracy, Jean Monnet rejected the model of delegated and temporary seconded national civil servants at the centre of the Community executive (Shore 2000: 177). Monnet's vision largely collided with the wishes of the French government in the 1950s and 1960s. The French government 'had made a strong case for the Commission to be comprised solely of temporary officials seconded from national administrations' (Cini 1996a: 120–121). For federalists, like Monnet, secondments represented the opposite of an independent civil service at the EU level, and therefore the parallel administration of the Commission represented a 'Trojan Horse' threatening the coherence and autonomy of the core executive body of the emerging European Community.

However, initial recruitment to the High Authority of the Coal and Steel Community and to the Commission(s) of the EEC was mainly based on national officials on short term contracts (Nugent 2001). Today, few international organizations have institutionalized a parallel administration to the same extent as the European Commission. Reflecting increased workload, functional differentiation and a need for external assistance, the non-statutory staff of the Commission has increased to about 30 per cent of the current Commission's workforce (European Commission 1999b: 18). The Council of Ministers, the Council Secretary and the European Parliament have 'practically no temporary staff' (Bodiguel 1995: 451). However, different EU institutions often second officials amongst themselves (Christiansen 2001). The size of the current parallel administration of the European Commission has even forged counter-reactions from the Commission, highlighting that 'the high percentage of non-permanent officials in the Commission cannot be justified' (European Commission 2000d: 37). The parallel administration of the Commission makes up a considerable part of the institution, rendering the Commission a multi-faceted organization with respect to recruitment practices, personnel, career paths and perhaps even institutional allegiances and individual loyalties.

Largely being an understaffed institution, the Commission is heavily dependent on external assistance. This assistance is brought into the Commission through the web of EU committees and more permanently through the non-statutory staff. However, whereas 'comitology' has grown into a big 'research industry', secondments have been given only scarce scholarly attention. At present, about 16,000 permanent officials work on established posts in the Commission (Nugent 2001: 164; Stevens and Stevens 2001: 17). Additionally, the Commission has about 4,200 non-permanent officials on various short term contracts (European Commission 1999b: 9). This system of non-permanent staff is divided into three different sub-groups: temporary agents (N = 2,400), auxiliary staff (N = 1,000), and seconded national experts (N = 760) (European Commission 1999b: 9; Stevens and Stevens 2001: 17). This study focuses particularly on the latter, that is civil servants from member state administrations 'loaned to the Commission for up to three years' (Spence 1997: 9). Temporary agents and auxiliary staff, by contrast, come from various research institutes, interest organizations, etc. Indicative of the increased salience of seconded personnel in the Commission, these officials numbered 200 in 1989, 250 in 1990, about 600 in 1994, and in 1995 the number was 650 (Bodiguel 1995: 442; Edwards and Spence 1997: 79). At present, seconded national officials number 760, accounting for 15 per cent of all A-grade staff of the Commission and probably for about 25 per cent of A4 to A6 staff (Nugent 2001: 165; Stevens and Stevens 2001: 20). Hence, the parallel administration of the Commission has increased by about 250 per cent in the 1990s, especially in the top ranks.[2] Moreover, this part of the Commission will be extended substantially by EU enlargement in 2004. The Commission has estimated a need of over 5,000 new recruits from the candidate countries, mostly based on non-permanent posts (EUobserver 2003).

According to the official line, seconded national experts have a potential for generating system integration across levels of governance 'by allowing [national] civil servants ... to learn about [EU] procedures and administrative culture' (Spence 1997: 79). To cite the Commission directly (1999b: 63), seconded national experts 'are a way of forging stronger links between national administrations and the Commission'. From a more analytical point of view, studying the emergence of supranational loyalties amongst temporary national experts within the Commission can identify mechanisms of re-socialization at the heart of the European Union. According to Shore, for example (2000: 152), 'they find it a wonderfully mind-expanding experience: most who come here want to stay after their secondment has finished. Like the *agents temporaires*, once they get one foot in the door they want to get the rest of their body through'.

Two concepts of system integration

This section outlines a weak and a strong concept of system integration. A weak concept views system integration as the web of contacts, networks and relationships that emerges between politico-administrative systems. A strong concept measures system integration as transformational change – that is, the basic dynamics of governance, decision-making, and individual roles and identity change.

System integration, both in the weak and strong sense, is a relatively embryonic field of study, remains under-studied and poorly understood. System integration or *engrenage* may be understood as processes and not as fixed states of affairs (Held *et al.* 1999: 27). The mutual relationships between politico-administrative systems constitute ever-changing phenomena in political-administrative life. Just as single organizations are in constant states of flux, the relationships between organizations are constantly evolving. Moreover, system integration is relational – covering the relationships, interdependencies and interconnections between different systems and between the members of these systems (Spinelli 1966). Finally, system integration is a continuum, not a dichotomy, ranging from weak to strong modes of integration (Trondal 1999). As discussed more thoroughly below, weak system integration requires that actual contacts occur between at least two systems. A stronger notion of integration requires, in addition, that these contacts mutually affect the systems and the individual members within them.

Several suggestions as to how to conceptualize system integration have been addressed in the literature. Rosenau (1969: 46) defines system integration as penetrative processes whereby 'members of one polity serve as participants in the political process of another'. March (1999: 134) gauges system integration by measuring the 'density, intensity and character of the relations amongst the elements of [different systems]'. Moreover, '"integration" signifies some measure of the density, intensity and character of the relations among the constitutive elements of a system' (Olsen 2001: 4). Referring to system integration in the EU, Scheinman (1966: 751) sees system integration as the 'intermingling of national and international bureaucrats in various working groups and committees in the policy-making context of the EEC'. Similarly, Majone (1996) 'refers to the idea of *copinage technocratique* to denote the interaction between Brussels officials, experts from industry, and national civil servants' (quoted from Radaelli 1999b: 759 – original emphasis). Common to all these conceptualizations is an emphasis on the mutual relationships and contacts between systems and the members of these systems. In this sense, these conceptions of system integration represent fairly weak definitions of this phenomenon, emphasizing that different systems actually come into mutual contact of some sort.

Advocating a stronger notion of system integration, Barnett (1993: 276) asks, 'what happens when state actors are embedded in two different institutions ... that call for different roles and behaviour?' Similarly, Olsen (1998: 2) asks, 'what happens to organized political units when they become part of a larger unit?' More assertive, Eriksen and Fossum (2000: 16) argue that 'integration, in the true meaning of the term, depends on the alteration, not the aggregation of, preferences'. System integration thus denotes processes whereby organizational dynamics and behavioural logics are transformed amongst European institutions and decision-makers (Held *et al.* 1999: 18). This represents a stronger definition of system integration by emphasizing how governance systems are mutually affected due to increased and intensive interaction.

From the late 1960s onwards, a growing literature on system integration emerged in the wake of accelerating processes of European integration. Studies of public administrations discovered how domestic administrative systems became increasingly embedded within international political orders. Consequently, the open-ended and multilevel character of domestic politico-administrative systems attracted increased attention from scholars of public administration. Early scholarly contributions to system integration demonstrated how the domestic-international distinction became increasingly blurred due to the intermingling of national and international bureaucrats (Cassese 1987; Egeberg 1980; Feld and Wildgen 1975; Hopkins 1976; Kerr 1973; Pendergast 1976; Scheinman 1966: 751; Scheinman and Feld 1972). Highlighting 'bureaucratic inter-penetration' across levels of governance, this literature emphasized that the descriptions of the Community as 'above', 'alongside' or 'outside' the member states were oversimplifications (Rosenau 1969; Scheinman 1966). The national level and the Community level were described as mutually interwoven and intermixed in fundamental ways (Demmke 1998: 15). This body of literature highlighted that national government officials became regular participants at the EU level of governance (Rosenau 1969). However, only scarce attention was devoted to how such cross-level participation affected the 'inner selves' of the participants, let alone their actual decision-making behaviour (see, however, Feld and Wildgen 1975; Kerr 1973; Pendergast 1976; Scheinman and Feld 1972). As such, a weak notion of system integration underpinned these early studies. This chapter advocates a stronger definition by focusing on the political/ transformative dynamics of system integration.

Going beyond a *sui generis* notion of the European Commission, the next section suggests a middle-range institutionalist approach to system integration. First, assuming that the Commission shares important characteristics with national bureaucracies, three general institutionalist arguments are outlined to render intelligible system integration through the parallel administration of the European Commission. Second, I propose five hypotheses that specify five institutional conditions under which seconded Commission officials are likely to evoke supranational allegiances.

Towards a middle-range account on system integration

Departing from three general institutionalist perspectives suggested below (STEP I), I suggest a middle-range institutionalist account on system integration (STEP II). STEP II identifies conditions that are conducive to the emergence of supranational roles and allegiances among seconded Commission officials. Through this endeavour STEP II also specifies conditions under which pre-established national and sectoral identities and roles are sustained among these officials. Our principal aim is not to theorize the various micro-foundations that underpin the three institutionalist approaches, only to suggest conditions under which seconded Commission personnel evoke supranational roles and identities. STEP II thus aims at making conditional assessments of the political dynamics of the parallel administration of the Commission services.

STEP I: Three institutionalist arguments

STEP I introduces institutional arguments from Simon (1957), Selznick (1957) and March and Olsen (1989) which emphasize the *transformative potential of organizational structures*. The first perspective is a cognitive perspective on organizations (Simon 1957). According to the bounded rationality approach in organizational science, the attention of actors is limited. Humans have cognitive limitations, rendering them vulnerable to the systematic selection of decision premises and stimuli offered by organizational structures. Moreover, assuming that actors are multiple selves, organizational arrangements contribute to activate and deactivate particular repertoires of decision behaviour, identities and role percep-tions. Political and administrative life is portrayed as multi-faceted, contex-tualized and endogenous. More particularly, formal structures are pictured as political agendas that contribute to a mobilization of bias (Hammond 1986; Schattschneider 1960). The identities enacted by organizational actors reflect their rational choices, even if these are biased and skewed in systematic ways by the organizational structures within which they are embedded.

Formal organizations are sometimes '*infused with value* beyond the tech-nical requirements of the task at hand' (Selznick 1957: 17 – original emphasis). Value-laden organizations acquire strong potential for socializ-ing the organizational members into loyal trustees. At the same time, however, actors affiliated to organizations with a strong institutional core are often disposed to resist changing pre-established identities and roles (Knill 2001). Accordingly, processes of socialization over time make actors take particular identities and roles *for granted*. Actors become norm- and rule-driven as a result of the internalization of roles and identities. A cul-tural perspective on organizations emphasizes the 'pre-packed' character of governmental actors. When seconded into the European Commission, national civil servants will thus retain and sustain pre-established national and sectoral affiliations and evoke role perceptions that deviate only mar-ginally from past roles. Processes of re-socialization into supranational loyalties are subject to the logic of recency (March 1994: 70).

A related institutional perspective views actors' identities and alle-giances as reflecting logics of appropriateness (March and Olsen 1989). Actors often have several institutional affiliations simultaneously that provide different cues for action and senses of belonging. Based on the following questions, actors make *deliberate* choices as to what identity and role to apply in particular situations:

1   Who am I?;
2   What kind of situation is this?;
3   What should a person such as I do in a situation such as this? (March and Olsen 1989: 23)

According to the logic of appropriateness actors are basically rule- and identity-driven, however, not in the sense of taken-for-grantedness (cf. March and Olsen). Actors are consciously geared towards evoking identities they associate with particular situations and that have several points of resemblance. According to a logic of novelty, actors tend to evoke new identities and roles that deviate only marginally from past identities and roles (March and Olsen 1989: 34).

We have now addressed three supplementary institutional arguments. First, a bounded rational argument emphasizing that organizations have a transformative potential with respect to the identities and allegiances evoked by the organizational members. According to this perspective, organizational structure bias and skew role and identity perceptions in systematic ways. However, the impact of socialization processes is modest both with respect to *depth and permanence*. Actors' roles and identities are pictured as contingent and endogenous, but at the same time malleable and not very deep-seated. The second and third institutionalist approaches envisage a stronger transformative potential for institutionalized organizations. Officials not only 'go native' in Brussels, they tend to 'stay native' in the sense that new supranational loyalties are internalized and/or considered appropriate. However, this transformation and re-socialization process easily becomes subject to inertia, path-dependencies and a logic of recency (March 1994).

Bearing these different institutionalist insights in mind, the next section suggests an institutionalist middle-range research agenda that specifies *the conditions under which* seconded Commission staff are likely to evoke or construct supranational allegiances.

STEP II: Towards a middle-range approach

Despite arguing that the European Commission socializes Commission officials into supranational agents and 'European elites' (Christiansen 2001; Shore 2000), less effort has been put into studying under what conditions Commission officials evoke supranational loyalties. Based on the above institutionalist arguments, this section suggests five conditions to account for the political dynamics of system integration in general, and the emergence of supranational allegiances in particular. These conditions are:

- The primary and secondary institutional affiliations embedding seconded officials,
- The organizational dynamics underpinning these affiliations,
- The length and intensity of affiliation towards secondary institutions,
- The degrees and patterns of pre-socialization within primary institutions, and
- The social milieu embedding civil servants.

Suggestively, supranational identifications are likely to be strengthened and fostered amongst seconded Commission personnel under the following conditions. That is:

H1 if the officials have the European Commission as their primary institutional affiliation;

H2 if the European Commission is governed by dynamics that challenge the core dynamics of national government systems;

H3 if the seconded personnel are employed in the European Commission for long periods of time and participate intensively in the day-to-day decision-making processes of the Union;

H4 if the seconded personnel are weakly pre-socialized before entering the Commission;

H5 if the seconded personnel are strongly integrated into the social milieu of the Commission.

This section elaborates theoretically and substantiates empirically these five hypotheses. Due to the present lack of *systematic* empirical studies of seconded personnel in the European Commission, the discussion benefits from secondary empirical material on seconded officials from different EU member states and Norway (CLENAD 2003; EFTA Secretariat 2000; Smith 1973; Smith 2001; Statskontoret 2001: 17). In the following we analyse this body of empirical material to help illustrate the above hypotheses.

Upon arrival in the Commission, seconded national officials are supposed to work for the Commission (EEA 2002: 6). However, despite being under Commission instructions (Staff Regulations Art. 37), seconded civil servants retain their primary institutional affiliations to their national ministries and agencies (EEA 2002) (H1). When seconded to the Commission these civil servants continue to receive most of their income from their national employer. Moreover, their stay in Brussels is only temporary. When the secondment period reaches its end most civil servants return to prior positions within their national civil service (CLENAD 2003: 6). Seconded officials are thus heavily 'pre-packed' and pre-socialized when entering the Commission (H4). They also anticipate potential future career paths within the national civil service after their stay in Brussels. Consequently, the Commission should be considered a secondary institutional affiliation to the seconded personnel. Even when staying in the Commission, their national ministry or agency remains their primary institutional affiliation. Accordingly, the identities and roles evoked by seconded personnel are likely to be more national than supranational. They are likely to attach weight to their national identities and roles while working as non-statutory staff in the Commission. An early study of 36 former seconded Dutch officials to the Commission reveals that all of them retained a national loyalty when working in the Commission and 'none indicated that [they] had ever come into a conflict of loyalty' (Smith 1973: 565). A study of seconded officials from the Scottish Office of the UK central administration to the European Commission supports these arguments (Smith 2001). Smith also observes that seconded officials reinforce their national administrative cultures and allegiances rather than becoming more supranationally oriented during their stay at the Commission.

I argue that the internal organizational structures of the European Commission are conducive to weakening national allegiances amongst seconded personnel (H2). The dominating organizing principle of the Commission is sector (Egeberg and Trondal 1999). This organizing principle challenges the dominating territorial principle in international relations and inter-state politics. The sectoral organization of the Commission is especially strong at the DG and the unit levels. Most seconded personnel are employed at the A7 and A8 levels within the DGs. Reflecting the general low level of inter-DG co-ordination and mobility, seconded personnel mostly work within *singular* DGs during their short Commission careers (Edwards and Spence 1997; European Commission 1999b: 57–58). According to a survey conducted by the EFTA Secretariat (2000: 1) among 18 Norwegian national experts to the Commission, 'all but one had been working in the same unit during their contract period'. Hence, seconded personnel are affiliated to organizational units within the Commission that are organized according to a sectoral principle. Prolonged and intensive exposure towards sectoralized decision-making premises within the Commission DGs increases the likelihood that the role and identity perceptions of the seconded personnel become denationalized and strongly sectoralized (H2 and H3).

Egeberg (1996), McDonald (1997), and Shore (2000) support these propositions empirically. Egeberg (1996) shows that *permanent* Commission officials put only marginal emphasis on national allegiances (H1). Moreover, Cini (1997: 86) observes that institutional identities among the statutory staff of former *DG Competition and Environment* are directed more towards the DG level than towards the Commission at large (H2). Hence, the horizontal organization of the Commission affects the identities of the incumbents. Moreover, officials employed in top rank positions within DGs having broad horizontal mandates and portfolios are likely to identify with the Commission as a whole more strongly than officials employed in medium or lower rank positions within DGs having specialist task descriptions. Overall, sectoral allegiances are likely to precede national identifications amongst permanent Commission officials. However, Egeberg (1996) also reveals that the nationality of permanent Commission officials affects their decision-making behaviour. This stems partly from the territorial principles of organization underpinning the Commission machinery (the cabinets, national quotas, etc.) and partly from their national institutional affiliations. Accordingly, seconded personnel to the Commission are *likely*

555

to put particular emphasis on pre-established national and sectoral roles due to their primary domestic affiliations and their sectoral affiliations within the Commission DGs (H1 and H2).

Most seconded personnel have lifelong careers in the national civil services. Hence, they are heavily pre-socialized before entering the Commission (H4). Most of them also return to prior positions in the national civil service after finishing their stay in Brussels. Furthermore, the European Commission is a relatively young and small institution compared to national central administrations. These factors render it difficult for the Commission to instill new identities and roles into officials with pre-established loyalties. Hence, supranational allegiances are likely to be modified and conditioned by pre-existing national and sectoral allegiances (Franklin and Scarrow 1999; Hooghe 2001; Kerr 1973; Scully 2002). Supporting these arguments, national officials attending EU committees tend to evoke national roles more strongly than supranational roles (Egeberg 1999; Egeberg, Schaefer and Trondal 2003; Trondal 2001; Trondal and Veggeland 2003). This is due to the fact that the national government machinery represents their primary institutional affiliation. However, it also reflects the fact that only a segment of the EU committee participants attend the EU committees with a high degree of commitment and intensity (Trondal 2001).

Most of the officials seconded to the Commission are national experts from sectoral ministries or agencies (EFTA Secretariat 2000). These officials have permanent positions within national government institutions that are mostly organized according to sectoral and functional principles. Most seconded Commission personnel are therefore accustomed to the organizing principles of the Commission apparatus. Accordingly, these officials are likely to put particular weight on sectoral identities, considerations and interests. Together, the above arguments suggest that officials seconded to the European Commission are likely to enact a mix of national and sectoral allegiances.

However, Shore (2000: 131) observes that an *esprit de corps* and a 'community method' emerge among new recruits to the permanent staff of the Commission. Similarly, some national officials who attend EU committees tend to evoke supranational loyalties – especially among those who are based at the Permanent Representations in Brussels (Lewis 2000; Egeberg, Schaefer and Trondal 2003). Similar observations are likely in the case of seconded Commission personnel, because these officials are affiliated to the Commission for longer periods of time than the EU committee participants. Seconded personnel are also likely to be involved in the social milieu within the Commission services more extensively than the EU committee participants. Moreover, studies indicate that seconded officials retain fairly weak formal and informal ties to their national employer while serving in the Commission (CLENAD 2003: 12 and 21; Statskontoret 2001: 17 and 34). According to CLENAD (2003: 21), 57 per cent of the 230 seconded officials studied report that they receive insufficient communication from the home organization/employer on relevant home issues and developments. Together, these factors render it likely that seconded Commission personnel evoke supranational identifications more strongly than national officials who participate in EU committees.

Re-socialization in the EU is likely to happen mostly among those with long term careers attached to the EU institutions (although see Franklin and Scarrow 1999). This is the case more at the bureaucratic level among Commission civil servants than among the commissioners (Lewis 2000; Smith 2003: 142). Seconded officials on long term contracts are likely to become re-socialized into supranational actors more strongly than officials on short term contracts. Acknowledging this, the Commission argues that secondment contracts 'can be so short that they sometimes make it difficult to incorporate the expert effectively into a department or for them to adapt to the working environment in the Commission' (European Commission 1999: 63). Seconded personnel are also de-coupled in time and space from domestic institutions and decision-processes, providing circumstances under which additional roles and identities are more easily evoked (Egeberg 1999: 461). In the EFTA survey the potential conflict between national and supranational loyalties was acknowledged (EFTA Secretariat 2000: 4). This conflict was reinforced by the fact that seconded officials had little contact with their domestic constituencies.

The potential for being affected by institutional dynamics relates to the duration and intensity of exposure towards certain organizational structures (Checkel 2001a; Risse and Sikkink 1999). The potential for being socialized and re-socialized increases with protracted memberships within organizations (Berger and Luckmann 1966; Checkel 2001b: 26). This general argument rests on socialization theory that emphasizes a positive relationship between the intensity of participation within a collective group and the extent to which members of this group take the world for granted (Meyer and Rowan 1991), become victims of 'group think' (Janis 1982), or develop particular 'community methods' (Lewis 2000). Socialization is seen as a dynamic process whereby actors come to internalize the norms, rules and interests of their government institution and task roles. Socialization processes are uni-directional in the sense that the 'socializator' educates, indoctrinates, teaches or diffuses his norms and ideas to the 'socializee'. The potential for socialization to occur is assumed positively related to the duration and the intensity of interaction amongst the organizational members (Berger and Luckmann 1966: 150; Kerr 1973; Pendergast 1976).

According to Ernst Haas (1958), participants become 'locked in' and socialized by the sheer intensity of interaction. Similarly, present neo-functionalist scholarship assumes that the emergence of supranational allegiances is 'a function of the *duration* of the socialisation impact' (Niemann 1998: 437 – emphasis added). 'The relative intensity of transnational activity . . . broadly determines variations [in supra-national-ism]' (Stone Sweet and Sandholtz 1998: 4). According to Deutsch, 'common identities are the product of intensive transactions and communications' (quoted in Rosamond 2000: 46). Accordingly, national civil servants on secondment in the European Commission are likely to identify with EU institutions due to 'daily reinforcement' and intensive exposure towards information, stimuli and decision premises at the EU level.

Most Commission officials have long working days. According to the EFTA Secretariat study (2000: 1–3), 'all 18 EFTA secondments confirmed that they were involved in the work of their respective unit in the same manner as their colleagues from the Member States'. They interacted often with officials from other nationalities, experienced 'cultural differences with regard to working habits' and applied 'Euro-speak' (EFTA Secretariat 2000). According to Shore (2000) 'Euro-jargon' and 'Commission-speak' characterize the working language used by most Commission officials. Over time, seconded officials are likely to adapt to the same set of grammar and semantics as permanent Commission officials. 'Euro-language' may represent an identity-mark that establishes buffers towards the 'others' and underscores shared practices among themselves (Bellier 1997: 95). A shared vocabulary contributes to bind actors together and assist in the construction of a distinct European elite (Christiansen, Jørgensen and Wiener 2001: 15).

As a consequence of interacting frequently with fellow colleagues within the European Commission, seconded civil servants are likely to take on supranational identifications (H3) (Christiansen 2001). However, some seconded officials also have prior experiences from international organizations, trans-governmental committees and boards, and from the permanent representations in Brussels. Moreover, some seconded officials are pre-socialized through their educational background (e.g. the *College of Europe* in Bruges), or through a multi-national family background. Suggestively, prior international experiences are conducive to supranationalism (H4). Hence, seconded personnel may have constructed supranational loyalties prior to entering the European Commission. According to Page (1997: 60), seconded officials generally have contacts with the Commission prior to entering it. Frequently, they 'indicate a wish to spend three years in Brussels' (Page 1997: 60). This indicates that supranational identities may reflect processes of pre-socialization as much as processes of re-socialization (cf. the self-selection argument (Kerr 1973: 76–77)). However, studies of EU committees indicate that supranational allegiances reflect processes of re-socialization more than processes of pre-socialization (Trondal 2002), even if such conclusions are plagued with methodological difficulties of causality. Further empirical studies are warranted to 'verify' the different pathways to supranationalism among permanent and temporary EU decision-makers.

Finally, supranational allegiances may reflect the social milieu embedding seconded personnel while staying in Brussels (H5). The physical symbols and artefacts dominating the Commission buildings remind the seconded staff of their current supranational embeddedness. The blue flag with the golden stars in the reception area, in the corridors of the Commission buildings and in the meeting rooms constantly remind the officials of their current 'European' affiliation. Seconded personnel live in exile in Brussels, talk several non-native languages, often applying 'Euro-talk' or 'Commission-speak', socialize with other nationalities, and live in 'EU-ghettos' in Brussels. Commission bureaucrats and the Belgian population of Brussels 'constitute two parallel social universes' (Abélès, Bellier and McDonald 1993: 26). Hence, the social environments surrounding seconded officials may be conducive to the evocation of supranational identities. However, many Commission officials also socialize with colleagues of the same nationality and take weekends off in their home country (Stevens and Stevens 2001: 132). Hence, they are reminded of their national origins on a daily or weekly basis. However, a high level of cross-border mobility may also be conducive to the construction of supranational identities and roles. Hence, a blend of national and supranational identities and roles is likely to be evoked by seconded Commission personnel.

Conclusion

Few studies have empirically penetrated the inner life of the European Commission. The dynamics that govern this supranational executive have attracted minor scholarly attention. The current study had a dual goal: first, to identify the political nature of the European Commission at the bureaucratic level of DGs and units. We asked, under what conditions are Commission officials likely to construct or activate supranational roles, identities and loyalties? Second, determining the political nature of the European Commission is warranted when studying system integration across levels of governance. Arguably, studying the political dynamics of the parallel administration of the Commission is important for understanding system integration in Europe.

Going beyond a *sui generis* view of the Commission, the current study applies institutional arguments to account for the transformative power of the European Commission. According to the institutional approaches outlined above, organizational members often have multiple institutional affiliations that generate multiple cues for action and role enactment. Seconded personnel to the European Commission have two major institutional affiliations: the national central administrative system and the European Commission. The former is considered primary to these officials, even after being hired on fixed term contracts within the Commission (H1). Commission DGs are deemed secondary to most seconded personnel, however, more among newcomers than among senior secondments.

Hence, national and sectoral allegiances are likely to exceed supranational allegiances amongst the vast majority of seconded personnel.

However, under certain conditions seconded personnel are likely to evoke supranational allegiances more vigorously. This is the case among officials employed within national ministries and agencies which are organized according to a sectoral principle (H2), officials on long term contracts with the Commission (H3), officials who have prior socialization experiences from international organizations and universities (H4), who interact intensively with officials from several other nationalities, who apply 'Commission-speak', and who live in typical 'EU-ghettos' in Brussels (H5).

The hypotheses advocated in this chapter are not exhaustive, only suggestive. Making explicit references to operational dimensions are vital in order to determine the conditions under which institutions matter generally, and in order to identify the conditions under which the political dynamics of the European Commission contribute to system integration and transformation in particular. Further empirical studies, however, are needed to test the conditional validity of the hypotheses developed here.

Notes

1 The financial support of the ARENA programme (The Norwegian Research Council), Agder University College and 'Sørlandets kompetansefond' is gratefully acknowledged. Earlier versions of this chapter have been presented at the ECPR Joint Sessions of Workshops in Grenoble 2001, at a publishing seminar at ARENA in 2001 and at the Biennial EUSA conference in Nashville 2003. Thanks to the participants who attended these seminars. Special thanks go to Jeffrey T. Checkel, Thomas Christiansen, Michelle Cini, Helen Drake, Tore Grønningsæter, Virginie Guiraudon, Johan P. Olsen, Cécile Robert, Helene Sjursen, Andy Smith and Ulf Sverdrup.
2 Seconded personnel are also *parachuted* into top positions of the Commission (A1 and A2 positions). Reflecting both individual aspirations, a need for technical expertise from outside the Commission, informal national quota systems, as well as new states joining the EU, 'nearly half of senior appointments [in the Commission] are recruited through *parachutage*' (Hooghe 1999: 399 – original emphasis). The vast majority of those parachuted to the Commission are national civil servants (Page 1997: 85).

5 The invention of a Directorate General for development (1958–1975)

Véronique Dimier

Ideas which are found in some (African) circles on the relationships between Europe and Africa are often basic. The creation of a Euro-Africa, in the spirit of the Treaty of Rome, must be backed by political action and day to day propaganda. It is a long term task, an urgent one. Indeed, Europe and the Association of overseas territories will only be built through an act of faith which needs to be backed up by reason.

(Chauler 1958: 2472)

This article will analyse this propaganda as a form of political action designed from 1958 by the Directorate General responsible for the 'Association' (development policy) with African countries: the DG VIII. Its main objective was to enhance the legitimacy of the European Community in what was soon to become its first international mission. It was also part of the larger process of the institutionalization of DG VIII (Dimier 2002, 2003a, b, c). 'Institutionalization' refers to the process whereby an organization – and the officials who operate therein – develops its own identity or culture (Selznick 1957). The success of that institutionalization much depended on the capacity of DG VIII to identify itself with a mission, specific values and principles, but also to convince the actors it had to deal with of the benefits and necessity of that mission, in sum to make it acceptable in order to gain some legitimacy. This legitimacy can be referred to as the process by which an institution becomes respected, 'desirable, proper, or appropriate within some socially constructed system of norms, values, beliefs and definitions' (Suchman 1995: 574). The problem concerning DG VIII is that its mission, as formulated in 1958, became less and less desirable for the world in which it was acting.

As defined in the Treaty of Rome, the Association included trade agreements and foreign aid to be channelled through a European Development Fund supervised by the European Commission, more precisely the Directorate General VIII. At first, it only concerned countries which had 'specific' links with member states, e.g. African territories which were still colonies in 1958. Soon after decolonization in the 1960s, this 'Association' led to several conventions (in particular the Yaoundé and Lomé Conventions) with the newly independent African states. Because this policy had been imposed by France during the negotiation of the Treaty of Rome, conceptualized in the typical French colonial word, 'Association', and copied on its colonial policy (Dimier 2001), and at a time when everything colonial became politically incorrect, it did not have much legitimacy for other member states (Belgium excepted) and the African territories concerned. Germany and the Netherlands only accepted the financial 'burden' because France made it a necessary condition for signing the Treaty. Located in Rue du Marais in the popular quarter of Brussels, DG VIII was not considered a serious matter by other members of the Commission which used to disqualify it as the DG responsible for 'dealing with Negro kings'. The Negro kings themselves were quite uncomfortable with an Association which had been decided on by France without their ever having been consulted and which was considered by many of them as a new kind of colonialism. Even those who had fought for the creation of a kind of 'Euro-Africa' such as Leopold Senghor, Senegal's representative to the French National Assembly, had warned that 'we may agree in this marriage of convenience to be the servants who carry the veil of the bride, but we do not want to be the wedding gift' (Senghor 1953: 124). Last but not least, some parts of the 'Association' policy were considered by other international actors (the GATT, the United Kingdom and the USA) to be the extension of the old colonial preference and in conflict with general trade agreements.

Given this hostile environment, the main task of DG VIII during the first years of its existence (1958–1970) was to 'sell' the Association in order to gain some legitimacy for its mission both outside and within the European institutions; in short, to transform what was soon to be considered as the 'mere perpetuation of a historical context' into a *'grande oeuvre de solidarité'*. This necessity was clearly recognized by the European Assembly after one of its delegation's trips to Africa: 'the delegation has remarked during its trip that the idea of Association was fought against by propaganda and actions coming from different sides. The Association will be able to resist these attacks and opposition only if positive action is organised by those who have competence to give life to the Treaty'.[1] These 'positive actions' also came to be referred to as 'propaganda', a word that no one would dare use nowadays.

Using propaganda proved to be a difficult political task, a real magic trick, especially as the magicians who handled it were former French colonial officials who had played a major role in the institutionalization of the DG by infusing it with their colonial methods (Dimier 2002, 2003a, b, c). The 'potion' used included several artefacts, especially colonial ones: besides the usual advertising instruments, it was based on a well-organized dramatization of power, ritualized touring, official visits and ceremony, protocols similar to those used by the French Republic or the English

Monarchy to build their legitimacy and reinforce their political order (Hobsbawm 1983; Deremez, Ihl and Sabatier 1998; Déloye, Haroche and Ihl 1996).

Based on archives and interviews,[2] this article will focus precisely on this set of political ceremonies as part of the efforts of the early European Community to gain legitimacy. Following the main hypothesis of this book, it shows how important this process was for the new EC political project in order to gain ground amongst the member states and the African states, and all of this at a time when that order was still to be built, when power relations between those states and the diverse institutions within the EC were not yet established. DG VIII is a very interesting case in that it seems to constitute a caricature of what may have happened in the European Commission as a whole. Indeed, because of its contested mission, its place as an institution within the European Commission was very weak, its quest for legitimacy all the stronger, and the fervour of its top civil servants in their 'propaganda' all the more obvious. Following the approach developed in this book, we will focus on senior civil servants as political actors in their dealings with other political officials in Africa and in Europe. In particular, their networks and strategies will be examined. Our first argument will be that this strategy was mainly designed for the elite, whether European or African. The idea was to reach a larger public, a kind of indirect method for legitimacy which very quickly reached its limits. Indeed, it seems that despite its ambition, the propaganda of DG VIII, as well as that of the Euro-African project it had to sell, remained a small family business. Our second argument is concerned with the key to the success of DG VIII in its propaganda with respect to African elites. The hypothesis defended here is that in order to be efficient, a set of political ceremonies must correspond to the expectations and political culture of the public to which it is addressed. Since the EC political order was multi-national and the mission of DG VIII international, its strategies had to be adapted to a very diverse political public.

In charting the attempts by DG VIII at coping with diversity, this chapter deals separately with the strategies used by the two sides of the family (African and European). It begins with the instruments designed for those associated territories which were quite reluctant in accepting what was presented to the world as the new 'European burden' in Africa. We will see how it allowed DG VIII to test methods and tools which were also to be used in Europe. Indeed, in the second part, we will focus on the huge efforts deployed by DG VIII to convince other member states and other parts of the Commission that 'Africa could help to build Europe'.

Africa as a 'European burden'

Convincing African leaders of the benefits of the 'Association' was the most urgent task because in 1958–1959 many of their countries were clearly verging on independence. Consequently, 'the Association' could no longer proceed without their consent. The personal networks and colonial experience of the main leaders of DG VIII were to be of great importance here. They played on references that were known by their African friends. They transferred back to Europe their method of touring and negotiating with the African elite. Indeed, the irony of this episode is that this colonial 'art' was used in order to get rid of any remaining prejudice against the colonial aspects of EC development policy.

The need for such an action was very quickly recognized. As the French ambassador in Belgium, M. Bousquet, remarked:

> the Commission is determined to refute any accusation of neo-colonialism ... We have to fight misunderstandings on this point, and make an effort on information, especially as regards the overseas territories associated to the Common Market, in order to clearly specify the intentions of the Community, which are peaceful and positive.
>
> (A.M.A.E., Box 721)

This was recognized by other commentators as well:

> Here lies the necessity for a vast action of contact and information on one side, and of consultation of the opinions and interests of the Africans on the other side. All means have to be used to inform the Africans, meet their prejudice and obtain their adhesion. Constant links have to be established between Europe and Africa, through contacts with politicians, the media and the universities. Trips and missions of officials and technicians, information meetings, conferences and organisation of a large diffusion of information are means to reach that objective: inform and convince our interlocutor of the usefulness of a dialogue, then of an agreement and cooperation.
>
> (*Marché Tropicaux* 1958: 2473)

This speech was made during a conference on Euro-Africa (The Gand International Fair) where two major officials of DG VIII were present.

As early as 1958, several 'information-seeking' delegations led either by the Director General of DG VIII, Helmuth Allardt, or the first commissioner in charge of the Association, Robert Lemaignen, went on tour in Africa. Following his trip and his disillusions, the latter promised that a visit by the officials of the Commission would be organized at least every two months. From that time on, touring in Africa became a ritual for the Commissioner in charge of Development and Directors General of DG VIII. Each trip was organized around visits to the 'most characteristic parts of Africa', inspections of projects funded by the Commission, official meetings and cocktail parties with African ministers.[3] Inauguration of

projects became the highlight of these visits and a way for DG VIII to celebrate its work in front of, and with the applause of, the African population. This may also be one of the reasons why huge and prestigious
projects were encouraged at that time by members of DG VIII. As one ex-
official put it to me: 'at least we were visible'. Henri Rochereau (commissioner for development 1963–1969) apparently spent his entire tenure in
the Commission going into the bush, the only way to get 'practical knowledge of the local reality' (A.C.E., Bac 25/1980/1344 (1)). Heinrich
Hendus, the Director General from 1960, also indulged in several of these
trips, in order 'to develop personal contacts with the population' (A.C.E.,
Bac 25/1980/1344 (2)).

In the opposite direction, invitations to Brussels for African heads of
state or their ambassadors also became common. Very early on it was
decided by the Commission that 'representatives of administrations, trade
unions and Parliaments would be regularly invited to visit the six states of
the EC and to discuss with the European states and institutions about the
consequences of the Euro-African relationships' (A.M.A.E, Box 721).
Following the guidelines set by the Director General, H. Allardt, these
'informative' visits were:

> aimed at informing members of the associated countries and at
> getting them acquainted with the ideas and the work of European
> institutions and organisations. In order to reach that objective, these
> members need to have a deeper knowledge of Europe in general and
> of the Six in particular as well as of their achievements in every field,
> their internal cooperation and their desire for a real and moral co-
> operation with the associated countries.
>
> (A.C.E., Bac 25/1980/1332 (1))

However, participants had to be chosen with care:

> In order to have concrete results, we need to select Africans who,
> once back in their home country, will make the most of the idea of co-
> operation between the Associated states and the Six. Besides, the
> people chosen should constitute in their countries, a wide range of
> specialists in political, economic and social problems created by the
> Association.
>
> (A.C.E., Bac 25/1980/1332 (1))

It was thought that 'with their help, a network of correspondents could be
established in the associated countries. They could be used as contacts, as
a means for mutual information, as centres of distribution of documentation and information about the evolution of the EC and as centres of
diffusion for the ideas of the Association in general' (A.C.E., Bac
25/1980/1332 (1)). Not only representatives of the African government,

but also representatives of the countries at large (from trade unions, the private sector etc.) had to be selected. In any case, in their home country they 'had to have' some responsibility, authority and enough contacts to exert influence in the economic, political, social and cultural fields (A.C.E., Bac 25/1980/1332 (2)). The idea was clearly to use them as potential relays and intermediaries to reach a larger audience; what is known as 'public opinion'.

For the first of these trips in March 1959, it was thought necessary to invite around 20 important African politicians. They were to be received by the Commission and, together with some EC ministers, would take part in a conference on Africa and Europe organized in Brussels before embarking upon a two week trip around the EC countries where they would be exposed to 'the greatest social and economic achievements' of the West (the Ruhr, universities, polders, Renault's plants, large dams, co-operatives, chambers of commerce, etc.). Given the 'importance of that first trip', tremendous energy was spent by DG VIII and especially by John Van der Lee, the head of the Direction A (Affaires Générales), to organize this event. Every single detail, from collecting the flags of the African states approaching independence, to preparing officials' cars, telephone facilities and security was arranged by Van der Lee himself. As the practical organization of the conference was sub-contracted to some associations, and 'as any confusion in the heads of the African visitors had to be avoided', it was made clear in every official statement that 'DG VIII was the sole initiator' of this event (A.C.E., Bac 25/1980/1332 (3)). The trip eventually took place from 2 to 24 March 1959 with 25 African officials, most of them ministers, (amongst others; Mamadou Dia, Prime Ministre of Sénégal; Apithy, Prime Ministre of Dahomey) who visited France, Italy, and Belgium. During this trip they were taken to see, 'the way African products were transformed in Nestlé factories' (A.C.E., Bac 25/1980/1333 (1)) and given the Pope's blessing in Rome. Apparently the trip had the intended results: most of the visitors returned home 'interested, impressed and reassured as to the future of the Association' (A.C.E., Bac 25/1980/1333 (2)), as to the 'desire of co-operation which unifies African and European peoples. Great hopes can be envisaged. The tasks which await us are huge but exalting. We will cope with them together, in the same enthusiasm and the same spirit we will determinedly ensure the promotion of HUMAN BEINGS' (A.C.E., Bac 25/1980/1333 (3)). 'The memory of this trip will remain in my head for a long time ... I am convinced that our various discussions have paved the way for the beginning of a lasting agreement for the sake of our peoples' (A.C.E., Bac 25/1980/1333 (4)). The only reproach made by the latter was that the trip 'was much too short'.

Subsequently, such trips were renewed every year, but became increasingly designed for students or young civil servants, seen by the DG VIII as their future 'interlocutors' and collaborators, and whose opinion about the Association was seen as so important. Young African journalists were especially welcome. Internships for African top civil servants were also organized by the European Commission with the clear objective of socializing them into adopting EC principles, or at least informing them of the diverse opportunities offered by the Association.

Over and above these specific arrangements, many individual visitors or official representatives from the African States came to Brussels to meet different members of DG VIII. Given the flow of official visitors, a specific protocol had to be written down to receive them and rituals were set up which were copied on those used by the French President. Such contacts were made easier by the fact that R. Lemaignen, a former businessman in Africa and the most important representative of DG VIII, was also a former French colonial administrator who knew many African heads of state or their representatives personally, some of them being close friends. The main leader in the institutionalization of DG VIII, Jacques Ferrandi, was Lemaignen's *chef de cabinet* from 1956–1962, before becoming Director of the European Development Fund (1963–1975). Ferrandi had formerly been Director General of the *Afrique Occidentale Française's* Economic Service, and as such had been responsible for implementing the first French development projects in West Africa. In this capacity, he had worked in close collaboration with those who became the leaders of the newly independent states and had 'gained their respect and esteem' (Marchés Coloniaux 1963: 1234) and we may add, their friendship. According to Jean Chapperon, another former French colonial administrator in Africa who later became *chef de cabinet* of Henri Rochereau and Jean François Deniau (the French commissioners in charge of the Association from 1962 to 1973), no African representatives, from Bokassa to Senghor, would come to Brussels without being personally invited to dinner by J. Ferrandi. This is confirmed by the programmes of the visits to be found in the archives of the Commission. This is also evidenced today by the range of photographs of African heads of state on the wall of Ferrandi's villa, all signed 'to my dear friend J. Ferrandi', or by the ivory tusk given him by Bokassa which apparently was as long as the one he had given Charles de Gaulle, or the 'Ivoirien knighthood' granted by the President of the Ivory Coast.

Within DG VIII, the official responsible for the information services was Pierre Cros, a seconded civil servant from DG X (Information) and yet another former colonial administrator in Africa. In the 1950s, he had been seconded to the French parliament by the French colonial Ministry and, in this capacity, had become acquainted with many African representatives in the French National Assembly. Most of the time, commissioners or Director Generals were guided in their African tours by a former colonial administrator working in DG VIII. As a method drawn from colonial experience, these personal relationships gave DG VIII a specific identity (Dimier 2003a, b, c) which was clearly recognized outside, and summarized in the expression: 'the DG dealing with Negro kings'.

Later on (Yaoundé I, 1962), the setting up of common consultative institutions made up of African and European representatives and the creation of delegates of the European Commission in each African state made these contacts more institutionalized, but not less personal. The renewal of each convention (Yaoundé, then Lomé) also became an opportunity for officials of the member states and the associated states to meet, celebrate the greatness of the Association, this 'act of friendship and co-operation, through specific ceremonies (Le Naëlou 1995). Large conferences such as 'The Economic Conference of the French Economic and Financial Zone' (Marseille 1959) were presided over by R. Lemaignen and other DG VIII officials. A useful relay was also found in the media. The European Commission did not have its own journals before the 1970s. But in the former French Empire its action was popularized and publicized by a French journal specialized in colonial economics which was reputedly read by the African elite as well as by French business circles and whose director was a close friend of J. Ferrandi's: *Marchés Coloniaux du Monde* (renamed after decolonization, *Marchés Tropicaux*). The review of the Journal regularly gave full records of the different projects financed by the European Development Fund and had a specific page on the European Community and Association called '*courrier de Bruxelles*' or '*A la Communauté Européenne*'. Indeed, following a trip to Africa by a delegation from the European Assembly in 1959, a special issue (18th December 1959) on the Association policy was published. Featuring an introduction by R. Lemaignen himself, the issue was clearly meant 'to contribute to the mutual information of African and European'. Regular press conferences by Ferrandi or Lemaignen were reproduced, and their speeches in the European Assembly and their trips or actions commented upon because it was recognized that 'a conference by R. Lemaignen is always an event which has some echoes in Africa' (*Marchés Tropicaux* 1961: 255).

In these conferences and speeches, the Association came to be presented by H. Rochereau as 'a unique phenomenon in the world', a 'rare example of success, perhaps even the only one amongst European common policies' (*Marchés Tropicaux* 1969: 175). As J. Ferrandi put it: the specificity of the Association 'was its innovative aspect and its challenge to the past', ie. the colonial past (Ferrandi 1973: 230). The idea was repeated over and over again and in the end seems to have been convincing enough to be repeated by African representatives themselves. The campaign was apparently successful since all African states, with the exception of French Guyana, agreed in 1961 to renegotiate their association with the EC. At least, it succeeded in making them aware of the material benefits they could gain from such a linkage. For the actors involved it was easy to conclude, as J. Van der Lee did in 1962, that: 'this highly established relationship has greatly contributed to mutual understanding between the associated and the Six' (A.C.E., Bac 79/182/4). By 'associated', however, it seemed to mean mainly the elite of the African states. Speeches and attempts at information were of course addressed to 'African public opinion' at large. Indeed, to measure the efficiency of its policy in that matter, to test the knowledge that 'common' people in Africa may have about the Association, DG VIII even commissioned a survey from IFOP (Institut Français d'Opinion Publique).[4] However, despite reassuring figures, as P. Cros recognized in 1970, this information scarcely reached the population. The African elites and governments often played the role of a screen, if not that of a censor (A.C.E., Bac 25/1980/1325). But this conclusion could also be extended to Europe itself.

Africa as a means of helping to build Europe

Indeed, efforts by the European Commission to make the Association policy more acceptable to member states and public opinion other than that of France and Belgium ran up against similar difficulties. The strategy used was the same as in Africa: personal networks and touring, mostly designed to please a certain elite. The discourse and the cultural references used had to be adapted since the aim was less to show what Europe could give to Africa, but what Africa could give to Europe.

Ironically, J. Van der Lee, the man who became the main propagandist for the Association in Europe came from the EC country which was the main opponent to that policy: the Netherlands. But was this pure chance? As a top civil servant trained in Amsterdam, Paris (Sorbonne) and Cambridge, Van der Lee participated in the negotiation of the Treaty of Rome and in 1958 was chosen as *chef de cabinet* by Sicco Leenderdt Mansholt, Vice-President of the Commission. In 1959, he was then appointed head of the Direction A (Affaires Générales) of the DG VIII and was therefore responsible for dealing with external relations.

From 1959, J. Van der Lee began touring EC countries, and even beyond, to 'hostile' Great Britain, in order to combat any criticism against the EC's 'neo-colonialism'. He would speak in any conference or seminar where the Association policy could be presented. Other members of DG VIII were encouraged, whenever they could, to advertise the European Development Fund. The most important officials of DG VIII, especially J. Ferrandi, R. Lemaignen, H. Rochereau (commissioners for development) and the new Director General from 1961, H. Hendus, also toured European capitals (German and Dutch in particular), especially in 1961–1968 when the conventions with the associated states had to be renewed and the intentions of the more reluctant member states had to be gauged. Visits to Brussels by groups of students, academics, technicians from EC member states, also became common and were always accompanied by discussions or seminars organized by DG VIII. The flow of visits was such that eventually it became difficult to find officials from DG VIII available to give the talks. Given the rising numbers of invitations, the Director General H. Allardt also insisted as soon as 1959 that talks from DG VIII officials 'should be coordinated and reflect a unique policy', and so had to be approved by him or the commissioner, which in fact came to be the general rule (A.C.E., Bac 25/1980/1546).

Each of these trips or visits became an opportunity to reaffirm how much the Association contributed to the 'external influence' of the European Community, how much the newly independent African states 'appreciated' and were thankful for EC financial help. Sometimes films were arranged which showed the implementation or results of the projects financed by the European Development Fund. To solve the German 'dissatisfaction' and the Dutch 'hesitations', every tool was used to demonstrate that 'the Association was one of the most favourable means, even though the least expected one, for reinforcing the European spirit ... Africa must help to build Europe' (A.C.E., Bac 25/1980/1323). The public addressed through these talks was very diverse but consisted mainly of chambers of commerce, academics, students, youth organizations, members of parliaments, business circles, technicians, and top civil servants of the ministries concerned. In sum, the target was groups (be they private or public) which might have an interest in Africa and could put pressure on their home government for a more active development policy. These efforts seem to have been successful at least for the elite directly concerned by the Association. Following his trip to The Hague in June 1961, where he met several Dutch officials concerned with the renewal of the Association agreement, R. Lemaignen came back satisfied with 'the evolution of the position of the Dutch government towards the Association' (A.C.E., Bac 25/1980/1376). This may explain why the renewal of the Association in 1961 and later in 1968 (Yaoundé I and II Conventions) was accepted by the reluctant member states with much less criticism. It is also worth remembering that the issue became so important as to be one of the main elements in the discussion concerning Britain's entry into the EC.

However, DG VIII's plan to reach public opinion at large through these specific elites quickly reached its limits. This was clearly recognized by André Auclert, J. Ferrandi's assistant, himself a former French colonial administrator:

> European public opinion, although informed about the gradual construction of a common market which has an impact on the main aspects of its daily life, ignores almost completely that, since her birth, Europe has kept specific relationships with more than thirty developing countries, amongst which eighteen independent states. In Paris, Bonn, or Rome you would surprise people in the street, but also professors and politicians, if you asked them to enumerate the eighteen independent states associated to the European Community.
>
> (A.C.E., Bac 25/1980/1324)

Hence, it was considered that more efforts had to be made through the media to reach the masses: speeches by officials to specific audiences, press conferences came to be organized. For example, in Hamburg in November 1961 the main German newspapers (especially those specialized in Africa), as well as TV and radio, arrived to listen to J. Van der Lee and 'gave the conference a great deal of publicity' (A.C.E., Bac 79/182/4). Contacts with radio stations were fostered. Events, like the signature of financial conventions for development projects by the commissioners and the representatives of the African states, were good opportunities to mobilize the press. Tours in Africa were also organized for journalists of different EC countries, with the clear aim of 'getting them involved in informing not only the specialized circles but also – and maybe especially – public opinion' (A.C.E., Bac 25/1980/1330).

Last but not least, specific tricks were devised by DG VIII officials to arouse the interest of colleagues within the other Directorate Generals or other commissioners. The European Commission being a collegial body, their support was essential for any decision to be taken. The solution was found in the organization of tours and safaris in the African bush, the only way to allow them to 'have a precise view of the day to day reality in the associated states, and of the complex and varied problems of their social and economic development', to 'show them our action' (A.C.E., Bac 25/1980/1422 (1)). As the *chef de cabinet* of J.D. Deniau and H. Rochereau (J. Chapperon) explained:

> In order to have a proposal accepted by the entire Commission, we needed to have the Commissioner for Agriculture on our side. We decided to take him on a grand tour in Africa. I came with him and served as a guide. He came back totally convinced by the greatness of our task and of course voted with us.
>
> (Interview, 1999)

The same could be said for the then President of the Commission, Jean Rey: 'I spent the entire trip explaining to him that there were only two common policies and only one foreign common policy, the Association. I succeeded in convincing him'. Given the importance attached to these trips, preparation for African tours became a full-time occupation for DG VIII: finding a development project for the commissioner to inaugurate became an absolute necessity. For example, in one of his letters, J. Chapperon asked H. Hendus to see to it that the inaugurations of development projects in the three African countries visited by J. Rey should be delayed for the occasion (A.C.E., Bac 25/1980/1389). These inaugurations became a way to convince the visitor, as much as the African populations, of the greatness of the European task in Africa. Precise documentation on the economic, social and political situation of these countries, of the projects implemented etc. had to be prepared for the commissioner with, if possible, positive quotations from African politicians about the Association. Receptions for former African *stagiaires* of the countries visited were also organized. The results of such actions seem to have been positive. For example, a note reporting on A. Sassen's trip in 1968, remarked that 'the many interviews and visits to the projects had convinced him' of the importance of the European Development Fund for those countries (A.C.E., Bac 25/1980/1422 (2)). The logical consequence of this tropical frenzy, what R. Lemaignen called 'a real working tool',[5] can also be measured financially: DG VIII came to draw for itself the main part of the funding reserved for the travel expenses of the officials of the Commission.

Conclusion

This amount of money shows the utmost importance granted to artefacts, ceremonies and other modes of dramatization in the strategies used by DG VIII to enhance its legitimacy. In this sense, it was not so different from any national institution. Our main argument in this article has been that the adaptation of this strategy to the public it tried to reach, along with the personal relationships of the officials of DG VIII with the African and European elite, account in part for its success with respect to those elites. In line with the main theme of this book, it shows how important the political role of the top civil servants of DG VIII was in their dealings with African and European political officials and in their contribution to the construction of a new political order whose ambition was also to be international.

However, two questions remain which cannot be dealt with at length here. The first concerns the specificity of the strategy used by DG VIII compared to other parts of the Commission. Research on the institutionalization of DG Culture (Ludlow 1998; Shore 2000) suggests that the example of DG VIII is far from being an isolated case. More generally, the growing irritation of Charles de Gaulle with regard to the protocol used by Walter Hallstein, President of the Commission, and of its administration highlights the sensitivities this form of dramatization can provoke (de Gaulle 1970, T 1: 195). Given that de Gaulle considered protocol to be the 'expression of order in the French Republic' (quoted in Deremez, Ihl and Sabatier 1998: 11), he feared that a European protocol would build up a superior political order and the emergence within the EC bureaucracy of new political actors.

The other question concerns the efficiency of the propaganda launched by DG VIII with respect to 'public opinion'. As this chapter has suggested, the effect of this administration's 'indirect strategy' was not what had been expected. Based on a survey of more than 200 practitioners, a report written 30 years later under the supervision of the European Parliament recognized that despite the intensive information campaign of

DG VIII, African actors – not to mention the population – knew little about European development policy (Calame 1999: 18). This policy is still described as 'clandestine and known only by the small number of actors (administrations, NGOs, enterprises, consultants) who know how to draw the most they can from that money' (Calame 1999: 38).

We will conclude on this point by underlining the similarity between this strategy and that used by the French colonial administrators to build up their legitimacy. Through what was then called Indirect Rule – specific and personal relationships with the African chiefs who supposedly had the confidence of, and authority over, the African peoples – French colonial civil servants in Africa had attempted to get their policy accepted by those they had colonized (Dimier 1998). In reality, because it remained 'a small family business', the Association, just like Indirect Rule, never succeeded in developing the legitimacy necessary for its survival.

Notes

1 See Report by the European Assembly, document no. 67, October 1959.
2 This paper is drawn from a research project started in 1999 on the 'institutional-ization and bureaucratization of the European Commission: the case of the DG VIII, 1958–2000', financed by Oxford University (St Anthony's College) and the European Commission (Marie Curie, EURSSIF programme, European Institute, Florence). It is based on the archives of the DG VIII and of the French Ministry of Foreign Affairs, as well as 30 interviews with former officials of the DG VIII.
3 A.C.E., Bac 25/1980/1344, letter from H. Hendus to H. Rochereau, 25 June 1967, sending him the programme of his visit to Chad; letter from H. Hendus to the Director General in charge of the administration, 27 January 1967, asking him for 2,000 Belgium francs to organize a cocktail party in Fort Lamy for African politicians and officials. Note on his mission to Chad by H. Hendus, 2 March 1967.
4 A.C.E., Bac 25/1980/1678, note on the information designed for the EAMA without date and signature. It includes a survey made by IFOP during the year 1964 in several African countries. This survey shows that in Senegal, 33 per cent of people living in Dakar, 29 per cent in other towns and 14 per cent in the countryside had some knowledge of the EC. These figures have to be taken with caution: no indications were given as to the methodology used.
5 A.C.E., Bac 25/1980/36, meeting of the group 8 (DG VIII), 2 October 1958. A.C.E., Bac, 25/1980/1611, Poste 802 (travel expenses) for the year 1967, 7,260,000 *unités de compte* (out of a total of 32,250,000). In comparison, DG I, the other main consumer, accounted for only 4,000,000 *unités de compte*.

6 Institutionalizing public health in the European Commission

The thrills and spills of politicization

Sébastien Guigner

The food safety scandals of the 1990s have partly brought to light the 'ignored history' (Lefèbvre 1999: 16) of EU intervention in health by putting both a political and a media focus on this subject.[1] However, by concentrating on food safety, a large number of Community activities in the health field have been overlooked. Right from its beginnings, the European Community has in fact been involved in health issues. First in the field of health and safety in the work place, then in the pharmaceutical area and the area of health professions and, to a lesser extent, in disease prevention.[2] These first actions were linked to the construction of the common market (Berthod-Wurmser 1994). Towards the end of the 1980s, however, the Community engaged more directly in health matters by establishing public health programmes. The programmes entitled *Europe against Cancer* and *Europe against AIDS*, respectively set up in 1987 and 1991, were established and applied even before the Maastricht Treaty introduced any Community competencies in the field of public health (article 129), or before these were extended by the Amsterdam Treaty (article 152).

However, by provoking a questioning of the Commission's role and its reorganization, the Bovine Spongiform Encephalitis (BSE) crisis emphasized the limits of the institutionalization of public health within the Commission. Indeed, a social space can only be considered to be institutionalized when: 'there exists a widely shared system of rules and procedures to define who actors are, how they make sense of each other's action, and what type of actions are possible' (Stone Sweet, Sandholtz and Fligstein 2001: 12). The institutionalization of a social space therefore appears as 'normal' as it does 'legitimate' to those involved with it (Alink, Boin and T'Hart 2001). Thus, the institutionalization of public health, as for that of many sectors, faces problems of political legitimacy referring both to contestable democratic grounds and to the reluctance of member states to yield control of this sector to the EU. More precisely, intervention by the member states gave rise, in this case, to a restrictive and tardily adopted legal framework. While the Amsterdam Treaty conserved the article 3-o from the Maastricht Treaty which set the Commission the general aim of contributing to the realization of a higher level of health protection, this clause only slightly altered the former article 129 that became article 152. The latter is the only clause which directly refers to public health. Although there have been a few improvements, the Amsterdam Treaty still defines public health in a restrictive manner by enumerating a list of possible actions. Furthermore, the area of application of EU measures has been narrowed and the dispositions set up to prevent the expansion of Community activities are substantial.

Governments pay particular attention to the preservation of their competencies in public health due to the strong legitimizing potential of health, in particular public health, that corresponds to social and public imperatives which legitimize state control. Thus, public health is a significant part of the material and symbolical resources of any government (Fassin 1996). The vigilance of the states against moving public health activities to the Community level is also due to the current orthodox definition of public health which, following the Acheson Committee report on the future of health in the UK, can be considered to be 'the science and art of preventing disease, prolonging life and promoting health through organized efforts of society' (Acheson 1988, quoted in WHO 1997: 67). Public health is therefore not only concerned with the control of transmissible diseases.

Indeed, in the industrialized countries the main health risks are no longer linked to epidemics but rather to socioeconomic effects of development and to behaviour and lifestyle (WHO 1997). In this setting, the 'new public health' emphasizes health promotion rather than disease prevention. Therefore, intersectoriality is one of the characteristics of public health policies. For example, it is impossible to intervene over tobacco, alcohol or food consumption without interfering with agricultural policies. Likewise, the fight against the effects of poverty on health involves actions at the level of social, employment and economic policies. This intersectorial aspect nurtures reticence from the member states to hand over public health competencies to the EU as it could be followed by a functional spillover effect because public health policies 'can be assured only by taking further action, which in turn creates a further condition and need for more action, and so forth' (Lindberg 1963: 10).

In order to get around the constraint imposed by the member states and the challenge of political legitimacy linked to it, the Commission has turned to its usual emancipation strategies such as bench-marking or soft law (Guigner 2001). To make up for deficient political legitimacy, the Commission makes use of other available instruments. Among these, the instrumentalization of technical legitimacy is often mentioned. The capacity of the Commission to mobilize external or internal expertise (Radaelli 1999b) and to depoliticize issues by deploying a technical register (Mazey and Richardson 1996) is sufficient to enable it to legitimize most of its actions. One would therefore expect the EU and the Commission to function in a more technocratic way, where decisions are made based upon their efficiency and scientific arguments, rather than in a political way, where decisions are primarily based on values and electoral arguments (Radaelli 1999a).

Health is indeed an eminently technical field where decisions that are not scientifically sound can, perhaps more than anywhere else, have irreversible consequences for the general public. Scientific argumentation is therefore particularly influential in this sector. This could suggest that in the field of public health the Commission benefits from its capacity to mobilize expertise. However, this is simply not the case. Indeed, this chapter shows that in the sector of public health the Commission has, in spite of its efforts, not yet been able to use the potentially political role of expertise, that is to say exploiting the legitimizing capacity of expert advice, in order to make up for its own lack of political legitimacy. In reality, the institutionalization of the handling of public health by the Commission is confronted with a lack of both political and technical legitimacy, the latter resulting in the existence of competing expertise both within the Commission and outside of it.

In making this argument, this chapter is divided into three parts. The first shows that the legitimacy of the Commission to intervene in the field of public health is challenged within the Commission itself due to the interdependence of health and other sectors which oppose and impose an economic logic and a health logic. In the second part we will see that the use and development of scientific legitimacy in the Commission also suffers from interdependence, or even dependence, that links it to other international organizations also active in the field of public health. If the Commission has tried to surpass these obstacles in different ways, the last part of the chapter puts the effectiveness of such strategies into perspective. Rather paradoxically, due to its lack of legitimacy in the field of public health, the Commission has often in fact been compelled to act from political rather than technical imperatives.

Internal competition: the Commission's expertise versus that of others

Although, following a neo-functionalist logic, the development of economic activities in the Community has favoured the emergence of EU actions on health, this logic also highlights the limits of the institutionalization of this type of task. In order to get out of the situation of domination and exclusion in which they find themselves in relation to the economy, the health units in the Commission use two parallel methods. On one hand they *economicize* health in order to insert it into the EU economic matrix. The current aim is to transform the technical register that links economy and health into a political register, and thereby into an instrument for legitimation. On the other hand, the administrators in charge of health in the Commission try to insert health matters into other policies through involving themselves in a variety of different committees.

Public health subordinated to the economic nature of the European Community

If it is undeniably simplistic to systematically put economic development and health protection up against each other. As the BSE crisis showed with a vengeance, the EU has long prioritized an economic logic little concerned with health consequences. A multitude of other examples show how economic activities promoted by the European Community have also been harmful to the health of European citizens. For example, through the structural funds, the building of road infrastructure has increased intra-community traffic and, as a result, the emission of toxic gases, thereby indirectly degrading the health of European citizens (Guyomard 1995). Certain measures of the Common Agricultural Policy (CAP) also illustrate the contradictions between the economic activity of the Commission and its obligation to protect public health. Thus, alcohol that is commonly considered to be a health threat is seen at the Community level as an agricultural product and its production is therefore subsidized as such. Finally, the frequently used example of tobacco can be mentioned to emphasize the contradictions and priorities of the Commission. Indeed, as the Court of Auditors have highlighted, like alcohol production, the growing of tobacco is subsidized by approximately one billion euros whereas the project *Europe against Cancer* only receives 0.15 per cent of this amount (Rougemont 1999: 69).

Member states protecting their sectoral interests are the most determined opponents of the organs of the Commission that try to make health considerations prevail over economic considerations. However, these organs must also regularly face another actor: the Commission itself. Within this organization, there is thus a considerable imbalance favouring an economic logic over a health logic. Rather than stemming from institutional division, it is the different dynamics of action at play within the Commission that gives it its 'multiorganizational' nature (Cram 1994). More generally, public policy analysis has shown that, seen up close, 'an agency that appears to be a single organization with a single will turns out to be several suborganizations with different wills' (Pressman and Wildavsky 1973: 92). Consequently, 'the DGs have a tendency to want to preserve what they consider to be their own political influence sphere' (Cini 1996b: 460). Conflicts of competence certainly exist, however, the most common problem is due to differences in the political and technical priorities of the DGs. As a result of this, and due to the strong contradiction between the economic logic which dominates the Community and a health logic, the health organs of the Commission are often faced with resistance to their projects from within the Commission: 'Virtually all the

decisions taken by DG SANCO [DG of health and consumer protection]
are contested by DG Enterprise or DG Agriculture' (Interview, DG
SANCO official, March 2001).

Moreover, the difficulties in leading concerted and co-ordinated
actions in the health field are increased by geographical fragmentation on
one hand, with some units in Brussels and others in Luxembourg, and a
fragmentation of health between the different DGs on the other hand.
Indeed, until recently, health services within the Commission were not
specialized and did not have the necessary size to be heard and carry out a
coherent approach to health in the Community.

The economicization of health: adapting health policies to the EU matrix

M. Cini has shown that in the 1980s DG XI ('Environment') had a weak
position compared to the other DGs. This was due not only to its reduced
financial and human resources, but especially to the fact that its priorities
were distant from the main goals of the Commission on improving economic competitiveness. In order to reach its goals, this DG had to fit into
the economic environment surrounding it by proving itself compatible
with the other policies of the Commission. In fact, as A. Héritier explains,
'by linking an issue with another issue which enjoys wide support, or by re-
labeling it, its prospects of being accepted in the political arena may be
improved' (2001: 67). The organs in charge of health within the Commission have found themselves confronted by the same obstacles and power
distribution as those in charge of the environment had done before them.
They have faced them in the same manner, be it in the area of health
systems, health in the work place or, more surprisingly, of public health.

The Commission has no competence to intervene in the organization
of health systems in the different member states. Article 152 of the Amsterdam Treaty clearly condemns any Community intervention in the field.
Yet the Commission regularly addresses this subject in relation to a recurrent idea: 'the economic viability of health systems in the Member States is
threatened, the Community can save them by improving their efficiency'
(for example, European Commission 1997: 5). In this case the *economicization* strategy is very close to soft law, it can even be considered a special
type of soft law. In this specific setting, it is not a question of integrating
the economic environment but of setting the scene for future action. The
significance of these declarations is explicit:

> In any case we do not have any competence in the health area, so
> when we talk about health systems it is just a way to get noticed ...
> We use the financial crisis angle because it is what they are worried
> about.

(Interview, DG SANCO official, March 2001)

The civil servants in charge of health and safety in the work place have a different way of using *economicization*. The issue here is no longer to increase competencies but, more timidly, to use those that already exist without being confronted with the opposition of an 'economic DG'. Although these officials sincerely believe in the economic virtues of health protection policy in the work place, they still knowingly transform this argument into a strategic instrument:

> We have always favoured the stand that good management of health and safety in the work place is very cost-effective . . . However it is true that we insist on this a lot, too much according to some, because it is a good strategic tool. When we are told 'beware of the economic reality' we can say that on the contrary we contribute to the economic development of Europe.
>
> (Interview, DG employment and social affairs official, March 2001)

The link between public health and economic achievements is less clear than for health in the work place or for the health systems. The *economicization strategy* of health has nevertheless also been applied to public health as one of the public health representatives of the Commission confirms:

> To link health and economy in a virtuous circle facilitates the acceptance of our policies without changing their aim which gives us space. Without that, the member states and the rest of the Commission would spend their time blocking our suggestions.
>
> (Interview, DG SANCO official, March 2001)

In the first Communication of the Commission concerning public health the following statements were made:

> An efficient action can prevent premature deaths within the working population, as well as infirmary and chronic diseases with the consequences that these result in non-attendance and incapacity to work; it can improve health and allow the control of healthcare demand. In short, the productive capacity of the Community can be maximized and at the same time disease related costs can be reduced. Finally and most importantly, apart from the economic advantages, health protection can also improve the quality of life, which would be an invaluable contribution both at the individual level as well as for society as a whole.
>
> (European Commission 1993a: 7)

The fact that this strategy has not yet been abandoned is a sign that the legitimacy of Community intervention in the field of public health is still fragile. Indeed, David Byrne, the European Commissioner responsible for public health, recently gave the following statement:

> Despite all the legal difficulty, economic anxiety and institutional concerns, this is a moment to turn what currently looks like a problem, into a real opportunity. An opportunity to set out a positive political concept of health as fundamental to the fulfillment of our personal and economic well being . . . A concept of health as both the driver of our economic prosperity and as a source of renewal for citizenship and governance alike.
>
> (Byrne 2001)

If we make use of the distinction made by Hay and Rosamond (2002), it is possible to state that the *economicization* strategy consists in transforming the economic performance of the health policy theme from the speech form, i.e. conviction, into the rhetoric form, i.e. the strategic use of speech. The technical and political registers are therefore in reality two separate but interdependent registers.

This strategy can have two different objectives. It can be used first of all as a form of soft law in order to attain new competencies. Then, in most cases, this rhetoric can be used by administrative units which have weak resources or are marginalized within the Commission due to their objectives being remote from the EU's economic matrix. These units must integrate into their environment in order to become independent of it. The weakest DGs cannot afford to jeopardize the ostensible coherence of the Commission because they do not have the means to impose their political or technical views. In this case the strategy of *economicization* is no longer an offensive strategy aiming at increasing competencies, as in the case of soft law, but rather a defensive strategy used to develop the autonomy of the units that use it.

The tools of co-ordination: adjusting the EU's economic matrix to health policies

In parallel with the *economicization* strategy and its accompanying auto-integration logic, the Commission has set up two informal working groups with more ambitious objectives known as the High Level Committee on Health (HLCH) and the Interservice Group on Health (IGH). Founded in 1991, the first groups together high level officials from national ministries of health. This group is responsible for advising the Commission on health matters; it can thereby help the Commission to co-ordinate its policies by giving suggestions or opinions. For its part, the IGH was funded in 1994 and is constituted of representatives from the different DGs that have an interest in the points touched upon by the different sub-groups of this committee. As prescribed by the Treaty, its direct objective is to co-ordinate Commission policies in order to avoid overlaps and to integrate health requirements into other policies. Within this framework the IGH has already carried out several reports on the integration of health requirements in other policies and has recently distributed a practical guide on the evaluation of the impact of different policies on health to all the DGs (European Commission 2001c).

As their members all agree, the importance of these groups should not be over-estimated. Neither of these entities have any constraining powers and the efficacy of the information, co-ordination and integration of health with other policies can only rely on the goodwill of the members and their respective DGs. For this reason evaluation of the impact of health policies is carried out by the sectoral DGs and not by the units responsible for health matters. Even if this analysis is made public and is carried out based on the guide provided by the IGH, these DGs still retain a lot of flexibility for their actions due to a shortage of human resources in the health units of the Commission which prevents them from carrying out detailed control of these auto-evaluations. In reality the formal procedure of the Inter Service Consultation (ISC) often remains a much more efficient tool than the HLCH and the IGH whenever the Commission's health units wish to introduce health requirements into other policies.

Nevertheless, the members of these groups still believe that they can play a mediating role. By providing a meeting place for representatives of different DGs, these groups lead to the establishment of a network of people involved in health matters in different DGs. The regular contact that results from meetings in these groups allow the health representatives to have faster, more precise and more constant access to information and decision-making in other DGs. More than the groups themselves, it is these informal contacts that can favour better co-ordination and better integration of health matters into other policies. For the time being, however, it is health that integrates economic considerations rather than the economy integrating health matters.

External competition: the Commission's expertise versus that of others

As has already been emphasized, knowledge is an essential resource in the health sector, but in this respect the Commission is in a situation of inferiority compared to other international organizations. By being more legitimate than the Commission at the scientific level, these organizations also have more legitimacy to act in the health sector, since any health policy must be based on scientific grounds. The link between science and politics goes both ways, however, since the Commission's ability to develop its scientific legitimacy in public health is restrained by political elements. The scientific aspect can therefore be interpreted from a technical or a political point of view.

This part of the chapter will expand upon this hypothesis by showing that, after having been in unbalanced competition with the World Health Organization and the Council of Europe, the Commission has recently begun to undertake far-reaching collaborations with these organizations. As in the case of its economic relations, the Commission seems, consciously or unconsciously, to 'phagocyte' its opponents: it first uses them for mutual support before breaking away and even dominating them wherever possible.

The Commission and the saturated space of international health organizations

The EU does not develop itself *in vitro*, it evolves at the heart of a larger international political system in company with other international organizations which influence it and that it, in turn, influences. In areas where several international organizations are active, the EU must develop advantages compared with the other organizations in order to become a reflective and decision-making arena chosen by the member states. Among the several international organizations active in the health sector (Koivusalo 1998), the World Health Organization (WHO) and the Council of Europe (CoE) set a problem for the extension of the EU's role in the public health arena. The EU, the WHO and the CoE are in fact in implicit competition on several levels. First of all, competition takes place on a geographical level. The WHO is subdivided and organizes its action according to regional offices. Based in Copenhagen, its European office has a geographical activity area which, like that of the CoE, approximately corresponds to all the EU member states and the accession countries that will soon join it. Competition over competence adds to this geographical competition. In this case, competition from the CoE seems much more limited than that of the WHO. The CoE is above all an international organization that deals with ethical questions (Eberhard Harribey 2002). Its activity in the health area is therefore primarily directed at the ethical aspect of health policies.[3] On the contrary, the WHO covers the entire health field and it encompasses very similar competencies to those of the European Commission.[4]

If these organizations seem to be competitors to the European Commission, this is especially so because their scientific legitimacy is much more important than that of the Commission. While the Commission's intervention in the field of public health is relatively recent, the CoE and the WHO have been active in this field for a long time. Compared to the Commission, these two competing organizations have had time to prove themselves capable of dealing with public health matters. The legitimacy of the WHO is also derived from the prestige of the United Nations, of which it is a specialized agency, and which enables it to recruit the best specialists. Having initially entrusted generalists with health matters, more recently the Commission has also acquired very competent specialists. However, the weight of the bureaucratic structure and the legislative procedures of the EU often force the Commission's specialists to act like administrators and therefore their technical skills are not fully utilized.

Furthermore, the legitimacy of the Commission still suffers from its approach to health that has long been based on economic logic criteria:

> For people in the European Commission the WHO is a Scandinavian thing, a puritans from the North thing. For the WHO, the Commission tries to develop a commercial approach.
>
>   (Interview, public health lobby president, February 2001)

The Commission officials in charge of health are indeed torn between becoming integrated into the economy-centred Community environment and the desire to prioritize a genuine health logic. In short, they struggle to be accepted, in the same way as the WHO clearly is, as a true international actor in the field of public health. Meanwhile, as shown above, the integration of health concerns into other policies still largely relies upon a declared objective rather than a solid fact. In concrete terms, this means officials from the health units therefore have to compromise with the actions of their colleagues from other services. The difficulty in convincing the international health field of the Commission's credibility is also made more arduous by the fact that it appears to be a monolithic entity because differences in opinion between the different DGs are never made public. In any situation where one DG prioritizes economy over health the entire Commission is associated with this negative decision. On this question, M. Koivusalo (1998: 68) explains how a conflict between a recent WHO resolution on the regulation of basic drugs and the interests of the pharmaceutical industry, an industry actively supported by certain 'economic DGs', has been detrimental to the credibility of the Commission services concerned with health matters.

Finally, the technical credibility of the Commission suffers from 'being a supranational construct' (Mossialos and Permanand 2000: 46). Due to the power of constraint of EU decisions, the Commission is much more under pressure from the member states that wish to maintain their prerogatives than the WHO or the CoE are. Since the opinions or recommendations of the latter two organizations have no automatic constraining power, they do not endanger the prerogatives of their member states. The CoE or the WHO are therefore more rapid than the EU in taking decisions. Furthermore, these decisions are often more ambitious and more precise than the suggestions made by the Commission which has to take the reticence of the member states into account and therefore promote lowest common denominator and imprecise decisions. As a result of this:

if you ask a scientist whether he prefers to work for the European Commission or the WHO, he will always chose the WHO, it is an achievement for the most gifted to go and work for the WHO, here [at the European Commission] we have not yet reached that point.

(Interview, DG SANCO official, February 2001)

As numerous examples testify, when there is a discrepancy between the European Commission and the WHO or the CoE, non-governmental organizations or member states invariably support the latter two.

Construction of a technical legitimacy: the creation and infiltration of legitimate technical forums

The first tactic used by the Commission to face this situation was to 'go it alone' (Mountford 1998: 33) and build its authority by force. This approach was disastrous in every aspect, leading to overlaps of public policies between the organizations where the policies of the Commission turned out to be less pertinent than those of the CoE and especially the WHO. This strategy came to threaten the very existence of an intervention from the Commission in the field of health and was abandoned in favour of active co-operation between the Commission and its two competitors. This co-operation is carried out through the participation of Commission representatives as observers to decision-making in these organizations, through regular exchanges of information, through formal and informal meetings and, more recently, through staff exchange.

This pacification of the relations between the Commission and what can now be referred to as partners, can also be seen by the use and frequent re-use of technical research and opinions of the WHO and the CoE in the preparatory or official work of the Commission. Moreover, the official documents of the Commission make increasingly explicit references to these two organizations and to the co-operation that is now in place. For example, in the justification and the presentation of a recent proposition for a Directive, representative of this situation, the following details are provided:

This proposal for a Directive takes account of the most recent progress made and agreements attained at international level, particularly within the World Health Organization and the Council of Europe ... These specific provisions take into account international standards (e.g. Council of Europe, World Health Organization) ... The Commission intends to collaborate closely with the Council of Europe when the adaptations are developed, in order to ensure coherence with the recommendations it develops in the same field.

(European Commission 2002c: 15–17)

The concept of epistemic community developed by P. Haas (1992) can help to understand this cognitive and institutional reconciliation. Epistemic communities are networks of professionals who have a strong capacity for expertise and well-renowned skills in a particular field, which enables them often to be solicited by decision-makers. The WHO, and to a lesser extend the CoE, can be seen as epistemic communities. By joining these communities the Commission can take support from a pre-existing scientific legitimacy and thereby increase its own legitimacy that is still limited in the eyes of the non-governmental health organizations and the member states. In this way, the Commission hopes its propositions will be less contested and that, in the long run, it will increase its autonomy and even its competencies.

While taking support from the WHO and the CoE, the Commission has also been building itself a support network which could help it to become emancipated from its tutors. In the image of what has been done in numerous other sectors (Mazey 1995; Jabko 1999), the Commission has tried to create what one of our interlocutors calls 'positive lobbying' (Interview, DG SANCO official, March 2001). By organizing seminars, forums or meetings, the Commission fits itself into networks of actors, or creates these networks if they did not exist. In a logic of political exchange, these groups provide the Commission with expertise that is autonomous from that of national governments and, where possible, vis-à-vis that of the WHO and the CoE. In turn, the Commission provides these groups with access to decision-making and in some cases to funding. The EU Health Forum, of which the first session took place in November 2001, symbolizes this phenomenon since this forum serves to inform and to consult public health stakeholders on the public health activities carried out by the Commission.

However, it should also be mentioned that certain advantages of the Commission, in conjunction with the above-mentioned strategies, can modify the equilibrium of relations between the Commission, the WHO and the CoE. The first of these advantages is the financial superiority of the EU compared to the two others who have only limited budgets and thereby limited actions. Second, the possibility of forcing governments to change their policies which is so often a disadvantage, can also become an advantage in certain circumstances especially in the case of a health crisis. For example, the BSE crisis would have been much more difficult to solve without the constraining legislative instruments of the EU. Finally, as a regional integration organization, the EU has the potential to deal with both new public health issues and the transversal dimension when integrating health into other policies. In contrast, the WHO in particular does not have the possibility to interfere directly with any policy other than health. The Commission has therefore been able to stamp out the rumours that once circulated in its own corridors according to which 'the WHO has brains but no money and the Commission has money but no brains'. Certain members of the WHO even expect that in the very long term the Commission could be used as a regional office for the WHO, in the same way as the Pan American Health Association (PAHO) is for North and South America.

The politicization of public health: a necessary evil?

In this final part of the chapter it will first be shown that, due to the lack of legitimacy presented above, the main driving force behind the EU's public health activities is not the Commission. Incapable of turning expertise into political resources the Commission is in fact not able to hold a leadership function that, according to March and Olsen (1984: 739), can be conceived as: 'that of an educator, stimulating and accepting changing worldviews, redefining meanings, stimulating commitment'. The Commission is, on the contrary, regularly consigned to the position of a follower. As a result of the spillover effect, and especially its accompanying political logic, the EU's public health policy therefore consists only of a random agglomeration of policies limited to narrow issues instead of a well-founded global strategy.

A second point concerns change in the organization of the Commission for dealing with public health. Studying the instability and the incoherence of the 'health organigramme' underlines the chaotic development of the Commission's role in public health and the institutionalization process that it has been engaged in.

Political rationality versus technical rationality

Due to the fact that the Commission is not well rooted and accepted in the health field, it is difficult for it to resist exterior pressures and take a lead on producing coherent public health policies. The commissioner responsible for this portfolio, David Byrne, recently implicitly confessed his fears about this situation:

> I made very clear at the time of my appointment that our policy on health protection must not be guided by the latest newspaper headline or the most recent crisis. Instead it must look at the full range of policies which impact on health.
>
> (Byrne 2000)

As a result of the growing politicization of health matters the interventions of the Commission in the public health field are frequently determined by national political preoccupations rather than technical considerations. This in turn feeds a vicious circle since it is harmful for the Commission's credibility, and thereby to the development of its legitimacy, to act in the sector in question. This legitimacy deficit then favours the permeability of the public health community policy to external and contingent solicitations.

There are many examples which show that the public health activities of the EU are largely governed by different elements based on calculations or political crisis. In this regard, specialists agree that the revision in the Amsterdam Treaty of the former article 129 on public health was a political reaction to the BSE crisis:

> The prognosis for a modification of article 129 of the Treaty that founded health policy was bad: being too recent it had not delivered all its possibilities. Its impreciseness and shyness were not enough to put it back on the case.
>
> (Ernst 1998: 10)

While this new article is unanimously recognized as a significant opportunity for improving the quality of the public health actions carried out by the EU, it was not conceived for that purpose but rather to make a visible response to the BSE crisis. This led Padraig Flynn, the commissioner in charge of public health matters at the time, to declare:

> I must confess to a certain degree of disappointment on the text . . . Yes, the draft Treaty does confer new Community competencies in the field of public health. However . . . in my view, the new Treaty provisions do not provide the Commission with an adequate legal basis to address future concerns.
>
> (Flynn 1997: 2)

This very restrictive legal base has indeed prevented the Commission from developing a global approach to public health issues and constrained the EU to adopting instead a disease-based approach with no overall strategy or general coherence (Mossialos and Permanand 2000). Moreover, a certain amount of the diseases that are dealt with at the Community level depend on a 'political insertion' (Mountford 1998: 15), which has led certain Commission officials that we have interviewed to talk about *political diseases*. In this case, the public health actions undertaken do not have clear-cut 'Community added-value' and are not structural public health priorities because they have been adopted under political pressure. In the best case scenario, it is possible to come up with an a posteriori technical justification for such actions.

The report entitled *Priorities for Public Health Action in the EU* made by the French Society of Public Health with Commission funding, confirms these statements in a striking manner (Commission (SFSP) 1999). Based on a questionnaire distributed to many members of the public health community, this study concluded that in the list of top priorities 'neither Cancer, accidents or AIDS, all of which are the subject of major European programmes, were included' (Weil and McKee 1998: 258). Furthermore, a lot of the people interviewed, as well as academic specialists, consider that the setting up of the programmes *Europe against Cancer* and *Europe against AIDS* was primarily due to the personal commitment of François Mitterrand. For some this was due to the state of the former French President's own health (Randall 2000), whereas for others it was a consequence of the French contaminated blood scandal. In no case has decision-making been based upon rationality or the existence of a genuine 'Community added-value'. Many other activities are based on a similar logic. For example, Mossialos and Permanand (2000) emphasize the counter productive aspect of the introduction of a programme against Alzheimer's disease by the European Parliament. This uses an already low public health budget without demonstrating the 'Community added-value' of such a programme. Another example is the extreme caution of the research carried out following a recommendation from the European Council on the impact of electromagnetic fields on health. The latest of these 'political insertions' is the programme against bio-terrorism and the task force with the same name rapidly set up following the terrorist attacks in the United States on 11 September 2001.

The long road to organizational coherence

It is interesting to study the organizational structure of the Commission since it reflects what the Commission does and how it does it. Such an analysis sheds light on the competencies, the priorities and the performance of the Commission (Nugent 2001; Nugent and Saurugger 2002). Indeed, historical analysis of the organizational structures within the Commission that deal with health matters confirms the essentially random and chaotic role the Commission has played in this sector.

To this day, two thirds of all the DGs are involved with health matters and particularly public health: DG Environment deals with the impact of the environment on health; DG Information Society deals with tele-medicine; DG Industry deals with matters concerning pharmaceutical drugs, etc. (Merkel and Huëbel 1999). This scattering of competencies is the perfect image of the first steps of Europe in the health field: health was not a goal in itself but a necessary step to reach the essentially economic objectives of different DGs. As health was being inserted into other policies, none of the parts of the Commission were specifically designed for this sector, with the exception of the health and safety at work Directorate based in the former DG V. Although for years the latter was the only Commission service specialized in dealing with health matters, its influence should not be over-estimated. On one hand the title of this Directorate: *Health and safety at work* reflects the priority of its activity concentrated on developing safety standards rather than focusing on public health protection. On the other hand the motivation of this Directorate was not very different from economic considerations because it was supposed to fight to reduce 'social dumping' by the member states.

Not only did this fragmentation present an obstacle to the development of a coherent public health policy, it also reduced the capacity of the organs concerned with health to be heard by the other DGs, and sometimes even by their own DG, because of its lack of symbolic power or its limited human resources. Consequently, health was condemned to exist only as a side issue entirely dependent on the necessity for economic integration. Only an exogenous shock seemed likely to change this situation.

This impulsion came from the programmes *Europe against Cancer* and *Europe against AIDS* which launched a long, still unfinished, process towards the development of a cohesive health organigramme. The establishment of these programmes was carried out by a unit that was specially set up at the end of the 1980s in the Directorate for health and safety at work due to the lack of any other health-related services within the Commission. This process continued with the coming into force of the Maastricht Treaty which for the first time provided the EU with explicit public health competencies. This event allowed public health to emancipate itself from health in the work place and thereby from economic considerations. In concrete terms, this change lead to an inversion of the proportion of units involved with health in the working place compared to units involved with public health. The name of the Directorate logically changed from health and safety at work to *public health and safety in the working place*, thereby taking into account the public health element. The 'mad cow' crisis then further emphasized proportional differences. Since the crisis, health and safety in the working place have been dealt with by only one unit.

In parallel to this evolution, units of the Commission were restructured in order to deal with the food safety crisis and the increased visibility of these issues. Following criticisms of the monopoly of DG agriculture on food safety, this question was placed under the authority of the DG for consumer affairs (the former DG XXIV). The name of DG XXIV became *consumer policy and consumer health protection* in 1997, thereby emphasizing the new importance given to health. On 29 October 1999, the Prodi Commission adopted new organizational charts and a distribution of competencies between the DGs. Public health was then removed from the competence of DG employment to begin a new life – as a public health Directorate – in the renovated DG XXIV. Organized around health activities, the DG XXIV then became the health and consumer protection DG (DG SANCO).

The BSE crisis and the politicization of public health resulting from it have thereby led to the reorganization of the Commission and given rise to a DG almost entirely devoted to the management of health issues. This has had both a symbolic effect by showing that health was at last completely part of the European Commission's preoccupations, as well as a remarkable material effect since DG SANCO is now one of the DGs with the most personnel. However, despite appearances, DG SANCO is far from being a 'DG Health'. In fact, two out of three intervention areas of DG SANCO do not directly depend on the health activity area:

> Food safety and consumer protection are not in a first instance aimed at health in itself, even if they have indirect effects on health, they are first of all aimed at safety.
>
> (Interview, French ministry of social affairs official, February 2001)

In other respects, a quick look at the organigramme of this DG shows an important imbalance between the way these different activities are treated within DG SANCO. Four Directorates out of seven are almost entirely assigned to food safety and one is still allocated to consumer issues. Therefore, we can observe that in the same way that public health had 'phagocyted' the health and safety at work Directorate, food safety has swallowed up consumer affairs. Concurrently, public health has been stifled by food safety since it is only represented by one Directorate, namely the public health Directorate. In addition to this imbalance in manpower, the political resources of DG SANCO are focused on food safety issues. This is symbolized by the nickname of D. Byrne, the DG SANCO commissioner, who is often called 'the BSE commissioner'. In this regard, a head of unit in the public health Directorate told us:

> When Byrne arrived he was very interested in public health matters but he was immediately trapped. Dioxin, BSE, foot and mouth disease, he is only dealing with food safety ... he is dominated by events.
>
> (Interview, DG SANCO official, March 2001)

A final element can be mentioned to underline the *bricolage* (patching-up)[5] logic that is characteristic of the management of public health by the EU. Although the setting up of the public health Directorate in Luxembourg has often been criticized – especially by the European Parliament (Mountford 1988) and by the Commission itself (EC 2000e) – the creation of DG SANCO has not modified this fact.[6] This situation is indeed detrimental to public health officials because it makes them remote from their political representative, i.e. the commissioner based in DG SANCO's headquarters in Brussels, as well as from the EU's decision-making centre and from access to informal discussions that constantly take place there. This situation would be detrimental to any sector, but it is particularly so for public health and its 'capability-expectation gap' (Hill 1994, quoted in Cram 2001: 774). This is due to the intersectorial dimension of this field which necessitates constant relations with other DGs.

It can therefore be claimed that the creation of DG SANCO has not favoured the handling of public health matters. Rather, as some authors have feared (Lefèbvre 1999) this reorganization, at least initially, has led to a slow down in the expansion of this sector. Public health has been subordinated to food safety issues hereby illustrating 'the permanent co-presence in the Community sphere of the immediate topics of the day and of the long term project that has yet to be carried out' (Lequesne and Smith 1997: 175).

In reality, the window of opportunity (Kingdon 1984) that was opened by the health crisis was opened in two stages. The crisis had to disappear from the agenda of the media and then the political agenda needed to be alleviated in order for the Commission to give meaning and coherence to its new role in public health. On the legal side, important Directives have been adopted or are in the process of being adopted.[7] Moreover, a new public health programme (Decision no. 1786/2002/EC) was passed for the period 2003–2008 with the explicit objective of ending the vertical disease-based approach in favour of a more strategic approach based on three general and horizontal strands.[8]

Furthermore, from summer 2003 the Commission will undertake a slow but significant reorganization in order to improve the coherence of its public health policies. This reorganization will start by the creation of one or even two new units in Brussels that will be in charge of horizontal legislation. This refitting may, however, generate some confusion since the units in charge of the management of the public health programme will remain in Luxembourg, at least in the beginning. They will be assisted in this by a new executive agency that should allow Commission civil servants to abandon a certain number of administrative tasks in order to do more specialized work. The creation of an independent European centre for disease prevention and control is also intended for 2005–2006.

However, it should be noted that this agenda could be turned upside-down if any new unpredictable political events occur. For instance, in a rather cynical way, one might expect that just as food safety policy benefitted from the BSE crisis, public health at the Community level may benefit, or at the very least be influenced, from Severe Acute Respiratory Syndrome (SARS) if the latter continues to influence the media and political agenda. The work of the Convention is also to be taken into consideration since it has come out in favour of a strengthening and an expansion of the public health competencies of the EU. The coming enlargement of the EU could also have an impact on the public health policy of the Community. Despite the Convention's opinion, the amount of commissioners will probably also increase so that each nationality is represented (Nugent 2001: 104). It will therefore also be necessary to increase the number of portfolios. The creation of a health DG is therefore increasingly mentioned in the corridors of the Commission.

Conclusion

This chapter leads to two conclusions concerning the relationship between the Commission and politics. The first is that the Commission is not 'beyond politics'. The decisions taken by the Commission rarely rely solely on a technocratic mode. In fact the choices of the EU policies and of their contents depend on more political elements, as the Commission is simply not able to oppose technical arguments to political ones. If the focus here has been on the influence of external political elements on the policy led by the Commission, it should nevertheless be recognized that the Commission itself can deliberately include politics in its policies. For example, in the case of tobacco, the efficiency of the general information campaigns at an international level has been questioned due to the differences in perception according to age, gender and regions. The justification of the campaign '*feel free to say no*' launched in 2002 by the Commission therefore does not depend so much on the expected effectiveness of the campaign, as on the mediatized visibility that the Commission would benefit from. The Commission is therefore a political actor which interacts with other political actors.

The second conclusion is both analytical and normative: political and technocratic ways of functioning should not systematically be opposed. Their combination is necessary. The integration of fields of public action where values play an important part, as is the case for public health, is complicated by the diversity of European cultures. Resulting from the mediatization of a subject or from political strategies, politicization is therefore essential to break through the barriers that technocracy alone would not be able to overcome. The risk is to leave the institutionalization of fields of action where expertise is essential open to the randomness of politics. Without going into an ideological discussion about what shape the political system of the EU should ideally have, the case of public health constitutes a perfect illustration of the point made by Radaelli when he specifies:

> The new challenge of the EU is ... how to combine an increased politicization with the need for more expertise. Politics and knowledge, which the conventional literature on technocracy sees as polar opposites, are indeed needed at the same time for developing public policy in the EU.
>
> (Radaelli 1999a: 9)

Notes

1 This chapter is mainly based on observations made during an internship in the public health Directorate of the European Commission (October 2002 to February 2003) and on two rounds of interviews (winter 2001 and winter 2003) with approximately thirty observers and actors involved in the Europeanization of

health. I would like to thank all the people I have interviewed as well as those who made me so welcome in the public health Directorate.
2 For an overview of the Commission's activities in the field of health see Randall (2001). For an historical presentation see Cassan (1989).
3 In terms of health protection the CoE has four main objectives:

- bringing together human rights, social cohesion and health agendas;
- harmonising the health policies of Members States with regard to safety and quality;
- developing prevention and health education;
- promoting fair access to health care, patients' rights, citizen participation and the protection of vulnerable groups.

(Council of Europe 2002)

4 Article 2 of the WHO constitution declares: 'In order to achieve its objective, the functions of the Organization shall be:

c) to assist Governments, upon request, in strengthening health services;
f) to establish and maintain such administrative and technical services as may be required, including epidemiological and statistical services;
i) to promote, in co-operation with other specialized agencies where necessary, the improvement of nutrition, housing, sanitation, recreation, economic or working conditions and other aspects of environmental hygiene;
n) to promote and conduct research in the field of health;
o) to promote improved standards of teaching and training in the health, medical and related professions;
u) to develop, establish and promote international standards with respect to food, biological, pharmaceutical and similar products . . .

5 The *bricolage* concept is close to the garbage can concept developed by J.G. March and J. P. Olsen (1986) since *bricolage* can be defined as 'the activities that aim at resolving specific problems . . . arising in relation to a fixed calendar . . . by means of know-how, tools, available technologies, that are more or less appropriate, even uncertain' (Garraud 2000: 224).
6 The geographical position of the public health Directorate is the result of political negotiations that led to a decision on the 8 April 1965 of the heads of state requiring that health protection be based in Luxembourg (Decision 67/446/CEE, 67/30/Euratom, *Official Journal no. B 152* of 13/07/1967: 18–20).
7 For example, the Directive 2001/37/EC on the fight against smoking and the Directive 2002/98/EC on standards of quality and safety of human blood.
8 These three strands are:

1 to improve information and knowledge for the development of public health;
2 to enhance the capability of responding rapidly and in a co-ordinated fashion to health threats;
3 to promote health and prevent disease through addressing health determinants across all policies and activities.

Part II

The media, the Commission and its legitimacy

7 Was it really just poor communication?

A socio-political reading of the Santer Commission's resignation

Didier Georgakakis

This chapter analyses the political processes which led to the European Commission's resignation in March 1999. The chronological development of the crisis is well known: the scandal originated from a number of embezzlements revealed in the Belgian press in August 1998. Following the disclosure of these crimes, the scandal gradually took shape in the press and in the European Parliament. The Parliament took a vote of no-confidence, which was finally rejected in mid-January, but at the same time a committee of independent experts was appointed to shed new light on the subject. Made public in mid-March, the Committee's report called into question Edith Cresson's personal credibility and accused the college of commissioners of mismanagement. That night, the Santer Commission resigned.

One interpretation of the resignation was that the Commission was unable to deal with the crisis especially because of its 'poor communication' skills. On the one hand, I will show that this interpretation is wrong. At the root of the crisis lay not a communication problem, but a legitimation problem. Moreover, this legitimation problem is linked to a more general transformation of the European political game wherein the usual alliances of the Commission disintegrated. However, on the other hand, one could say that the poor communication thesis is interesting in a very particular way: the Commission's communication was wrong-footed by the politicization of the European institutions which occurred during the crisis. In other words, this crisis provokes reflection about the link between legitimation and the construction of an order of political practices. For this reason, and after a few words about the analytical framework used to structure these thoughts, this chapter focuses upon the dynamics of the multi-sectoral mobilizations which led to the Commission's resignation.

The sociology of political crises as an analytical framework

The resignation of the Commission is often treated in anecdotal fashion by social science. However, some more precise studies have tackled the origins of the resignation (Stevens and Stevens 2001; Meyer 1999).

Despite their respective qualities, these publications suffer from a number of problems when looked at from the angle of the sociology of political crises.

The first comment to make on the existing literature concerns its objectives. Most interpretations have in common the search for causes or the 'factors' which led to the resignation. Although this approach appears scientific, it leads one to seek reasons for the resignation 'after the event', to the detriment of what was actually played out at the time of the resignation. In this sense, this approach suffers from the typical defects of what history and political sociology call a 'retrospective illusion'. The central hypothesis of these publications is the idea that the resignation of the Santer Commission is the product of an a priori deficit of legitimacy. On a general level, this proposal is not false: it is well known that Jacques Santer was designated by default and invested by only a narrow majority in the European Parliament. However, this interpretation neglects the fact that the Commission was in rather good shape a short time before the resignation. On the one hand, the results of the intergovernmental conference were judged disappointing, which tended to strengthen the Commission in the definition of its leadership role. On the other hand, the Commission had just been successful with two important issues: enlargement and the euro. For this reason, the legitimacy deficit of the Commission should not be taken for granted but seen as an integral part of a progressively unfolding crisis.

The second comment on this research is that it focuses on the 'problem' of the Commission as an inefficient organization. For Stevens and Stevens, for instance (2001), the crisis is thus the product of the incapacity of the Commission to conform to its own procedural rules. As proof, the authors frequently quote the report of the Independent Experts Committee which stresses the defects of political direction or of management within the Commission. However, in reality it was more the publication of this report and its strategic interpretations which had key effects rather than the problems it underlined. More generally, while focusing on analysing the 'non-management of the Commission', to quote the title of Stevens and Stevens' article, the authors are led to neglect the conditions which made this problem of non-management into a political issue. This is also the case for communication when it is studied outside the context of the political crisis. These arguments can be sustained from the point of view of a specialist of administration (Stevens and Stevens' work is probably one of the best informed on the administrative realities of the European Commission). But at the same time, it leads the authors to neglect the *political* construction of problems (Edelman 1988) and to simply repeat the clarion call for 'good management' so often heard within the Commission.

Christoph Meyer's article (1999) presents a different, and to a certain extent more political, point of view on the affairs and the development of the crisis. It develops the hypothesis that the crisis stemmed from an insufficiency of public communication and of skills within the Commission. Fragmented political authority, a technocratic vision and a lack of know-how in terms of political communication opened an opportunity for the member states to profit from public dissatisfaction with the European Commission. According to Meyer, this absence of policy and, correlatively, the longstanding absence of political communication in the Commission, are at the root of the crisis. This approach has the merit of bringing us back to fundamental problems, in particular the historical depoliticization of the Commission and its consequences in terms of political communication, but it nevertheless has two defects. According to this interpretation, the organization of public communication and its malfunctioning are, once again, seen as the source of the crisis. This reading is not incorrect, but it neglects the relational context into which public communication fits. If communication is not 'good', this is not only owing to its content or organization. It is also because those who are its usual recipients or relays are not, or are no longer, willing to be satisfied. Meyer's reading of the crisis also presupposes a definition of what 'good' political communication practices are in the European context, and moreover, in a European context of politicization. However, most evidence indicates that this context is new, which partly explains the difficulty actors had in finding the right tone and message. The crises that the EU had previously experienced were due more to blockages by member states (think of the image of the empty chair, for example) than to political dynamics such as the ones which led to the resignation.

If I share some of the conclusions of the above-mentioned research, I advocate a different central hypothesis: the resignation is the result of a process of politicization which knocked off balance the actors who normally dominated the European political game. Consequently, this led to a situation which was not easily readable and controllable. In other words, I do not seek to evaluate in a normative way what charisma, political know-how, or administration problems in the Commission are. Rather I set out to highlight the multisectoral dynamics which allowed the crisis to emerge and its consequences on the political judgements made during the heat of the interactions that followed.

This approach is inspired by the sociology of political crises initiated by Michel Dobry (1986). Constraints of space forbid a summary of the principal contributions of this research tradition. However, some of its main points can be sketched out. First, it invites one to be wary of causalist interpretations and to observe instead what actually occurs during a crisis and how it occurs. Nothing about the resignation of the Santer Commission was inevitable, indeed it would have been highly improbable to forecast its demise only a few months before its renewal. If this resignation came about, it was therefore because the protagonists' calculations changed abruptly and the resources of the college of commissioners had already been deeply devalued.

Second, this posture invites one to observe changes in the political alliances which characterize routine situations. This means analysing the effects of political 'hits' on the structure of the political game, and particularly the relationships between the various sectoral components which had previously contributed to its stability. In this case, the relations between the Commission and the press, the sub-committee and Parliament, the college and the administration of the Commission were all strongly transformed. Indeed, this occurred to such an extent that one can talk about a process of desectorization of the European political space. Where, usually, the European political game seems to be fragmented, the revelation of the affairs became a focal point which contributed, for a short time and in a very new way, to the development of a permanent European political space, endowed with issues with a single temporality that were shared by the majority of those involved.

It is in this context that the Commission came to be called 'corrupt' or 'racked by bad management' and that resignation could represent a way out. This observation invites us – and this is the third contribution of the sociology of crises – to be attentive to what interactionnist sociology calls 'the definition of the situation' and 'labelling effects' (Becker 1985). If the Commission was labelled corrupt this was the culmination of a number of political mobilizations, played out in several sectors, which came to define the crisis for a large number of protagonists. It is these mobilizations that I will present first before observing their effects upon the Commission's political communication 'problems'.

Internal 'policies' and the management of the affairs

For something to exist and to turn into a scandal, a fact must be qualified or labelled as extra-ordinary and then this definition must become shared in order to create a mobilization (Dobry 1986; Garrigou 1992b). The question of why these affairs were made public reveals a number of frustrations within the administration of the Commission. These frustrations do not relate to the redistribution of material resources, but more directly to a coincidence between the power of individual commissioners and the pressures which the reform of the organization of the Commission were seen as imposing upon its civil servants. Under the effect of these changes, solidarity between the college of commissioners and the European civil servants was ruptured, thus creating the climate in which the 'affair' came about and was then defined as a 'scandal' (Lascoumes 1997).

The origins of the affair are of a political nature. Before the scandal, cases of fraud were secrets heavily guarded by the Commission's internal arrangements. This secret and technical arrangement was underpinned by the existence of a group of specialists from UCLAF (unit for co-operation on fraud prevention), made up of about 150 agents, most of whom are in some way attached to the national administrations (customs agents, magistrates). UCLAF was designed above all as an audit office for the use of European subsidies in and by the member states. Looked at it in this way, it is no accident that we know so little about the affairs which preceded those of 1998–1999. To be more specific, these affairs never became 'affairs' of any great concern. On the one hand, UCLAF monopolized the investigation into fraud, and on the other hand the circulation of information was directly linked to the college of commissioners. Given the way these entities were structured, the economy of the relations involved was also influenced by the civil servants' duty to preserve secrecy. Moreover, over and above their legal obligations, European civil servants usually had a particularly strong attachment to the Commission.

However, under the Santer Commission modifications were applied which became a determining feature in the creation of the very special 'climate' in which the scandal took place. For many, Jacques Santer's arrival signified a re-balancing of the Commission towards Nordic and managerial matters. This idea was held by two Scandinavian commissioners in particular who acted as Santer's 'guardian angels'. The first of these was Erkki Liikanen, a Finnish socialist commissioner and ex-Minister for the economy who had prepared the Finnish accession, who was placed in charge of the Commission's budget and personnel. From this position he became the source of many projects for the reform of the internal organization of the European Commission. Given the post of commissioner responsible for curbing fraud, Anita Gradin, a Swedish socialist, took on the task of dealing with the 'southern' practices of the Delors Commissions and bringing things back into line, in particular by accentuating the pressure applied by UCLAF.

From their nomination onwards, the intention to 'change the regime' through a number of internal reforms became obvious. The presence of these two commissioners was considerable throughout successive endeavours to reform the Commission's structures. Liikanen also became the driving force behind many reform projects, including the reform of staff regulations, sub-contracting to external companies or even the possibility of giving 'under-performing' civil servants the sack. These reform projects were also dramatized using a deliberately 'modernist' attitude ('high-tech' events to preview the reform, use of consultants, etc.) and interpreted within the Commission as a challenge to its internal social dialogue and to the very status of European civil servants. Indeed – and this is where the climate comes into play – these reform projects provoked an unprecedented level of mobilization. A day of action in April 1998 represented a breakthrough in the division that had been developing between the college and the administration of the Commission. For the first time ever, the Director Generals, a very senior level of authority close to the college, expressed opposition to the Commission. As readers' letters published in the Commission's internal review show, the day of action was followed by several 'internal debates' which pitted the

Northern 'modernists' against the 'traditionalist' representatives from 'Southern' Europe.

However, this was not the only change brought in by the new Commission because it sought to tie internal reform to a moralization of the practices of European civil servants. For example, the reform of the statute was connected to the issue of fraud. This policy of moralization was pushed in particular by Gradin. Having discovered the debate about transparency of the European Union initiated by Finland and Sweden during the Amsterdam intergovernmental conference, this policy came to involve a number of highly symbolic measures, such as the project to suppress privileges like the right to tax-free alcohol and tobacco, which were often evoked during the strike against the project to reform the statute. Above all, this policy took concrete form through the reinforcement of UCLAF and its mission to initiate more internal enquiries into allegations of fraud. In doing so, this policy stigmatized the 'Delors approach to public management' and a combination of 'Southern' practices, whilst applauding more Nordic ones.

The strengthening of anti-fraud policy therefore allowed a whole series of 'problems' to be transformed into 'affairs' (Lascoumes 1997). By intervening in the conflicts associated with the internal reform of the Commission, the denunciation of fraud by UCLAF and the college contributed to a growing feeling of dispossession amongst European civil servants. At the same time, internal struggles over administrative reform opened up a space for a number of previously unthinkable counterattacks (Georgakakis 2002b).

The effects of this moralization and dispossession are particularly apparent at the beginning of the affair involving the French commissioner, Edith Cresson. The rupture with previous practice and sidelining of EU officials led them to turn against the Commission and leak information to the press and the Parliament. In his book on this affair, the journalist Jean Nicolas shows well how civil servants collaborated with journalists. Along with information from other leaks, a case was put together and activated by the press. If it was almost impossible to identify the authors of these leaks, they were nevertheless largely attributable to the new internal divisions between the college and Commission civil servants. This split was accompanied by a modification of the thin line between what can be voiced and what should remain unspoken. This modification was observed in my interviews with European civil servants where freedom of speech suddenly became much greater; a 'freeing of tongues' which contrasted sharply to what happened during interviews after the resignation. The extent of the modification was also visible in the vicious nature of the leaflets distributed by staff unions on the internal reform and their veiled threats to inform the press (Georgakakis 2002b).

The press's anti-institutional attitude

Of course, analysis of these internal ruptures is not sufficient to understand the process of crisis. If the affairs were leaked, this was also because they found an external audience. As Olivier Baisnée's contribution to this book underlines, the changing relation between the Commission and the press is a major reflection of this change, as can be shown by examining the convergence between several journalistic strategies.

The disclosure of the Cresson scandal by the *Lanterne*, followed by additional articles published by a group of journalists and then by the entire press was characterized less by a desire to bring a European 'public space' into existence, than by the encounter between journalistic strategies driven by very different motives. For years journalists had been little more than a relay of information for the European Commission. The federalist vocation common to civil servants and journalists tended to merge the press corps into a larger movement of European activists. The increase in the number of journalists and the arrival of new journalists seeking to be more 'professional' (Baisnée 2002; Bastin 2002), along with the growth of the Commission's missions and authority, were contributing factors to changes in the political order. The channelling of information and its technical dimension began to be increasingly criticized. However, explicit tensions were yet to exist between the Commission and journalists. At the beginning of the Cresson affair, institutional connivance made the Commission's management 'problems' impossible to attack. In addition, journalists shared the views of the dominant actors within the Commission. Indeed, the Commission's practice of resorting to 'submarines' (temporary Commission personnel paid from the budget for Community programmes instead of from a frozen personnel budget), was part of the inside knowledge which bonded the different actors together.

This is also what linked the development of the Cresson affair to the slow and progressive process of journalistic autonomy and encouraged the encounter between civil servant and journalistic strategies. Three types of strategy allowed the affair to be leaked and, simultaneously, accelerated the journalists' move towards autonomy: the first was initiated by a marginal journalist, specialized in 'Belgian' affairs, the second stemmed from a desire for more autonomous journalism and the third strategy is that of German newspapers concerned about their national economy.

The *Lanterne* and the journalist who brought the affair out into the open differ sharply from the definition of journalistic purity which has dominated commentary about the victory of the European public space. This right-wing Christian Democrat paper is well known for its criticism of affairs in Belgium and, more generally, for its approach to 'democracy'. Jean Nicolas, the journalist who brought the affair out into the open, is the author of many publications on 'scandalous' subjects: *The paedophiles are amongst us* on the Dutroux affair of 1997, *The protectors* about the procurers in 1998. Even if in his book on the Cresson affair, *L'Europe des fraudes,* published immediately after the resignation, he strongly denies his membership of the extreme right, a large number of journalists have little doubt over his true motives.

In this context, it could be seen as surprising that this 'disclosure' was then taken up by a newspaper like *Liberation*. In fact, the affairs were taken up in a context where they represented an opportunity for a new definition of European journalism to be made; a journalism more independent of the college now seen as the 'European executive'. This opportunity emerges when the mobilization of civil servants against the college takes place. Above all, for *Liberation*, publicizing the affair had the advantages of a no-risk coup: by inciting the college to maintain its opposition to the civil servants, at least initially, the terms of exchange between *Liberation* and the latter were not upset by this press exposure. Paradoxically, it was the principles of a number of European civil servants that led to the affair being exposed. These principles included a commitment to good management, the future of European integration and criticism of the 'charismatic deficit' of President Santer.

From the point of view of national journalism, the affairs offered increased recognition for journalists specialized in European matters. For a long time, such journalists had undergone a real struggle to get any recognition from their editors. European themes were seen as obscure and of no interest to the reader. On this occasion journalists also had the opportunity to look behind the scenes and learn more about European politics. Indeed, it was through a weekly column about 'backstage Brussels' that Jean Quatremer managed to bolster his position within *Liberation*. In a way, the revelation of the affairs simply followed on 'logically' from here, by conforming with more general models of journalistic excellence. Since the 1930s, and above all, since Watergate, this model was that of journalistic investigation.

This crossover between the strategies of journalists based in Brussels and national media market strategies took on very different forms in countries such as France, Germany and the United Kingdom. The difference between French and German journalists specialized on Europe, is that the German journalists have generally not had to work as hard at making a position for themselves as the French have had to. There are many more German journalists in Brussels and European politics had featured amongst the standard parts of newspapers long before the Cresson affair. However, this recognition is linked to the particular position of the German state in the EU. The German 'position' in the negotiations for the Agenda 2000, their demand for a re-balanced budget and criticism of the Commission's 'squandering of resources' were the object of a widely-held consensus amongst political parties and other actors. It must not be forgotten that this 'pressure' from the Germans had a major impact on the Commission. Consequently, it is not surprising that a journalist from the *ARD* and others from the *Frankfurter Allgemeine* were at the heart of the disclosures. An article that appeared in *Wirtschaft Woche* in November 1998 is a good example of the criticism levelled at the Commission. It criticized the high salaries of the European civil servants and underlined how the strikes against Liikanen and his performance criteria had been scoffed at by these same actors. A number of minor facts were also presented as symbolic of the Commission's poor management, such as the fact that economy class tickets were often reimbursed at the price of business class tickets, the doctoring of expenses slips, etc. A far larger number of examples of such practices were given in the British press.

MEP mobilization

If at the beginning these positions seemed far from reconcilable, very quickly the affair developed further within the European Parliament. Indeed, some commentators consider that the exposure of the scandal stemmed essentially from the Parliament's quest for more autonomy and power. In reality, at the start of the affair the European Parliament was relatively in line with the college due to its longstanding consensual relationship based largely upon the weakness of the Parliament. When inspected more closely, it becomes clear that the acceleration of the affairs in Parliament was more closely linked to a collective process of emancipation than to internal competition. Even with its increasing power, the parliamentary game did not really change, but the quasi-monopoly of the two large political groups, the ESP (European Socialist Party) and the EPP (European People's Party) was still a source of a number of frustrations.

When the affairs started to come out into the open at the beginning of September 1998, Edith Muller, an MEP for the Green Party, quickly backed up by the leader of her party, was very virulent and became the first person to describe the 'affairs' as 'scandals'. Speaking as a member of the budgetary control commission (COBUCO), she made herself renowned for her strong position against the opacity of the Commission's management. Indeed, when the journalist from the *Lanterne* came into possession of incriminating evidence files from a disgruntled consultant (Claude Perry), he went to Muller. Consequently, it was around the COBUCO that the affair developed in Parliament. Still, at this point, the COBUCO took a position that kept most of the 'frustrations' within the Parliament. The COBUCO was not the most prestigious parliamentary committee because it usually followed a budgetary orthodoxy that was largely set by the Commission. Operating in a technical register rather than the political one of the larger committees, such as Foreign Affairs Institutional Reform, the COBUCO had neither the budget nor the prestige of the Legal committee. The most prominent MEPs did not feature in the COBUCO and, consequently, many minority groups, such as the

Liberals and the Greens, were over-represented. Indeed, this Committee was chaired by a German MEP at a time when there was a lot of pressure on the Commission's budgetary affairs coming from the Germans. Moreover, the commissioners under attack (Cresson, and also Marin) were socialists. In short, all these points were important for generating the political climate within which the affairs subsequently developed.

The process of politicization

The scandal took its final form through the sum of these interactions rather than as a result of face-to-face confrontations. In so doing, actors had to use their political know-how in order to participate in a dynamic where the affairs had now become a 'focal point' (Schelling 1960). In its issues of 4 and 5 January, *Agence Europe* wrote in an editorial: 'the visible development of the events hides the manoeuvres, the intentions (which had not always been confessed) and sometimes even the manipulations and the intrigues'. This formula shows that the situation favoured an increasingly large number of political motives. It should be added that it is more the relatively new status of some actors in the European political game than their number, that influenced the disappointment, the surprise or the jubilation of their fellow protagonists. Nourished by the attempt to escape from crisis planned by the commissioners and the increasingly similar mobilizations of MEPs and journalists, these motives first took on the form of a left–right opposition, then one of an ordinary internal group struggle and, finally, one of an executive/legislative struggle. Indeed, this final act offered the different protagonists an opportunity to put their respective institutions back into the game of European politics.

Being very similar, the converging positions taken by the journalists and the Greens were highly influential. Erving Goffman has accurately described what happens when this structure of interaction is broken down: the mad smile, the tears, the violence (Goffman 1969). This rupture with the usual structure of EU politics can be seen behind Emma Bonino's public tears and her threats to register a complaint against the *Financial Times* (*Liberation*, 14th October). But it can also be seen in Edith Cresson's violent counterattacks.

Here it is necessary to make an inventory of all the strategies which played a role in the crisis. The journalist Jean Nicolas gives us a certain number of them, amongst which are misinformation, propaganda, secret pressures and manipulations, which all fitted in well with the increase in political motives and their inscription in the 'classical' frameworks of national politics (Nicolas 1999). On top of all that, at a later stage came the exposure of the plot. The plot can be seen from this point of view as something other than the product of paranoid scheming. By talking of 'the disclosures' rather than 'the affairs', many protagonists came to talk of a 'government system crisis'. It also corresponded to a political strategy which was still in its infancy in Europe: Liikanen applied this approach when the results of the investigations were leaked, while Jacques Santer spoke of a 'witch hunt'. Above all, at this point this strategy seemed particularly well adjusted to the complexity of the matter. Due to the precarious alliances and the many uncertainties which weighed upon the internal relations of the European Institutions, this strategy in fact presented the critics of the Commission as destroyers who made the situation incomprehensible. This was the case for the journalists who did not completely master the journalistic positions and the strategies of countries other than their own. This is also the case for the relations between the different national representatives at a moment when relations were tense between Germany and France over the negotiations for Agenda 2000.

This politicization of know-how also marked the Commission's counterattacks against the press and its relations with the Parliament. Looked at from this point of view, Santer's reaction could well be seen as a 'tactical error'. At the time of the vote to discharge the budget in December, Santer did not want to interpret the vote as anything other than defiance and it was he who initiated the first 'ascent to extremes' by the intermediary of a letter to the President of the Parliament. In response came an institutional innovation which has since been reinterpreted as a 'heated' moment in the competition between the two institutions. The Parliament refused to agree to the discharging of the budget by 270 votes to 230, with a few abstentions.

This situation changed its emphasis from November onwards as the Parliament took on a new tactic consisting of developing a power of decision-making over institutional matters. Here the vote of no-confidence should be put into context. Initially the vote was not exactly an act of democratic control, but more a transaction which took place between President Santer, MEPs and the socialists in order to make the overall institutional order legitimate once again.

However, this attempt at conciliation came too late. Worse, by unveiling an alliance between the college and the Parliament's majority group, it exacerbated latent oppositions. This change in the nature of the game can be observed around the second motion of censure which marked a genuine rupture with the tradition of EP – college relations. Through the intervention of Hervé Fabre-Aubrespy, a French right-wing 'villierist' MEP, the second motion deposed by the socialists was transformed into a confrontation between truth and falseness. In addition, this framing of the crisis was the result of a paradoxical alliance between monarchists, liberals and greens which gained momentum by superimposing national and European political logics. In France, the meeting of the national parliament for the revision of the constitution necessary for the ratification of the Amsterdam Treaty took place four days after the vote on this motion of censure. Similarly, the German position on agriculture influenced the posture of German journalists and needs to be interpreted in the light of preparation for the forthcoming European elections. This also happened at a time when Germany assumed the EU presidency and during important negotiations around Agenda 2000. In short, for the German delegates, the motion of censure was an opportunity to kill two birds with one stone: attack the Commission and France via Edith Cresson at a time when this member state was its principal opponent in the European Council.

This transformation of the game can also be seen in the results of the vote of this second motion and in its interpretations. As within the Commission, these show a very strong opposition between the countries of the North and those of the South. If all German MEPs voted for, all Spanish, Portuguese and Italian MEPs voted against. To this one should add intra-party divisions and the politicization of speeches and standpoints. Throughout the debates, 'electoral' arguments are constantly evoked. Verbal exchanges took the form of a political test where possible alliances for the future were experimented with. To give an example, a number of delegates who voted against the second motion of censure denounced 'the party-political and national interest' approach of the 'yes' voters, and advocated instead a more 'European' approach.

This transformation of the game can finally be observed from the angle of the distance that journalists increasingly took as regards the Commission. This distance was seen as a democratic control function that they now intended to embody. More precisely, the Association of the International Press issued an opinion criticizing the way the Commission operated. Jean Quatremer's article in *Liberation* on 31 January 1999 is a perfect example of the way in which journalists had become more vigilant. It reports a blunder by the Commission when it made public an internal note regretting 'the taking over of the press room by investigatory journalists'. This event echoed on and became another affair within the scandal, and this at a time when the effects of the 'committee of wise men' began to prompt discussion.

Independently of this particular issue, journalists also made use of interpretations of the crisis that were increasingly close to ones that had historically been used in national cases. This was the case when they adopted the 'heroic' form of the open letter (e.g. the article 'Long live eurocensure' in *Liberation* of 11 January 1999). As an illustration of the mechanisms of frustration and of the politicization of the categories used to interpret the affairs, journalists came to depict Santer as the opposite of Delors. To this one must add speculation over Santer's succession. Romano Prodi's name was actually put forward as early as November 1998, i.e. five months before the resignation and more than eight months before the normal replacement of the Commission. Similarly, eminent political 'candidates' were discussed in the press, such as Oscar Lafontaine.

With hindsight, one can see better how these new ways of playing the game took form. It is no coincidence if, by February 1999, all the actors, including advocates of a compromise solution such as Pauline Greene and Jacques Santer, came to see resignation as the only way out. In a very political way, they were all pushed to follow a movement which increasingly invoked 'European public opinion'. From this point of view, the resignation came to be seen less like a constraint and more like a resource redynamizing the college's communication strategy and thereby getting itself back in the driving seat.

The college's communication: wrong-footed then sidelined

In this fast moving context, the Commission's communication strategy was largely out of sync with events. Nobody in the Commission had envisaged what was going to occur. Actors were therefore overwhelmed by the events and the college's routinized approach to communication was caught on the wrong foot.

This occurred first because this approach to communication was based on a project of long term legitimation. This register was founded on the Commission's capacity to embody the Community interest, and in particular on its capacity to promote European integration via technical achievements. To borrow a hypothesis developed elsewhere (Georgakakis 2000), one of the specific characteristics of the European communication is its capacity to distribute 'assets of salvation, like other hierocratic groups', as Max Weber would have said (1947). This is typical of what Santer did at the beginning of the crisis. The context of the crisis was the launching of the euro, which was considered by everybody, at that time, as a major mission, an imperative for the future and a success. It was in this register that Santer and the college played in the beginning. All his speeches vaunted this success and devalued the crisis. Thereafter, other major issues of European integration (e.g. enlargement, Agenda 2000) served as a basic argument in the communication of the president of the Commission.

But the problem here is that this communication occured in a context of the politicization of issues and of European political practices. This context had no patience for 'technical' victories or the capacity to successfully and discreetly conclude major negotiations. Instead it called for the fundamentally political resource of 'charisma'. This observation should not lead one to evaluate whether Santer had charisma or not but simply to see how the reference to charisma added value to the context of the crisis. This was very new within European institutions and few actors have been comfortable with it. Moreover, in a context of strong oppositions, few observers are willing to recognize this charisma. In short, this was the first time the Commission had been wrong-footed into making 'poor communication'.

The second wrong footing action is linked to another, newer, process through which the Commission has sought to legitimate itself. As we have seen above, when Santer arrived as the head of the Commission he tried to introduce a moralization policy. Under the ideological heading of 'good governance', this policy was intended to achieve two things: distinguish the new Commission from the Delors period and position the Commission 'above' the 'interest-dominated' member states. However, what the Commission intended to be its strength actually ended up being its weakness. Given the college's collegial rules, paradoxical communication (Watzlawick 1977) was the end result. Either the college had to protect its members and drop its moralization policy, or denounce rogue commissioners and thus commit 'political suicide'.

These paradoxes of the Santer Commission certainly had an effect in terms of blurring its image for journalists and for the general public. But this blurring was also due to increasingly fraught relations with journalists mentioned earlier. Indeed, to complete the footballing metaphor, having been wrong-footed, the Commission ended up putting itself on the sidelines. Unlike many national cases, the journalistic field at European level is not a closed one and therefore any attempts at censorship are likely to be ineffectual. Nevertheless, in reaction to the initial articles on the affair, Edith Cresson tried to use a tactic habitually employed in French politics. Although the affairs had initially been revealed by the Belgium press, a group of journalists joined forces to carry on the attack, including French journalists from *Liberation, Le Monde* and *Le Nouvel Observateur*. Cresson immediately filed a lawsuit against *Liberation* and simultaneously gave an exclusive interview to *Le Monde* in an attempt to symbolically pay-off the latter. This tactic was designed to encourage *Le Monde* to distance itself from the affairs. It also led journalists from the left-leaning *Le Nouvel Observateur* to withdraw from the emerging group of European investigatory journalists.

In the French national situation, this tactic would probably have led *Liberation* to withdraw its attack because the newspaper would have been isolated. As prestige of the press in France is connected to its institutional dimension, falling out with politicians is seen as a form of downgrading. But here *Liberation* took support from a foreign press over which the commissioner had no influence. Exactly the same situation occurred for the Belgian journalist Jean Nicolas, who found support in the German and English press. The failure of the Commission's communication is therefore due to the fact that the game got away from the national journalistic field without engendering a structured European journalistic field within which censorship and/or self-censorship may have found its place.

Later this situation developed because the Commission's clumsiness had the effect of uniting the journalists. This unification occurred during a multitude of direct confrontations between Commission spokespersons and journalists. But it was also caused by the tactics adopted to try and manage relations between journalists and the rest of the administration as a means of curbing leaks. Once again, the Commission tried and failed to establish competitive relations between journalists as a means of regaining a position of power.

Unfortunately for the Commission, the game moved too quickly. For a while common ground did seem to be reached but the logic of journalistic autonomization soon led to renewed distance with political authority. The place and the role of the association of the accredited journalists in the conflict provides a good example of this trend. For instance, the International Press Association declared: 'Europe is now so important that we need stricter control over the Commission by the parliament and press'. A second example is that the rumour spread about Jean Nicolas and his neo-Nazi connections was interpreted by journalists as 'disinformation' and 'propaganda'. In short, all the communication transmitted by the college, or indeed by other parts of the Commission, ended up sidelining itself.

Conclusion

The story of the Santer resignation highlights the Commission's prior approach of non-communication. Previously all political problems were simply denied, which is a major explanation of the way the affairs were seen as a surprise and gave rise to such political mismanagement. Something changed during the crisis but in very unexpected ways that made the game largely uncontrollable, thereby beginning a trend that has been a major problem for the Prodi Commission.

More generally, the episode of the resignation is a good example of the way new ways of doing politics in a European space are invented. From this point of view, the crisis should not just be seen as a moment where the Commission lost its legitimacy. This clearly was the case for several commissioners, and more generally for all the Commission's staff in their relations with the outside world. Above all, however, as the Parliament's role, the emergence of new categories and perceptions or the idea that the Commission is 'the government of Europe' show, the crisis provides a window on how a European political space is being constructed. From this point of view, if it is certain that the Commission lost a great deal during the crisis itself, it is far from clear that this institution has not won itself other opportunities for the longer term. From the point of view of research on the Commission, this episode in its history underlines a particularly important challenge for the future: going beyond the analysis of who has won or lost, and deducing their causes, and observing instead precisely what happens during crises, such as the alliances and practices that are invented and tried out. Over and above the singular nature of the events under study, these are the sort of indicators which will allow research to really focus upon what structures Europe as an emerging space of politics.

8 The politics of the Commission as an information source

Olivier Baisnée

In order to study the political logics which govern the European Commission it is useful, for once, not to look within the institution itself but alongside or, to use the spatial metaphor of the press room, in front of it. Based upon a study of the EU press corps, this chapter deals with problems of crucial importance regarding legitimacy and the way the Commission deals with its own political ambiguity. If the European Commission is to be analysed as a political institution, it is beneficial to examine the way it communicates and attempts to gain both a visible and social existence.[1] While the themes of the democratic deficit and of the emergence of a European public sphere (for a critical approach, see Smith 1999) have become the topic of much scientific investigation, few studies have been dedicated to the Commission's communication practices (Consoli 1997; Meyer 1999), and this despite the fact that the ability of an institution to shape its legitimate social image is one of the key components of political power. In contrast, the attention paid to this question at the national level reminds us to what extent this relationship with the media is an essential political issue for most governments (Davis 2000, 2002; Franklin 1999; Legavre 1993). From the point of view of a sociology of journalism which studies relationships between journalists and their sources, I attempt to analyse the communication strategies of an institution which has to deal with one of the biggest press corps in the world (800 correspondents). The priority for the Commission, as for any political institution, is to try to persuade the media to share its interpretation of the current affairs of the EU. In this respect, the sociology of journalism is divided between a structuralist approach and a more competitive/dynamic conception of the interactions between sources and journalists.

The first intellectual tradition (Hall *et al.* 1978; Gitlin 1980) has depicted journalists as broadly dominated by the will of their socially powerful sources. Because of their social authority, or due to their social proximity to journalists or media owners, these sources are seen as able to ensure the diffusion and the reproduction of the 'hegemonic' ideology. Interpretations of the (socially, economically or politically) powerful thus only allow contestation within limits they themselves have fixed.[2] Interpretations deviating from their own would therefore be considered as oddities, deserving no attention or forced to respect the terms of debate imposed by the 'primary definers' whose initial framing of public issues cannot be challenged. From this hypothesis of the existence of 'primary definers', Hall *et al.* have stressed the dependence of journalists on the framing carried out by their official sources:

> The important point about the structured relationship between the media and the primary institutional definers is that it permits the institutional definers to establish the initial definition or primary interpretation of the topic in question. This interpretation then 'commands the field' in all subsequent treatment and sets the terms of reference within which all further coverage or debate takes place. Arguments against a primary interpretation are forced to insert themselves into its definition of 'what is at issue' – they must begin from this framework of interpretation as their starting point. This initial interpretative framework ... is extremely difficult to alter fundamentally, once established ... the primary definitions sets the limit for all subsequent discussion by framing what the problem is ... Contributions which stray from this framework are exposed to the charge that they are 'not addressing the problem'.
>
> (Hall *et al.* 1978) [3]

In this respect, a socially powerful institution is necessarily a dominant information source which is able to impose its own framing of events.

The idea of the ability of some sources to impose their interpretation of 'what is at stake' needs to be retained. However, other studies have tempered the conclusions of this structuralist intellectual tradition (Schlesinger 1992). For example, they have developed the idea that when the internal coherence of a source is undermined, their ability to impose a framing of the situation is challenged (Hallin 1989). Moreover, the competition that may take place between various official sources is also one of the factors needing to be taken into account because alternative definitions of public issues might be supported by institutions that are equally legitimate (Miller 1993). The main conclusion of these new theoretical approaches is therefore that it is quite impossible to decide a priori which institution will be able to impose its framing of the situation upon others. The relationship of an institution to journalists therefore has to be studied in a pragmatic and historical way. Indeed, the components which make up a 'good source' (Gans 1979) have to be analysed as well as the way this relationship has been historically constructed. Although the status of 'privileged source' is by no means flimsy, it can be lost or challenged under certain circumstances.

Historically speaking, and as far as EU news is concerned, the European Commission has long been the dominant source. Communicating in an environment that is characterized by an enormous amount of information, the diversity of competing sources and the need for journalists to select from the information they are given, the Commission emerged as the institution best able to make its own interpretation of issues shared by journalists. With respect to the general theories mentioned above, this relative dominance of the Commission over the EU's information is more the consequence of a relationship that has been constructed with journalists than of its political or social power. Indeed, at least outside the context of 'Brussels', the Commission is not such a politically and socially powerful institution that it would automatically become the primary source of journalists. Indeed, in general terms, the Commission is characterized more by its weak political legitimacy and social 'invisibility'. As this chapter shows, the particular characteristics of the Commission's relationship to the press corps serve to explain why it has long been favoured by journalists.

This chapter also studies the relationship between journalists and their sources in a dynamic fashion. As the political crisis that led to the resignation of Jacques Santer's team was going on, the internal coherence of the institution disappeared and informers provided investigative journalists with information. In a situation where the usual relationship between the Commission and journalists was no longer valid, competition between EU sources became very tough and sources usually marginalized by journalists (such as the European Parliament) were re-evaluated. Indeed, the latter managed to have their analysis of 'what was at stake' shared by the media. Finally, the chapter looks at the changes that took place in the Commission's communication strategy when Romano Prodi's team came into office. The overall failure of this strategy not only reveals the logic of the relationship between the Commission and the EU press corps, but also the difficulties encountered by an institution which has to face a 'public' with very diverse needs.

The characteristics of EU 'sources'

EU sources are characterized by three trends: their abundance and diversity, competition for access to journalists they are involved with and the hierarchy of sources established by journalists.

The diversity and amount of information

'It's a house made of glass', explains a journalist while pointing out the Breydel building through his office window. When asked about his relationship to the Commission as a source he indeed underlines how easy, especially when compared to his previous foreign correspondent's job, it is to contact senior Commission civil servants and even commissioners. 'Transparency', the buzzword of the Commission's communication policy

(Smith 2002), has accelerated the release of documents and increased the possibility for journalists to obtain explanations, answers, etc.

As we shall see, the amount of information it provides to journalists is one of the reasons for the Commission's domination as a source of information. Moreover, this is not merely the result of the commitment of just one institution since the profusion of sources is a characteristic of the EU. On a single subject, journalists can ask up to three institutional sources which have an interest in releasing information, thereby increasing the journalist's capacity to grasp the issues and problems at hand. Moreover, to these institutional sources one must add the thousands of lobbyists who inundate journalists' fax machines with their own news. The best example of this source of diversity is the Council where competing governmental sources have equal value and legitimacy; a situation which simply does not exist at the national level. As these two British journalists explain, there is always a source keen to release the information they are looking for, either because they aren't involved in the controversy and have no reason to keep it secret (which is often the case for small countries), or because they are involved in a controversy and want to embarrass their 'opponents':

> we complain and moan here, but actually, it's easier, and the sources of information are easier as well, probably because there are so many of them. So if I really want to find out what is happening, I can try here, but it probably won't come back to me, but then I can go to the UK representative, and the guy who covers chemicals there and say: 'well, what do you know about this?' He might not know anything, but he might, and then I'll go to France, I'll go to Germany . . . in the UK you wouldn't have a clue. In the UK, you would have to go to the press office.
>
> (British journalist, national daily newspaper)

> In Britain, and a lot has been written about it, the government has . . . tries to control the message a great deal. And it can do that if it's disciplined. Whereas here that isn't really possible because you have so many different other sources of information . . . If, for example on beef . . . If the British government says . . . you can crosscheck what they are saying by talking to the French delegation, to the Commission, to the German delegation if they've gone to the meeting . . . And that actually has a positive effect for a journalist on the way officials and press officers behave here . . . They can put their spin or their perspective on events but fundamentally they've got to provide more information than they would provide in London and be . . . make sure that it is factually accurate. It's more difficult to lie here as a press officer. It's a very difficult job to hold.
>
> (British journalist, national daily newspaper)

This abundance of available sources on the same subject and the fact that they have various interests in releasing information, makes the journalist's job easier in the same way as it makes it more difficult for spokespersons. Besides this diversity, sources are also involved in a form of competition which increases the capacity of journalists to crosscheck their information.

Competition between sources

This competition between sources can even be observed physically every day. Spokespersons from the Permanent Representations attend the daily briefing of the Commission. Standing discreetly at the back of the press-room, their task begins when the briefing ends by meeting 'their' national journalists in the bar of the press centre and providing the official position of their government about what the Commission has just said.

On the other hand, as the following example illustrates, Commission spokespersons can also encroach upon the member state's territory (the building of the Council) in order to promote the stance of their own institution.

14th December 1999.
In the bar of the Council press centre: 16h10, during an interview with a British journalist the British spokesman arrived, the interview stopped. The spokesman of the British Permanent Representation gathers together the British journalists who immediately form a circle around him. He quotes from a small notebook (reading with accents) comments made by Ministers Glavany and Brown. Journalists ask him for details and to repeat some points. Journalists discuss the implications together. The spokesman of the health and consumer protection commissioner then arrives: 'can I listen to you?'. The British spokesman then indicates that: 'I did not dwell on commissioner Byrne. I'm afraid I insisted on all the nasty things Mr Brown said about Mr Glavany'. Under pressure from a journalist, the Commission's spokesman gives an 'off, off, off the record' reaction, 'well, I'm listening to you'. Every journalist then gets closer. The Commission's spokesperson receives a phone call (everyone was waiting for the decision of the Commission meeting in Strasbourg about the '*avis raisonné*'). At the end of the call she tells a press agency journalist, 'I'm afraid you have to go'. The journalist asks 'is it five days?' When told 'yes', the journalist then runs to a phone. Indeed, the Commission had just decided to use a summary procedure which obliged France to answer for its decision not to lift a ban on British beef within five days.

This French journalist also confirms that information released by the Commission is a means of verifying what a minister has said whereas in the same situation at the national level, he wouldn't have had a means of checking what a minister has told him. In short, the availability in a single place of various sources enables journalists to know when a politician is not telling the truth.

> For example, . . . Pierret (French Minister of Industry) . . . It was about EDF, on the opening-up of the market. He said 'no, no, no I informed them, there was no problem'. We've been to others, I've been to commissioner De Palacio who told me 'Oh yes he has been given a shaking-up, etc.' so I wrote: 'It didn't go well'. Well, I found out too late to be able to say to Pierret 'wait a minute, the others say the contrary'. In France the contrary is true: political cant is everywhere. There must really be someone who wants to trip someone up to have an account of what goes on in the intimacy of the Council of Ministers or something like that. Here it's quite transparent.
>
> (French journalist, national economic daily)

Journalists' hierarchy of sources

Dealing with such an abundance of information and informers, journalists have to be selective in handling their sources. While for most European citizens the EU institutional system remains rather indistinct, journalists have to favour some sources over others, both for practical reasons but also because they are able to evaluate the respective political weight of each one. As the following example shows, sources not considered basic or interesting tend to be ignored by journalists.

On the 10 November 1999, quite unusually, numerous journalists gathered in the pressroom of the Paul-Henri Spaak building of the European Parliament (EP). To understand this unusual crowd, one has to take into account the importance of what was happening in the EP on this particular day. A French commissioner, Michel Barnier, and the president of the Commission, Romano Prodi, had come to explain to MEPs what the Commission's propositions were regarding the Helsinki intergovernmental conference. This was a big issue since it concerned the way the EU will adapt its functioning to the enlargement process. During the first few minutes of the meeting, only around 20 journalists came into the vast pressroom of the EP to watch the debates broadcast on a giant screen. However, as soon as the commissioner and his president (whose presence was not foreseen) were announced, the

> room suddenly filled up and MEPs' assistants were pushed out to free
> up space for journalists ('we have to do some cleaning' said one of the
> Parliament's civil servants). Representatives from the prestigious titles
> of national presses then settled down to listen to the Commission's
> propositions about a crucial issue.
>
> As the (short) press conference ended the president of the parliament-
> ary commission for institutional matters, Mr Napolitano, began his
> speech only to endure a mass exodus from the pressroom. Indeed,
> most journalists who came for the Commissioner's press conference
> left the room just as the Italian MEP was about to speak. This attitude
> is very revealing of the weak interest amongst journalists for the EP's
> position even when major issues are at stake. It provoked a humorous
> reaction from Mr Napolitano who seems to have understood that the
> institution he belongs to does not arouse much enthusiasm among EU
> correspondents. Speaking in French, he greeted 'all the heroes that
> have decided to stay'.

One can see from this episode the hierarchy that exists in journalists'
minds between the Commission and the Parliament. While the former is
attentively listened to and even provokes an unusual crowd in the Parliament's building, journalists appear uninterested in the thoughts of MEPs
about issues involving the enlargement process. In the cosy atmosphere of
'the European quarter' of Brussels, institutions struggle for the attention
of journalists. Often obliged to cover the whole of EU current affairs (and
sometimes those of NATO and Belgium), journalists have been obliged to
prioritize and therefore to favour certain sources above others.

Along with the observation of journalistic practices and analysis of their
output undertaken as part of my research, this example illustrates quite
clearly that the Commission is the dominant source for EU correspondents.
Through a historically constructed preferential relationship with accredited
journalists, the Commission has not only managed to receive considerable
coverage, but also to influence interpretations of EU current affairs.

Becoming the dominant source

Given the intense competition between information sources that takes
place in the European quarter, the ability of the Commission to shape
both the agenda and the interpretation of events of EU correspondents
has to be explained. As we shall see, its ability to produce abundant and
technically detailed information on a daily basis, as well as the dominant
way correspondents cover the news of the EU, are the principal founda-
tions of this decisive 'power to frame'.

The midday briefing as an institution: producing an information routine

While the social image of journalism depicts media professionals digging for information, most news actually arrives in newspapers through highly routine channels. This is why Léon Sigal (1973) used the metaphor of the pipeline in order to underline the role of sources in the news production process:

> like a pipeline carrying water from a reservoir to a city, it has some effect on what arrives at the end of the line. Not all droplets that enter the pipeline end up in the same destination; some are routed else-where, others evaporate en route. Yet the effects of the pipeline are minor compared to the source of the water – the reservoir. Similarly, newsmen, by adhering to routine channels of newsgathering, leave much of the task of selection of news to their sources.
>
> (Sigal 1973: 130)

Moreover, as most news comes from institutional and habitual sources, this enables journalists to have equal access from which no one benefits above others:

> Uncertainty loves company: the similarity of their stories provides some reassurance that newsmen understand what is going on in their world. For men who do not and cannot know what the 'real' news is, the routines of newsgathering produce 'certified news' – information that seems valid insofar as it is common knowledge among newsmen and their sources.
>
> (Sigal 1973: 130)

By providing journalists with a daily encounter, the Commission has been able to 'feed' correspondents with 'official' news through a routine channel. The main interaction between journalists and the Commission takes place every midday, during the '*rendez-vous de midi*'. Every day, at a few minutes before midday, between 200 and 300 journalists flock to the European Commission's presidency building. Most of them arrive at the Breydel on foot from nearby offices. However, the formal press confer-ence takes place only after the correspondents have finished queuing to get their documents. Then they enter the pressroom: a semicircle with barely 200 places. Indeed, these are cramped conditions in which to accommodate a press corps that has grown continuously since the early days of the European Community. The most striking point about this briefing is that sometimes a third of the press corp spend an hour of each day (a scarce resource) in the Breydel. During the hour-long conference, the official line of the Commission is made public. Spokespersons for the various commissioners come into the pressroom to make announcements of decisions already taken or to be taken, to expose the Commission's positions about events or processes that are taking place and to answer journalists' questions. During the whole interaction, spokespersons are also available for journalists in order to answer more precise questions 'bilaterally'. Indeed, particularly when the midday briefing attracted less journalists, it was a valuable occasion to obtain 'off the record' comments from the Commission.

This *'rendez-vous de midi'* remains the symbol of the control of the Commission over EU news. Whether they criticize its repetitive nature or recognize its usefulness, correspondents put up with the fact that this is the moment which organizes their whole working day. As such it acts as a kind of guide, enabling them to frame EU current affairs. By organizing the only daily encounter, the Commission is able to put its spin on EU news. The Commission defines the agenda and guides and influences further interpretations. Through background documents (speeches, data, etc.) and the words of its spokespersons, it channels the EU's informational flood.

Transparency: cluttering up timetables and offices

By filling up both the timetables and the very offices of journalists, the Commission's policy of 'transparency' constitutes another practice which tends to limit their ability to set agendas which differ from that of the primary source.

Apart from the ritual *'rendez-vous de midi'*, the Commission multiplies interactions where journalists are invited: technical briefings,[4] commissioner press conferences, receptions with foreign heads of state, etc. Obliged to cover these current affairs mostly on their own, journalists are literally inundated with possible encounters and information. Moreover, the huge press documentation released is, in itself, a problem journalists have to deal with. Piles of paper in offices are stocked for further reading or storage; the various press releases, speeches, files, data, etc., all reducing the time available for studying subjects 'in depth'. As journalists indicate, this amount of information prevents them from having their own work schedule. They have to 'go with the flow' as one of them put it, pointing to piles of papers around her office:

> You just have to look. And everyday you have that amount of documents [she points] and these are technical documents, you have to get into it. Our job, sometimes I liken it to the kind of analytical dissection I would have done at university . . . And that's very difficult.
>
> Qu: 'You were talking of the amount of press releases, and how you manage it?'
>
> It's horrible, it's horrible (laughs) It's awful, I sit on it. I try to do some filing. You must not be scrupulous or conscientious, anyway you

can't do it so you have to . . . it's empirical. Some people may have secretaries but most of the time it's like that [she points at her Italian colleague's office] It's not me, it's my Italian colleague, it defies description. I think he will never use it.

(French journalist, local daily newspaper)

On its own, the amount of available information is not sufficient to explain why the Commission can be regarded as the dominant source of EU news. First of all, journalistic interest for this information has to be explained. The crowd in the pressroom and the attention paid to documents (the queue to get press releases is a testimony of this phenomenon) cannot be explained mechanically from the fact that these papers are available. It is the historically constructed relationship between this institution and this group of journalists which better explains this interest.

A press corps which has supported the EU political project

Indeed, if journalists have an objective interest in a regular source which offers a landmark in the flow of information, its status of privileged source has to be explained. These two elements (dominant and privileged source) are linked to the kind of journalist the pressroom has long accommodated. Because of their biography and background, Brussels' correspondents have seen themselves as experts for many years, and just as often as advocates for the EU. Indeed, until the 1990s, the Brussels press corps was dominated by journalists with a particular profile.

For a time, accredited journalists were very few and far between. Well known by their peers, they were even more respected by European civil servants. Their longevity in Brussels is quite remarkable since some of them have been EU correspondents for more than 30 years. Year after year, they have come to know young civil servants intimately, some of whom have in time become Director Generals or even commissioners.

While this social proximity with senior civil servants has consequences on their daily work (it becomes rather difficult to criticize someone who addresses you by your first name), the reasons they decided to come to Brussels in the first place were twofold: to be close to Commission employees and others with a similar intellectual interest. Covering the EU in the 1960s or 1970s was indeed a sort of vocation. These young people, for whom it was often their first post as a correspondent, came to Brussels as true believers in the European project rather than as journalists. Indeed, before their arrival in the Belgian capital, some of them had belonged to learned societies or associations supporting the European ideal.

The other side of this 'institutional journalism' is its preference for an expert-linked definition of their job, one that is close to that of 'specialist journalism'. 'Quite assimilated to the institution' (Haegel 1992), these journalists come to look and act like civil servants. They are above all experts of European matters, 'fascinated by their subjects' and cover the way the institutions work in a very technical way. In particular, such journalists produce coverage more concerned with 'policies' than 'politics' and, consequently, are not very keen to dig up scandals and exclusives. The social and intellectual properties of these journalists have strengthened the domination of the Commission over EU current affairs. Seen as the only real European institution and the place where the European ideal is best represented, the Commission has therefore been given privileged treatment by these journalists. In comparison, the Council and the Parliament were considered to be institutions where struggles between national interests took place and tarnished the European ideal. For 30 years, the European Commission could expect to deal with a press corps which shared its preoccupations and, broadly speaking, supported the political project for which it was the symbol. By helping newcomers to the press corps and giving them precious advice, the first EU journalists were not only the 'grand elders' of the press corps, they also represented a professional model to be followed. As will be discussed below, growth in the number of the press corps and the arrival of journalists from more 'eurosceptic' countries, has changed the 'cosy club' atmosphere of the press room. It is now a place where numerous journalists have various interests and desires and not the place for 'pleasant chattering' that it used to be.

A crisis situation and the loss of internal cohesion

From an analytical point of view, the 1998–1999 political crisis that ended with the Santer Commission's resignation provides a privileged moment from which to study trends and phenomena which, except in exceptional circumstances such as these, tend to happen more silently. While it does not represent a definitive turning point in the life of either the press corps or the Commission, these events reveal tensions both within the professional group and the institution.

Changes within the press corp

If someone ever wanted proof of the Commission's belief in the loyalty of 'its' journalists, an internal memo written by Edith Cresson's spokesman which accidentally ended up in a journalist's hands would be a very crude example. As one of the solutions presented as a means of countering the 'attacks against the European idea and institutions', this memo explained:

> It is not true to say that all journalists have deeply changed. There is admittedly a 'takeover' of the press room by investigative journalists. But it is false to say that we don't have friends anymore. On the con-

trary: many journalists admit their confusion over what is going on; many disapprove – sometimes openly – of the excesses of their colleagues. I've seen journalists shouting openly at one of their colleagues. Instead of developing a general distrust of the press, this is why we must use our potential allies to restore a balance between background and investigative journalists.

(my translation)

This opposition between 'background' and 'investigative' journalists is very revealing of the confusion of a spokesman's service which now has to face a new 'breed' of journalism, to quote the term used in an International Press Association (professional association of EU correspondents) newsletter:

> Until the early nineties investigative journalism was an unknown species in Brussels. Most of the press corps, myself included, saw ourselves as fighting on the same side as the Commission to build up our common Europe ... Only a couple of years ago some journalists, given time and money by their editors, started to dig deeper and to look behind the daily press conferences, declarations and so-called 'background' briefings. Far away from mainstream reporting another truth saw the light of day.
>
> (Nathe 1998)

As the Maastricht Treaty was adopted and the EU's scope of activities enlarged, new correspondents arrived in Brussels to cover its current affairs that now appeared increasingly important to the politics of the member states. Unlike their elders, these journalists did not come to Brussels because of their own European activism or personal interest but to pursue a journalistic career they had begun in their own country. These journalists are younger than the institutional journalists but are in fact 'older' in terms of their journalistic career. They thus arrived with very different expectations. While 'institutional' journalists valued the local symbolic rewards within the Brussels microcosm (within which they are prominent personalities), these newcomers defended the 'professional values' that prevail in national journalistic fields. Put another way, these journalists have imported into the EU level the legitimacy principles of the national journalistic field, especially those of investigative journalism. This personal taste for in-depth reporting made them pay attention to things their elders ignored as part of an implicit refusal to undermine institutions and instead favour a journalistic style based on expertise and technical knowledge. When the internal crisis began to spread within the Commission, investigative journalists began to gain unprecedented access to informers within this administration, access which in turn provided major assistance for the production of their respective articles.

Leaks: the loss of cohesion within the college

Between August 1998 and the 16 March 1999, the Commission experienced the biggest political crisis of its history; a crisis which ended with the college's resignation. Meanwhile, many leaks undermined the communication of the institution and its apparent unity. Indeed, the very few investigative journalists who systematically pursued this story were only able to do so because of the informers who provided them with information.

As Didier Georgakakis (Chapter 7 in this volume and 2000) has shown, the administrative reforms and the 'managerial watershed' imposed upon European civil servants moved many of them to dissociate themselves from the college of commissioners. In this way the symbolic frontier between what can be said and what cannot was removed. A member of a commissioner's entourage related the following scene to me, a scene which is highly revealing of the incriminatory atmosphere that had come to exist within the institution:

> He recounts a meeting between a member of Cresson's entourage and four French journalists. The senior civil servant asks one of them what he is going to write about Cresson over the following days. The journalist answers that he's fed up with this story and will publish an article the next day and then give up. The civil servant replies 'well, what luck, you give up searching because Berthelot's son has a contract with the DG12, etc . . .' One of the journalists then leaves the room slamming the door. The storyteller then catches her up in the hall, she seems rather irritated and tells him 'this guy wants to knock Cresson down'. Effectively the day after, the journalist the civil servant was talking to published a new article about all the subjects he was told about, thus reigniting the controversy.

Journalists themselves are quite open about how such information was released:

> There were civil servants who were talking that's clear . . . so yes, leaks come from Director Generals and then officials within the Commission itself and within the spokesman service, there were . . . spokesmen or some of their assistants who had loose tongues. And so that's it . . . there were settlings of scores also. You have to know for example that Cresson was poorly thought of by her colleagues and . . . actually nobody thought well of her . . . enmities creating enmities well there has been a settling of scores and the time bomb could not be stopped

in time and that's it. At some time they wanted to stop it and try to offer an image of unanimity, of '*un pour tous, tous pour un*'. But it was just a front. The rot had already set in, the fruit was rotten and that's it. It was over.

(French journalist, national radio)

In the atmosphere of internal crisis, spokesmen in charge of ensuring the cohesion of the official line began to spread rumours and thereby keep investigations alive. As this young journalist explains, it was both because they wanted to protect 'their' commissioner (or put another in an awkward position) and because the warmth of the relationship between spokespersons and journalists is favourable to confidences.

> Well, at some point we forgot ... we forgot the boundary between the institution and the journalist ... At some point the Commission and its spokesmen lost control, forgot that they were talking to journalists and when ... When everything is all right, there's no problem at all. When everything is all right they say 'it's off', it's off. But when things are going badly, when there are revelations, the boundaries ... if such boundaries are abolished then ...
>
> (French journalist, national radio)

Moreover, the fragmented nature of the Commission played an important role. Its boundaries are very loose since it hires a lot of contract workers and often works with and through private companies. This fragmentation – while being one of the core problems evoked during the crisis – is also the decisive factor for the early leaks. Indeed, the first elements revealed by Jean Nicolas (a journalist from Luxembourg who did not belong to the EU press corps) were given to him by an entrepreneur who failed to obtain a contract with Mrs Cresson's services. When she refused to employ this company (Perry-Lux), Claude Perry then gave Jean Nicolas (with whom he also had a commercial relationship) information about Jean Berthelot, a friend of Edith Cresson, whom he in fact paid wages to as a means of obtaining contracts with Mrs Cresson's services (Nicolas 1999).

In short, the weak homogeneity of the Commission is not conducive to controlling information. As soon as a conflict appears between the Commission and one of the actors it hires, the latter may decide to release information. Yet, as we have seen, it is the arrival in Brussels of journalists with new profiles (compared to those of their elders) that enables informers to find journalists who will listen to them attentively. The loss of internal cohesion coincided with a change in the sociology of EU journalists which, together, resulted in the political crisis that ended with the resignation. Not surprisingly, Prodi's new team subsequently tried to define both a new communication strategy and a new relationship with the changing press corps.

Changes in communication strategies

As 'press campaigns' have been blamed (rightly or wrongly) for the resignation of the Santer Commission, the stability and ritual-like nature of the Commission's communication have been undermined. Belief in the power of press and the conviction that it provoked the departure of his predecessor, encouraged Romano Prodi to change the relationship between journalists and the institution he runs. In the name of the rather vague but politically significant notion of 'transparency', the new President set up a reform of the communication strategy of his institution. Thus, in a speech to the European Parliament on 14 September 1999, Romano Prodi explained:

> The Commission intends to become much more open. It is time for some glasnost here! I want to bring Europe out from behind closed doors and into the light of public scrutiny. I want people to be able to look over my shoulder and check that the Commission is dealing with the issues that most concern them ... And the new Commission will be putting much more efforts into communicating properly with the citizens of Europe, giving them open access to information.

This general announcement about a revised communication strategy entered the press room through diverse changes: the overall organization of the 'midday briefing' and the basis of this interaction were revised. By changing what was said and how it was said, the new team in charge of the media provoked the anger of part of the press corps who considered these changes were undermining their ability to do their job properly.

'An event a day': reforming the midday briefing

More attention will be paid to the way the 'midday briefing' has been transformed than to the overhaul of the spokesman service (now called the 'press and communication service'). This reform has been the subject of a major controversy between the new service and some journalists which is revealing of journalists' expectations and of their relationship with the institution. French journalists have been the most vociferous opponents, while their British counterparts, more used to the lobby system (Jones 1995; Tunstall 1970; Esser *et al.* 2000; Kavanagh 2000), have largely remained silent.

First, the 'stage' in the pressroom was significantly modified. Instead of the usual table where the spokespersons sat, lecterns were installed: one for the spokesman for Mr. Prodi, the other for spokespersons who are asked to answer precise questions or to communicate on a particular point. This modification of the set-up might seem anecdotal but it was interpreted by journalists as the sign of the 'Anglo-Saxon turn' of the service. As one journalist puts it 'they think they're in Washington'. Moreover, as the Commission asked Alastair Campbell (Tony Blair's then spindoctor) and the local BBC journalists for advice, the reform has been interpreted as Anglophile. When reforming its communication strategy, the new spokesperson service also tried to 'rationalize' and 'professionalize' its relationship with journalists. Based on mutual trust and social and intellectual proximity with journalists, previous practice was seen as obsolete by Ricardo Levi (head of the press and communication service). The new communication team decided instead to try to control and contain the communication of the European Commission. This reform concerned particularly the 'midday briefing' whose content and status have been revised.

> Clinton invented that during his 1992 campaign. In order to avoid having to answer questions coming from anywhere, about anything, you have to feed the journalists. You have to give them a big story each day to avoid them thinking of something else. That's the theory. And that's a bit like what the new Commission tried to do here. So, broadly speaking, Levi who is the chief spokesmen was arriving saying 'well, President Prodi wrote today to Clinton to tell him that there's a problem with the WTO'. That kind of stuff . . . What the new group of communicators did not understand when it imposed this policy of 'an event a day' is that it does not work. There isn't a single event that interests 15 nationalities on the same day. There are things going on and what they select as the event of the day is not often what interests most people.
>
> (French journalist, press agency)

As this policy was directed to a pressroom made up of media coming from 15 member states, but also of journalists from all over the world, it soon came to be seen as a failure. Given the various interests and expectations involved, it did indeed turn out to be impossible to put forward a subject that would be relevant for the whole pressroom, a situation which is very different from the national one. Because of the relative homogeneity of the hierarchy of information, when addressing a national press it is possible to select a particular event. While it is possible to predict the wishes of a national press it becomes much harder when there are 15 national presses with as many specific priorities and agendas. For example, whilst the EU is one of the main political issues in Great Britain (Wilkes and Wring 1998; Morgan 1995; Anderson and Weymouth 1999) it is not any longer in France. This leads to distinct ways of covering the same institutions because expectations from national desks differ. While most of EU current affairs are translated in terms of British internal political debate (with a particular focus on themes that can be explained in terms of 'victory' or 'defeat' for the national government), the French press never covers EU matters in its national pages. In the same way, countries where agriculture is only a marginal economic sector do not have the same expectations as those where this profession has greater political significance.

Undermining the 'off the record' basis for information exchange

However, another change has more definitively damaged the relationship between the pressroom and the spokesperson's service. Under the banner of 'transparency', the new Commission decided to broadcast the midday briefing both on *Europe by Satellite* (a TV channel that disseminates 'institutional' pictures of the EU) and on the Internet. By doing so, the new spokesperson service deeply changed the nature of the daily encounter. While it used to be 'friendly', 'informal' and based on the 'off the record' principle (which enables journalists, without quoting precisely any source, to go beyond the official line), it became a meeting point where only 'official' information was available 'on the record' (Legavre 1992). Indeed, because the midday briefing was broadcast through a media (Internet) available to anybody (even if the audience might not be strong) it became impossible to release 'off the record', background information.

This decision quickly became a major issue. The International Press Association (API), which represents a third of the press corps, soon reacted and set up a meeting with members of the spokesperson's service on 22 October 1999. This meeting was a failure since the head spokesman refused to change his decision. In its internal letter (La lettre de l'API, no. 6) the API underlines the fact that:

> The opinion of the majority [of the delegation] is that the current attitude of the Commission is likely to increase tensions with the Brussels press corps. It has been explained to Mr Levi that, unlike what he thinks, the upholding of the current line in the way the midday briefing is presented will be considered as a way to limit, rather than improve, the information flow. This is because the briefing can only be a useful information tool if, at any time, the use of 'off' information is possible. The fact that, as far as possible, information might be 'on' can't change anything on this point.

As negotiations reached deadlock, the IPA then convened the first extraordinary general meeting of its history in order to obtain a mandate from its members to reopen discussions with the spokesman.

The first extraordinary meeting of the IPA (25 November 1999).

In the International Press Centre, pressroom number 1.
50 seats. About 60 journalists were present.

During the debate, two issues are raised: the first one concerns the broadcasting of the briefing on EbS and Internet (which turns the briefing into an 'official' meeting where all statements will be 'on the record') and a more general one that concerns the failure of the new press relations' strategy introduced by the new team headed by Ricardo Levi. In fact, these two phenomena were closely linked, as the officializing of the '*rendez-vous de midi*' is an indication of the way the Commission considers the press corps as a public.

Jean Burner (president of the IPA and head of the AFP office in Brussels) speaks first: he points out the fact that EbS is only the visible part of the problem, 'the press office tries, in every which way, to give us ready-made information ... the 'on the record' cannot be used as such'. He suggests that 30 minutes of the briefing should be reserved for official announcements. A journalist then says that 'that's too long, they have nothing to say'.

Jean Burner then carries on, giving examples of every disfunction. A list, which he admitted, wasn't closed: 'the discontent has to do with all the mistakes within this press and communication service'. According to a British journalist since the arrival of EbS 'the outcome of the briefing has been reduced in the same proportion to which it has been made more public'.

A journalist from a German broadcasting service then indicates that he doesn't attend all briefings and instead uses the Internet broadcasting. He proposes to use the same system as with the German government where questions are divided into three categories: free information, restricted information and 'off' that can't be used. It is a technical regulation since the head of the press conference can switch the sound off when necessary. He points out that it has been working for ten years and that, concerning the Internet; a confidential code may be used. 'For those who can't attend the press conference, the Internet is wonderful'.

A French journalist underlined the difference with the German situation where journalists invite politicians to talk. 'If you invite people you can switch off ... Here we go to their place'. An American journalist later points out that in the White House there is a double briefing system: one is 'on the record', the other is 'off'. Two French journalists insist that the API's delegation refuse 'reverse angle shots' where journalists appear on television, they also want an 'on air' light to be installed.

A German journalist evokes the more general issue of a service that mistakes communication (which does not interest journalists) with a press relations department's role: 'we must demand a press relations office which knows how journalists work'. As a French journalist sums it up 'they behave as a communication service and not as a press relations one'.

The abilities of the members of the new service are then challenged: 'the problem is in their mind . . . they learned three weeks ago what 'off' means'. An Irish correspondent follows up, 'they do not understand how journalists work'. He recalls a briefing where 'there was absolutely nothing' and added that the problem was that 'they don't yet know how far they can go'.

Indeed, on 17 November 1999, Ricardo Levi spoke for an hour (after he indicated that what he would say would be 'unofficial, without EbS') to explain that on the beef issue, commissioners took a collegial decision! After this dull exposé, two journalists joked, 'it's rubbish, one hour of waffle to tell us the Commission took a collegial decision' and his colleague then followed up mocking Levi for saying '. . . that the Commission is formed of 20 commissioners'.

An American journalist said 'they tackle their job as civil servants do' and gives the example of a spokesman who 'still thinks he works as a EU negotiator'. He then wonders whether they should 'sit down with them and explain how the media work'. A German journalist then proposes an argument 'we will still get our information, we'll get it from the lowest secretary, but we will get it'.

Indeed, the main problem is the informational benefit that the attendance of the briefing represents. One of them says that within the present pressroom: 'I only get confirmed what I already know' and a Swiss journalist adds 'they think we're stupid, they think we don't know'.

Burner retains the proposition inspired by Germany saying, 'otherwise we go on strike'. He also summarized the major points of the talk: amateurishness, incompetence and finally, less information. In short, he sums up the conclusions of the meeting as 'a rejection of the method and of the content'.

Since this crisis, and after a short break, the briefing's broadcast resumed but now the sound transmission can be switched off when 'off the record' statements are made. Moreover, within the pressroom an 'on air' light has been installed for journalists to know in which kind of interaction they are being placed at any one time.

From an analytical point of view, the commitment of Prodi's spokesperson's team to broadcast the midday briefing represents a kind of official recognition that the pressroom plays the role of the European public. Turning what used to be a 'pleasant chat' into a much more official meeting is significant of its importance for the new President of the Commission. Furthermore, while commissioners almost never have any occasion to make speeches in front of a genuinely European audience, this pressroom and its inhabitants can ask questions relevant to their national situation in front of journalists from other member states, thus inciting them to take into account other national points of view.[5] In this sense, the pressroom can be described as the first and perhaps the only public for the European Union: a public socialized into the functioning of this political system, that knows its actors, that has direct contact with them and that, at least compared to the average European citizen, is well informed about it.

To journalists, however, the commitment to turn the daily briefing into a much more official meeting is seen as a significant mistake. As one journalist told an official after a very disappointing press conference: 'when you want to organize electoral meetings you should do it elsewhere'. The introduction of broadcasting, lecterns and the 'on the record' basis clearly show that Prodi's team wanted to use the briefing as an occasion to deliver political messages. This attitude is very revealing since it shows that they were convinced that the pressroom was made up of a public and not of a community of journalists present in order to obtain information. The reaction of the journalists, who do not consider themselves as members of the public but as professional reporters in need of information, highlights the ambiguous nature of this group. Because they are socialized into the EU political system and possess the analytical framework necessary to understand and analyse politics in Brussels, they function as a public. However, as long as they are journalists they consider that it is not their job to listen to political speeches which do not provide them with information.

Conclusion

This chapter has attempted to provide an account of the way the European Commission deals with journalists. Because it has dealt with a specific point of view, the picture presented is incomplete. To understand the production of EU news as a whole, one also needs to take into account the other main source for EU correspondents (the Council of Ministers), but also how editors in national capitals deal (in highly different manners) with the articles their correspondents send them from Brussels. Nevertheless, while incomplete, the present analysis provides some explanations of how, in a highly competitive environment, the Commission has become the main source for EU correspondents. This ability to shape news concerning the EU is a major political tool for the Commission. Yet, given its very weak political legitimacy this power is shown to be highly fragile whenever a crisis arises. In 1998–1999, the Commission's news routine that had essentially provided correspondents with technical information no longer fitted with their needs. In addition, the habitual discourse on 'collegial' decision-making was seen as anachronistic in the face of the intense conflicts raging within the very institution itself.

Moreover, the problems encountered during the 1998–1999 political crisis and when the communication strategy of the Commission was revised have called into question, at least temporarily, the Commission's status as a dominant source of EU information. As the Commission was undermined by its internal crisis, the European Parliament suddenly became one of the journalists' privileged sources. Both echoing and amplifying information coming from the Commission, the EP's press service began to provide investigative journalists with 'scoops'. As some journalists admit, this crisis led them to re-evaluate the parliamentarian source.

More generally, the arrival of journalists with new practices who stand more aloof from the Commission has probably contributed to 'making a whole generation take compulsory retirement' as one journalist jokingly put it. While it has been undermined, the Commission has not lost its ascendancy over EU news. Journalists continue to be interested in the 'midday briefing' for practical reasons, especially those who are bewildered newcomers in need of a 'lifeline'. Yet, the Commission is no longer regarded as a 'natural' and neutral source. In short, the Commission has become a source like any other; one that cannot dominate EU news as it used to do.

Notes

1 This chapter presents some of the initial results of PhD research on the logics of information production in Brussels. It is based on 63 interviews with correspondents and spokesmen and observations carried out during several stays in Brussels. (See also Baisnée 2000, 2002).

2 For Todd Gitlin (1980: 258) it is through socialization that ideological domination is organized:

> By socialization, by the bonds of experience and relationships – in other words, by direct corporate and class interest – the owners and managers of the major media are committed to the maintenance of the going system in its main outlines.

3 A similar hypothesis was also developed by Todd Gitlin (1980: 257) who explains:

> the economic system routinely generates, encourages, and tolerates ideologies which challenge and alter its own rationale ... But contradictions of this sort operate within a hegemonic framework which bounds and narrows the range of actual and potential contending world views. Hegemony is an

historical process in which one picture of the world is systematically preferred over others.

4 Directorate Generals or senior civil servants then provide journalists with 'off the record' information. These briefings are highly specialized and enable journalists to develop an in-depth knowledge of subjects.
5 For example, when a German journalist asked one day if the Commission might suppress regional funding to some Länder which don't respect an environmental directive, French journalists, who were not aware of this problem, immediately reacted by asking whether some French regions might encounter the same problem.

9 Advertising Europe

The production of public information by the Commission

François Foret

Every political authority has to deliver a legitimizing discourse in order to give meaning to the order its creates. This discourse may take various forms, of which the publications edited by the Commission for the general public in the 11 official European languages is one particularly meaningful example. These documents present the European Union to its citizens through the diversity of its sectoral policies and as an original institutional system or as a major historical process started by the 'Schuman declaration' of 9 May 1950. Through text and images, these booklets describe a political panorama assigning a place to every actor and emphasizing the 'necessity' of European integration. The Commission poses as both spokesperson for Europe and as the translator of the 'hidden truth' (Lagroye 1985: 408) who justifies the failures which mark daily practice.

From the point of view of research, the challenge is to discover whether the institution totally assumes the political dimension of European integration, or has been led to develop a more technocratic rhetoric because of its position and its functions within the EU.

On the one hand, the Commission's editorial policy undoubtedly has a political dimension if one compares this against the three criteria set out in the introduction to this book. First, the publications produced are a form of public intervention. The booklets are defined as 'collective writing whose edition implies a budget and is destined mainly for external use' (European Commission 1993b: 4). Second, this policy is a reflection of competition for power because, when producing European discourse, actors both engage in relationships of co-operation or opposition and must simultaneously dramatize this through communication exercises. Finally, this editorial policy involves dealing with sets of meanings founded upon values (Diez 1999). On the other hand, the political dimension of the Commission's publications raises some difficulties. As a spokesperson, this institution has severe limits. It manifests a propensity to search for consensus in order to protect itself against any attack. Reference to expertise is often the dominant means of closing any potential debate before it is allowed to begin.

In the first part of this chapter, I will show that when producing its publications, the Commission takes on the role of a locutor which has a vocation to speak in the name of Europe but remains hesitant in playing this role and does not easily manage to share it with other European institutions. The chapter's second part concentrates on how the form and the content of the discourse engendered illustrate the ambiguous position of the Commission, an organization which constantly oscillates between the behaviour of an accountable political actor and that of a neutral bureaucratic agent.[1]

The Commission as a locutor

The Commission is led by its functions to formulate a discourse for the general public. However, an analysis of the editorial process underlines the extent to which the institution suffers from a lack of skills and resources. More generally, the status of spokesperson for Europe is assumed with caution and, therefore, is shared only with difficulty.

An omnipresent but not all-powerful locutor

The Commission asserts itself as the spokesperson for Europe because of its four main functions (Cini 1996a: 14 ff.). First, it is the *inspirer of the integration process*, the ideas-machine, the force for new proposals which has to open up prospects for the future. As a consequence, it is enabled to elaborate general representations of the Union as part of the process of building long term strategy. Second, the Commission is in charge of the *management and the enforcement of European policies*, thus making itself the linchpin of the decision-making system and the first interlocutor of all social actors. Its civil servants are the daily interpreters of Europe. Third, the institution is the *guardian of the treaties and of the legal order*, playing the role of passive consciousness by controlling the implementation of European law and of active consciousness by promoting integration. In this way, the Commission is identified with the EU, any attack against itself calls into question the integration process as a whole. Finally, the Commission is the *builder of consensus* who has to reconcile positions of supranational, national, local, private and public actors in order to propose a 'common interest' from which its agents are able to create a technically viable modus vivendi.

Through these functions, the Commission has become the major historical agent of European communication. As the commissioner Rochereau said at the meeting of the Council on 23 September 1963, the founding treaties do not mention a common information policy but such an activity nevertheless fits with their fundamental objectives (quoted in Pourvoyeur 1981: 194) and it falls upon the institution which guarantees the Community's continuity and orthodoxy to perform this task. For this reason, over the years, the Commission has expanded its interventions in the public sphere (annual reports, speeches, articles, publications etc.) both in order to reach EU citizens, but also to make its partners more aware of its choices, to set the European agenda and to generate coalitions around its propositions (Cini 1996a: Chapter 5). In short, information is used both as a strategic weapon and as a pure resource for legitimation.

But the Commission has handicaps: its dual institutional nature, its complex way of working and its remoteness from the traditional expressive forms linked to universal suffrage. Its leading figures, the commissioners, have difficulties in catching the attention of the general public. Despite their very political mission and a supposedly collective decision-making process, their speeches remain individual, particularist and technocratic. They are too deeply associated with the member state they come from to claim to represent the EU and, in the eyes of the journalists, suffer from comparisons with national ministers (Joana and Smith 2002). For example, in October 1998, the Commission's President, Jacques Santer, was recognized by 31 per cent of Europeans, whereas 85 per cent claimed to recognize Tony Blair and 82 per cent Jacques Chirac or Helmut Kohl (Méchet and Pache 2000: 171–172).

Under these conditions, formulating a discourse for the ordinary citizen is a challenge. Indeed, the way the editorial process is carried out emphasizes the problems faced by an institution whose culture of the pioneer and whose history do not predispose its agents to give a publicly understandable account of its own actions.

A locutor hesitant about its role

During the period of our study, and therefore before the reform launched by the Prodi team at the end of 1999, the Commission's editorial policy was designed and implemented by the 'publications unit' (Direction D: 'communication'), located within DG X: 'information, communication, culture and audiovisual'. The mission of this unit was centred upon generality, both in terms of its audience and the subjects which were to be dealt with. The goal was to supply citizens with free information sources about the European Union, its institutions and its policies. As one civil servant underlined:

> The main objective, almost the unique one, of my unit is to provide information suitable for the general public. To spread the big political messages of the European Union to the citizens. There are other sectoral DGs which produce specialized information, for specific fields. Our mission is . . . everybody.
>
> (Interview, April 1999)

The documents elaborated by the 'publications unit' were divided into two categories. The Ordinary Publication Programme (OPP) dealt with all subjects for which a regular demand existed or which was considered to have long term strategic importance (booklets about the European institutions, maps, statistics). The budget (about three million euros) was managed by DG X. In contrast, the Priority Publication Programme (PPP) dealt with the main issues on the annual agenda of the Commission. The funds (about four million euros) were managed directly by the Secretary General of the Commission. In short, the publications linked to current events of the institution benefited from more money and were controlled at a more 'political' level than those aimed at satisfying public curiosity.

This predominance of the 'logic of supply' over the 'logic of demand' was deepened by the fact that the means available for anticipating the expectations of citizens about information remained scarce and imperfect. Eurobarometer surveys were not spontaneously cited by our interviewees as guides with which to choose subjects for publications. Instead, civil servants within the 'publications unit' more often mention the questions they receive from visitors to the Commission, press reviews, letters from readers and especially reports from the Representations of the Commission located in the member states or the delegations situated in the rest of the world. However, these different ways of taking public reception into account are not sufficient to have made evaluation of impact a decisive parameter. Rather the determinant element is the exposure and positional strategy of the Commission. Adapting to public demand is seen as the task of the Representations in the member states since these have the power to distribute a publication or not, to decide the number of copies and the distribution channels and to target specific social groups. In practice, however, the weakness of circulation-levels in comparison to the potential readership and the uncertainty of distribution by networks which are not directly controlled by the European Union, simply do not encourage any adjustments. The lack of any reliable indicator for the impact of these publications reinforces the image of a European message being addressed to citizens as if in a bottle launched into the sea.

If *ab initio* definitions of objectives of publications have never been paid great attention by Commission officials, the actual content has always been polished through a long editorial process. At least until the 1999 reform, first the 'publications unit' made a thematic proposal before sending it for approval and possible correcting to the decision-making authority (Secretariat General for the PPP or DG X for OPP). At this stage, reflection over the structure of the document began through interaction with all the competent services involved in the issue area concerned (sectoral DGs, commissioners' cabinets). The author is then selected with regard to the skills required by the subject and the availability of potential candidates. Representations and delegations were consulted to foresee demand and decide the print run. Once written, the text is first submitted to the criticism of the 'publications unit' which may suggest formal corrections, and to experts from other services for more factual verification.

Only then can the process of technical production and translation to all the official languages of the EU begin. The Official Publications Office of the European Communities (OPOEC) in Luxembourg undertakes contracts with private companies to print the publications. Finally, distribution to Representations and delegations is organized in such a manner that a unity of time, space and content is respected. Any booklet has to be available in the same form and at the same moment everywhere in the European Union.

In short, an 'executive troika' composed of the 'publications unit', the Secretariat General and the OPOEC, engages in a semi-formal, semi-informal[2] process of editorial production made up of numerous interactions between the different actors who contribute to modulating a final result which respects the overall logic of the institution, but without imposing a very constraining framework.

Indeed, the 'publications unit' has only very general control of this work. Producing booklets is one of the main tasks of the members of this unit, but their specialization is linked more to a particular object (publications) than to specific functions. Their daily practices (studying projects, preparing and implementing contracts, a posteriori audits) do not differ radically from the traditional bureaucratic routine of civil servants from other units. The price of this banalization is a transferring of the uncertain role of European symbolic producer to external authors.

Recourse to external authors is a necessity because of the small size of the 'publications unit'. It also results from a choice to hire professional writers, whose work is judged to be more accessible to a general public. Accredited journalists to the Commission are often solicited, whilst academics are more rarely called upon. As regards the authors of booklets from the 'Europe on the move' collection studied in detail in my research, they usually remain anonymous. This non-signature may appear logical, because the writer does not control the 'final cut' of their text. Moreover, authors are not asked to assume responsibility for their work since their names are not made public and they are not made available to answer questions. Indeed, many appear to be afraid of being misjudged by their professional colleagues because of their work for the Commission. To understand this attitude and climate of caution, it should be noted that this role was severely criticized, and even likened to corruption in a controversial article (De Sélys 1996),[3] which made considerable waves in the mid 1990s.

Only the authors of booklets from the 'European documentation' collection, aimed in a more sophisticated manner at an interested public, sign their texts. Being accountable for their discourse, they are far more autonomous as regards the Commission, even to the point of being placed in a situation which they themselves often define as 'anomic'. Without a clear status enabling them to speak in the name of Europe, they use the role of pedagogue as a substitute in order to give meaning to their work.

On their publications, they mention their academic titles and their teaching activities (e.g. at the College of Bruges, at Sciences Po Paris), which they believe to confer a 'presumption of objectivity' upon their texts. In reality, however, many of them are European civil servants. The writing of public communication documents for institutions is ill-perceived in the scientific world, preventing a lot of academics from playing this role. In any case, becoming a spokesperson for Europe has a cost in one's professional group of origin. This explains the Commission's difficulty in finding mediators who are both skilled, available and legitimate, without their involvement with the European institutions separating them from their initial environment, thereby weakening their capacity to spread their respective messages.

Indeed, this is a constant theme: speaking in the name of Europe remains a weakly legitimate and codified function. However, the Commission, which itself often plays this role in an ambiguous and doubting way, is not the only actor to blame. Instead, its action must be placed in the context of the European Union as a whole and of the Commission's interactions with other institutions.

A non-exclusive locutor

The internal and external co-ordination of communication policy is a chronic problem which has been constantly underlined without ever being solved. Even the very authoritative practices of Jacques Delors in managing the Commission's image never overcame the weakness of the centre's control over the other parts of the institution (Grant 1994: 142 ff.). DG X has always enjoyed little esteem from the top of the hierarchy (Ross 1995: 163) and, before disappearing in 1999, it had insufficient strategic power to impose its preferred options upon other services. Its attractiveness was mediocre; it was seen as a negative step in a career, as the number of posts left vacant in its organigramme illustrated (Smith 1998: 53–69). More significantly still, the organizational change of communication structures in 1999 follows a quasi-permanent series of reforms, which reveals the inability of the institution to establish satisfying practice in this field (Kaïpoulos 1992: 48). This change took place as part of a general revision of the Commission's institutional frame conducted 'to promote good governance principles': autonomy, accountability, obligation to report, efficiency and transparency (Livre Blanc sur la réforme de la Commission, COM 200, 1 March 2000, 8). Given its mission, DG X was more concerned by these transformations than with other services. According to Vice-President Neil Kinnock, the objective was 'to allow the Commission to speak with one single voice and to coordinate its communication actions in a more professional way' (Press release, 29 September 1999).

In the new organigramme a new DG for 'education and culture' was created to take charge of the activities of the former DG XXIII ('education') and of DG X. At the same time, the Representations in the member states, the audiovisual production unit and the Internet service were linked to a new press and communication service which replaced the former spokesman service (see Chapter 8 in this book). The ambition was to concentrate resources in order to create a 'critical mass' of specialists that was directly under the authority of the President and able to react quickly and skillfully to defend the Commission's positions in the media. The more structural and long term communication tasks, such as publications for the general public, remain managed by DG education and culture. As an actor said of the reform, 'it was necessary to split the urgent, hot information from the less political, slower, cold one' (Interview, September 2000). In the first case, the Commission has to be ready to assume potentially conflictual positions; in the second case, it has to collaborate with other European institutions and member states to explain Europe to the citizens. The separation had become increasingly inevitable because of the confusion and contradictions resulting from a mixing of the two activities. 'It was more and more difficult in a single service to denounce the policy of a national government in the morning and to negotiate an information agreement with it in the afternoon' (Interview, September 2000). This reform is still too recent to be evaluated in a definitive fashion, but the subject is very controversial. The change is perceived as too timid (*Le Monde*, 21 September 1999) or illogical because it dissociates different manners of addressing citizens. Moreover, according to our interviewees, the reform was seen as marginalizing the handful of communication specialists from the former DG X in a new organization where education experts are more numerous, in a position to impose their priorities and are overtly sceptical about persuasive actions other than teaching networks.[4] The professional cultures of the pre-existing services remain very strong. All actors agree only to criticize a badly prepared and led reform which they consider will contribute neither to rehabilitating the role of communication within the Commission nor to improving its efficiency.

The main problem, however, is the lack of co-operation between the internal services of the Commission and other institutions. The political imperative to make Europe speak with one voice, or at least to attain a certain harmony between the different messages expressed, is often thwarted by the conflicting interests of the actors involved.

From this perspective, the example of the EU's publishing policy is striking. As early as 1952, a desire to adopt shared information tools led to the creation of an Official Journal which has become the unique organ of reference. Only in 1969 was an Official Publications Office of the European Communities (OPOEC) common to all European institutions established in order to rationalize the production and the distribution of EC publications.[5] The creation of this structure clarified the issue of information supply by homogenizing classification systems and catalogues.

However, this did not lead to an overall publications budget, because each product was billed to its commissioning institution. Moreover, no actor was able to oversee the coherence and the pertinence of the overall editorial strategy (Hopkins 1985). At the end of the 1980s, the Andenna report continued to emphasize that, apart from DG X, four other DGs continued to produce booklets about nuclear energy and two others about agricultural policy (European Parliament 1988: 15–18).

The situation is not so different today as can be seen by the fact that insufficient co-ordination over communication is recognized by the Commission (European Commission 1994: 9 ff.) as much as by Parliament (Parlement européen, 'Résolution sur la politique d'information ...', 1998, AE; AF). Its development is presented as an absolute priority, and constant reference is made to the success of the European Citizen Information Programme associating the Commission, the Parliament and the member states. Nevertheless, the project of a unique inter-institutional communication office defended in 1993 by the De Clercq report (De Clercq 1993: 43), still remains utopic.

In summary, all these difficulties in producing a general discourse about Europe for the ordinary citizen reveal the limits of the Commission as a spokesperson for the EU. But it is also necessary to take into account the constraints resulting from the institutional system and the socio-political configuration of the European Union. In both the form and the content of its discourse, the way the Commission oscillates between the posture of the responsible political actor and the neutral bureaucratic agent confirms that its position is not well defined and must constantly be renegotiated.

The Commission and information blame

The Commission does not assert itself totally as the keystone of the Community political system described in EU publications. Neither does it unconditionally take responsibility for its discourse on the more polemical dimensions of European integration. Instead, the Commission avoids any excessively militant or ideological position and only accepts a mode of argumentation presented as rational, evident and pragmatic, thereby offering little possibly destabilizing interaction with its readers.

'Signing' discourse

In the booklets, the Commission speaks in the name of the European Union as a whole. Each publication is the property of the Community and not of one institution. 'Copyright belongs to the Community, not to each individual institution' (European Commission 1993b: 44).

As we have shown above, the Commission usually ascribes authorship to itself by not mentioning the identity of a publication's writer. However, for potentially more controversial documents it is common to give the name of the actual person who wrote the text. For instance, the leaflet 'Seven days which made Europe' is signed by its writer who is then deemed accountable for the militant tone and for the choices of some symbolic dates. What is more, a 'precautionary clause' may be added to attribute all the ideological dimensions of the text to the subjectivity of the author.[6] Thus, the Commission offers a plea in favour of integration without really accepting its paternity.

As the intellectual editor, the institution nevertheless keeps the copyright (European Commission 1993b: 25). The formula on the publication determines the degree of freedom with which the document can be used. This copyright formula reveals what is the priority: either the concern of imputing ownership to the Commission, which involves quoting its name as mandatory, even at the risk of putting off some potential users;[7] or the objective of developing the transmission of the European message, even if some mediators take excessive advantage of it or if the readers do not know who is addressing them. An overwhelming majority of publications are in fact submitted to a restriction that is twofold: the outlawing of economic use and the obligation to cite the source. A very clear change over time has been discernible because, since 1997, the documents no longer have any clause against possible commercial exploitation. But the imperative to identify the origin of the document remains, which strongly suggests that the promotion of the institution is considered more important than the transmission of the message.

Imputing responsibilities

In the imputation discourse that the publications constitute, the vision of the present contains no mistake. The Commission does sometimes give itself over to self-criticism, but always moderately and only about the past so it can legitimate its current acts. Confession of a failure is difficult to conceptualize because it would be the result of an inability to reach a predefined objective. But the integration process is presented as proceeding in big steps rather than through precise realizations, with a flexible calendar and constantly renegotiated methods. This leads the Commission to speak less of victories or defeats and more of dynamics or crisis, the results varying over time according to political conditions and the power relationships between numerous actors. In this way, a genuine discourse on accountability is prevented from emerging by the very workings of the European institutional system.

The consequences of the EU's polycentrism are nevertheless deepened by the reluctance of the Commission to show unconditional solidarity with its partners. In the publications, the institution looks to share the legitimacy of the European Council whose well-known members are assured of prestige and media success. But it also looks to share that of the

Parliament for whom universal suffrage provides a democratic aura. But this mechanism of mutual gratification between the European institutions can quickly turn into an affirmation of each entity against the others. Thus, the Commission often denounces the slowness or the excesses of intergovernmentalist bodies. The Council of Ministers is rarely mentioned in the booklets. The European Council is evoked only slightly more often, but every reference to its functions is balanced by developments about the Commission's role. On the contrary, the Parliament is often quoted and opposed to the Council of Ministers. To solve the problems of the European Union, the solution is unambiguously said to be a reinforcement of the former against the latter. In this multi-level game, it is by no means certain that such tactical logics and the expression of inter-institutional discord helps to reconcile the secular reader with an already complex and mysterious Europe.

Defending a position founded upon values

The European discourse transmitted in the Commission's booklets features a reticence to defend positions which could be considered too extreme. The ideological factor is reduced by using a flat rhetoric which presents European integration as a simple list of obvious choices inspired by common sense or rational interests. The objective is to present as little ammunition as possible with which to criticize the Commission, at the risk of weakening the political content of the message.

All the institutional mediators of Europe see themselves as working in the service of the European belief and, therefore, give themselves the mission of promoting it. Nevertheless, this does not mean that they are ready to openly assume options which could be called 'ideological'. For agents within the Commission, their discourse has the power of truth and can be criticized only in the case of occasional excesses. Exceptionally, the writer of a booklet (*L'Unification européenne. Création et développement de l'Union européenne'*, 1995) admitted that a British reader was right to have reproached him for his bias. The reader was indignant because federalist theories of integration were developed on more than one page, while intergovernmentalist theses were just mentioned in a few lines (Interview, May 1999). However, the *mea culpa* of this author departs from the official editorial rule of the publications which above all looks to strike a balance between different visions of Europe in the name of pragmatism and realism.

Any ideological arbitration which could be controversial is avoided. The choices expressed in the booklets are reduced to some supposedly consensual principles, whose means of enunciation tends to use unquestionable moral absolutes rather than arguable political factors. Free trade is one example among many others of how these fundamental principles are seen as transcending all opposition. The Commission almost invariably sides with liberalism without reserve (e.g. 'L'Union européenne et le commerce mondial', 1995). In the same way, this institution argues strongly against 'obsolete' Keynesian economic theories: 'The reduction of deficits is the only solution to create strong economic growth, the *sine qua non* condition for creating jobs and fighting unemployment in Europe' (e.g. 'Quand aurons-nous des euros dans la poche?', 1997: 10). The position is radically different, however, when a publication deals with more polemical subjects which still divide the major party political families. Community actors are then shown to be very careful in trying to find a moderate option. The presentation of 'social Europe' is an archetypal example:

> There are two schools of thought. The defenders of a neo-liberal economy want to strongly limit social and other restrictions to competition, in the hopes of reaching by this way a high level of prosperity ... At the opposite end of the spectrum, those who believe in a welfare state model consider that social taxes are necessary costs for preserving social peace ... The European Community has to develop a policy which is a compromise between these two poles.
>
> ('Pour une Europe sociale', 1996: 2)

The concern to adopt a low profile strategy explains that there are few theoretical developments. This laconism has the twofold advantage of offering little matter to criticize and seeming to reason from common sense, rather like a popular adage. Ideological prejudice in a position which is enunciated as 'obvious' looks improbable and thus can remain hidden. Indeed, this rhetorical style evokes the sparse and definitive formulas of Jean Monnet's *Memories* which, in the middle of detailed accounts of historical events, emerge like simple rules of behaviour which flowered in the heat of action.

This propensity towards the naturalization of the Community discourse is linked to a tendency to rationalize all the EU's problems in terms of interest. The way to deal with the problem of the external relations of the European Union is particulary significant here. What is preponderant is the economy (e.g. 'L'Union européenne et l'Asie', 1995: 1). The pledge of faith in free trade is not only the result of abstract reflection. 'If the European Union encourages international trade, this is not just through simple altruism' (e.g. 'L'Union européenne et le commerce mondial', 1995: 6), it is to reinforce its own growth in the long term. Even big universal causes, such as the protection of the environment, are presented under the light of the advantage the EU can take from them (e.g. 'Le marché unique européen', 1996: 40).

European discourse mobilizes the interest of the EU as a major argument, but also the interest of the reader as an individual. It appeals to their reason in order to solicit their approval. This strategy corresponds to a recommendation made in the De Clercq report, which suggested making individual argument an interest for legitimating integration. 'Ideas lead the world; but, in order that the ideal becomes the will of the people, the people must first perceive the concrete benefits that they will get from the ideal' (De Clercq 1993: 7).

The objective of this rhetoric is to protect the Commission against any accusation of proselytism. European publications are submitted to reproaches as soon as they do not deal with 'moral' subjects (human rights for example) but also with politically conflictual themes. In 1998, some criticisms were levelled at the Commission for 'Me, racist!?', a comic strip for teenagers which ridiculed racist stereotypes. But the protests remained moderate, even if the Representation in London decided not to distribute the document in Great Britain because of a supposed maladjustment of the discriminations as regards the local situation. On the other hand, attacks against the Commission were stronger over 'The Raspberry Ice Cream War' (1998), another comic strip promoting the common market and the single currency. In addition, members of the European Parliament asked several questions about the relevance of praising the euro in countries which had refused to take part in it.[8]

Quickly accused of propaganda when dealing with excessively polemical subjects, the Commission is prone to develop a technocratic and consensual rhetoric rather than a political one. This dominance of the technocratic register is also perceptible in the very unilateral dimension of the European discourse. The culture of compromises reached in small circles of actors that has been so central to 'the Community Method' does not facilitate wider dialogue where citizens might provide a potentially destabilizing input.

Structuring the relationship with the citizenry

In the Commission's publications, interactivity is limited. In three cases, 10 per cent of my sample, possibilities to come into contact with the European institutions are offered, but the reader is addressed each time as a taxpayer or a consumer. Interactivity is thus placed in a strictly utilitarian perspective and therefore remains limited.

In the same way, the use of interrogative or personal forms often sketch out the opening of a debate which thereafter is rapidly closed. The interrogative mode used in titles or headlines to simulate a dialogue with the reader appears in one third of the documents studied. However, the formula 'questions and answers' actually block exchanges by immediately proposing definitive answers to the questions asked. Personalized turns of phrase (for example, 'What can Europe do for me?', 'We Europeans' or 'Do you know your rights?') are restricted to 10 per cent of the sample. What is more, the model proposed to the reader is the consumer searching for his or her private profit rather than the citizen involved in a quest for general interest. As exceptions which highlight the 'rule', these timid attempts to promote an interactive reading of the publications emphasize how the usual tone is impersonal, neutral and cold. The discourse of the European institutions takes place in a very closed register where any risk of deviance is strictly controlled.

Conclusion

In summing up this short reflection about a particular but revealing example of the Commission's relationship to politics, the communication weaknesses of the Commission are clearly a structural factor. The reason for failure in this domain is above all the lack of a real communication sphere and of a common register shared by the citizens and the power at the European level. Nevertheless, the way the institution accepts – or fails to accept – responsibility for the political dimension of its activity in adjusting to its environment is also an element to be taken into account. The institution is unable to play the role of Europe's spokesperson in a direct fashion because of both its position in the political and bureaucratic game and its internal characteristics. In the editorial process, the specific logic of the European system prevails over the objective of producing an effective legitimation discourse.

The Commission has the mission of developing a general discourse about Europe for the general public, but neither its resources nor its political profile are up to this task. The division of labour is largely uncodified and remains heterogeneous and non-stabilized because of a lack of a clear political line and a well-defined framework. There is no real anticipation of public reception, 'supply' is more structuring than 'demand' and the complex editorial process involving numerous actors contains no entity capable of giving a strong lead and making choices in order to attain overall coherence. Finally, the Commission's organigramme shows that the very act of communicating is weakly valued and institutionalized.

The same can be said for the content of its discourse. As a locutor, the Commission does not embody an accountable political actor. Its rhetoric is defined as neutral and without ideology, without positions founded upon values. The objective is to avoid potentially conflictual postures, which also leads to limiting any possible interaction with citizens. Ultimately, in terms of legitimation, the Commission accumulates three handicaps within the European political order: it is structurally constrained, strategically self-circumscribed and politically subordinated.

Notes

1 This article tackles part of the symbolic policy of the European Union which is treated more comprehensively in my doctoral thesis (Foret 2001).
2 This mix between the formal and the informal is a constant in the general functioning of the Commission. The rigidity of procedures designed to ensure the

coherence of a multicultural institution is permanently counterbalanced by non-codified ways of speeding up work through personal relationships or the spontaneous organization of task forces (Bellier 1994).

3 The attack was considered harsh enough to justify an answer from Paul Collowald, an emblematic historical figure of European information policy (Collowald 1996).

4 Interview by the author, 21 September 2000.

5 Decision 69/13/Euratom, CECA, CEE, JO L 13 du 18/01/1969, 19, modificated by the decision 80/443/CEE, Euratom, CECA du 07/02/1980, JOCE L 107 du 25/04/1980, 44.

6 'The author is responsible for the content of the publication not the European Commission' ('Dix leçons sur l'Europe', 1998: 1). Increasingly, an author's signature has become a way of 'deresponsibilizing' the institution. This can be seen in many publications published since 2000. For example, the re-edition of the booklet 'A new idea for Europe. The Schuman declaration – 1950–2000' contains an unequivocal formula: 'Signed by its author, this text does not commit the European Commission' (2000: 1).

7 A civil servant from the 'publications unit' evoked the case of a journalist who wanted to use the document but was embarassed to have to quote its institutional origin.

8 Written question E-4078/98, Bulletin 03/C-99 (26 January 1999); Written questions E-0075/99 and P-0076/99, Bulletin 04/C-99 (19 February 1999).

10 Publicizing the euro

A case of interest maximization and internal fragmentation of the Commission

Jeannette Mak

Introduction

A combination of the following three statements sum up the rationale behind this chapter's research question. On 28 February 2002, the last day that national currencies were legal tender in the 'euro zone', Commission president Prodi stated that:

> The euro changeover has been an enormous success for Europe, for the European citizens, for our new money. All thanks to the enthusiasm of the European people who have shown themselves capable and ready to rally with resolve and determination behind ideas that make good sense for them, for their daily lives and for the future.
>
> (EC 2002b)

Furthermore, an evaluation of the introduction of the euro notes and coins by the Commission stated in April of the same year that 'The success of the changeover to the euro illustrates the ability of the institutions to bring to fruition a complex project and sends out an optimistic message for the continuation of the construction of Europe' (EC 2002a: 5). Finally, a Flash Eurobarometer shows that in May 2002, 60 per cent of respondents in the euro zone agreed with the statement that by using the euro, instead of one's national currency, one feels a bit more European than before. 79 per cent of the people regarded the changeover to the single currency as a major event in the history of Europe (Flash EB: 121/3). These statements suggest that the introduction of the single currency is capable of strengthening support for the EU and the European institutions, as well as reinforcing a European identity. Consequently, a question emerges as to whether the Commission has consciously and instrumentally used the introduction of the euro, and in particular its communication activities on the issue, to strengthen the direct legitimacy of the EU as a whole, as well as to improve its own status and position.

It could be argued that the Commission had the following incentives to play a major role in information and communication activities on the single currency. First, public support for the euro was of the utmost importance since the success or failure of EMU would be decisive for the future of both the EU as a whole and the Commission. Second, the Commission could have used this unique political momentum, which necessitated communication with every single citizen on a major European topic, to ensure that the information disseminated reflected its point of view as much as possible. Moreover, a currency is a symbol of identity which could be activated to contribute to the building of the public image of the EU and thereby bring the populations of the EU and its institutions closer together. Third, since most competences concerning EMU had shifted away from the Commission, it could use the information and communication activities on the euro as a way of remaining involved in the politically important field of economic and monetary affairs. Finally, there had been attempts to limit the abilities of the Commission to make and implement an information and communication policy. The Commission would be expected to aim for at least the status quo of its competences and, if possible, try to expand them. Given the salience of the policy area, the Commission could have actively strived for considerable involvement in the dissemination of information on the euro.

Examining whether the Commission has instrumentally used communication on the euro requires analysis of whether the institution can be regarded as a 'purposeful opportunist'[1] in this policy area. The term refers to the strategy of an organization which has a notion of its overall objectives and aims, but which is quite flexible about the means by which these are achieved (Cram 1997; Nugent 1997; Pollack 1998). It implies rational action and interest-maximization on the part of the Commission, dealt with as an actor in its own right. Although elsewhere in this book the Commission has been presented as internally fragmented, as having multiple identities and that its preferences need to be regarded as the result of internal politics (Page and Wouters 1994; Peterson 1995, 1999; Christiansen 1996, 1997; Drake 2000; Nugent 1997), it can also be argued that a certain common interest does exist within its ranks. Although the federalist rhetoric of the early years seems to have lessened, the existence of a pro-European ethos can still be observed (Shore 1995; Middlemas 1995; Cini 1996a; Pollack 1998). Moreover, it has been argued that the Commission is increasingly united by a common attempt to expand the competences of the EU (Page 1997). The aim of this chapter is to discover how these diverging and converging interests of the Commission interact. Its point of departure is therefore that the Commission is expected to deal with information and communication on the euro in a technical way if it aims for policy acceptance only, and in a political way if it equally aims for enhancing its own legitimacy, as well as for the EU as a whole. The technical approach would mean stressing practical and economic aspects of EMU and a strictly functional use of networks. The political approach would mean communicating on the economic, political and identity-related aspects of EMU and a more strategic use of networks.

This chapter uses interviews with Commission officials and numerous internal policy documents, in order to ascertain the relative importance of the interests of the Commission and reach conclusions on the nature of information and the networks involved in the issue. It first briefly explores what interests, limits and opportunities are involved for the Commission as a whole with regards to information and communication activities regarding the euro. Then the involvement of four DGs in the changeover to the single currency is examined and their respective behaviour on this issue analysed and compared.

The Commission: interest maximization

Lack of clarity in theories on the role and importance of the Commission can be partly attributed to recent developments, both external and internal to the institution, that have worked in opposing directions. On the one hand, the room for manoeuvre of the Commission has been limited in the last couple of years. The concept of subsidiarity has restricted the Commission's formal competences and both the Council and the European Council seem to have gained greater importance. Moreover, an increase in bilateralism in policy preparation can be observed, as well as an enhanced use of the open methods of co-ordination. This tendency can be explained by the fact that the focus of European policies and politics has shifted from the relatively politically neutral and technical regulations concerning the completion of the single market to more political issues. On the other hand, this interpretation of formal limitations has been undermined by convincing evidence that the relationship between the Commission and national governments has become increasingly 'fused' as a result of the progressing interdependence between national and European levels of governance (Peterson 1995; Marks, Hooghe and Blank 1996; Wessels 1996, 1997). As a result, it has been argued that the Commission may have lost direct and formal competences vis-à-vis the national governments but that it has won indirect and informal influence in highly salient policy areas. A second external, but more informal, influence that has arguably limited the freedom of action of the Commission is the increasing negative public opinion on the nature and activities of this institution. More than any of the other EU institutions, it has been the Commission that has become the focus of public discontent about what is wrong with the EU (Hall 2000).

Moreover, it can be argued that the Commission's ability to act forcefully has been limited by internal factors. Bureaucratic competition and fragmented public policy-making has increasingly led to the importance of coalitions along sectoral lines, rather than along institutional or national ones (Radaelli 1999a; Peterson 1999). Consequently, three main sources of conflict may be observed within the Commission: rivalry between DGs for influence and control within policy areas, competition on the distribution of scarce resources such as staff, money and status and, ultimately, ideological disputes over policy approaches and solutions (Stevens and Stevens 2001: 196–205). Intra-institutional cleavages are believed to be more likely in policy debates which concern trans-sectoral subjects, such as EMU, and when there is an absence of strong leadership within the Commission.

Notwithstanding the external formal restrictions and the internal fragmentation, it can be argued that the Commission has developed a common understanding of optimizing participation and influence as a way to maximize its interests. Both for external and internal relations, Commission officials seem to rely to a large extent on 'informal' methods in order to avoid formal limitations (Héritier 1999; Stevens and Stevens 2001). In this context, the role of the Commission is assumed to have shifted from initiator of policy to co-ordinator of national policies, and is believed to make active use of methods that are aimed at participation and mutual learning, such as bench-marking, 'best practices' and peer pressure. The Commission is regarded as being able to steer the final policy outcome in its preferred direction, by initiating and involving itself in co-operation between member states. With regard to sectoral interests, widespread use is made of consultation and the formation of networks is actively stimulated. Finally, the general public is approached by using a strategy of 'dialogue' and studies have shown that more participatory strategies in the making and implementation of policies are not just part of a new EU administrative discourse but are actually put into practice (Cini 2000; Rood 2000; Hall 2000). To what extent can this scenario be found in the case of the changeover to the single European currency?

The Commission and EMU

The Commission as a whole seemed particularly concerned about the wider implications of negative public opinion on EMU. It realized the impact this might have on its own credibility and regarded a successful introduction of the euro to be of the utmost importance. Within the Commission it was argued that the euro could not fail 'because the consequences of such a failure are simply too great' (Barkin and Cox 1998). An early Commission document states that the euro:

> will ensure that the single market lasts and that European integration will continue. Economic and political challenges are closely interrelated: future progress in European integration will depend largely on the achievements of monetary union.

(EC 1996: 9)

Furthermore, the Commission regarded dissemination of information on the single currency as crucial for attaining public acceptance:

> the transition to the single currency cannot succeed without the support of clearly defined communications strategies ... Their core objectives will be to win popular support for the single currency.
>
> (EC 1995: 73)

Initially, EMU functioned as a 'big idea' that was driving both European integration and the Commission. Yet, it gradually became the domain of the European Central Bank and national finance ministers (Featherstone 1999 Hall 2000). As a result, competences shifted away from the Commission. While the formal limitation of responsibilities has not affected the various DGs in the same way, retaining the status quo and possibly the expansion of the Commission's influence in this field was regarded as a common interest. On 3 October 2000, just after the Danish 'no' on the introduction of the euro, Commission president Prodi gave a relatively bold speech before the EP. He warned for the dangers of an intergovernmental approach and pleaded for a larger role for the Commission in EMU on the basis of formal grounds:

> In fact you only have to read the Treaty to understand that, while the European Central Bank is the pivot of monetary policy, the body responsible for the overall assessment of the European Union's economic policy can only be the Commission.
>
> (EC 2000b)

Have formal and informal instruments been combined in order that the Commission would remain involved in this policy area? The start of the Commission's official policy concerning information and communication on the euro is landmarked by the publication of a Green Paper on the practical arrangements for the introduction of the single currency. Published on 31 May 1995, its aim was threefold: to reduce uncertainties, to raise awareness of the key actors of the work to be done, and 'winning at each stage of the process, public acceptance and support without which the operation cannot succeed' (EC 1995: 5). In the years afterwards, the changeover to the euro would, together with preparations for enlargement of the EU, dominate the agenda and activities of all parts of the Commission.

The Commission and communication

In the past, the Commission as a whole has never regarded public information as very important. Commissioners saw it only as a partial and not very desirable portfolio. This has led to a lack of political leadership, which in turn led to a lack of strategy and co-ordination of the Commission's information and communication activities. Numerous reorganizations, aimed at resolving these problems, have only made this incoherence greater. Moreover, the former DG X (audio-visual, information, communication and cultural policy) has had a low status within the Commission for many years because of its limited vertical, executive and legislative functions (see Chapter 9). Finally, it lost even more credibility as a result of decentralization of its information activities.

Increasingly eurosceptic public opinion after the problematic ratification of the Maastricht Treaty was initially answered by a new information and communication policy intended to bring 'Europe closer to the citizens'.[2] This impetus was given by both the member states, who felt they had to react to the negative public atmosphere surrounding European integration at the time and the Commission, where DG X was used as a scapegoat for failures to raise public enthusiasm. However, as a result of the lack of political will from the college, absence of co-ordination and leadership from the commissioner and the fact that individual DGs and their commissioners wanted to hold on to their autonomous information activities, this new approach was not successfully implemented.[3] The 1999 reform of the Commission abolished DG X and distributed its various units throughout several DGs. While the new Prodi Commission proclaimed 'communication' to be a top priority, and announced 'a new communications strategy designed to ensure a continuous and interactive exchange with Europe's citizens' (EC 2000a: 14), little progress has since been made. It took this Commission more than two years to come up with an information document[4] that would, according to the accompanying press release, 'not propose at this moment a strategy for information policy' but instead 'launch a debate' on the issue (EC 2001b). In sum, it was thus nothing more than a 'dialogue on dialogue'. Therefore, it can be concluded that at the level of the services involved, importance has been clearly granted to information, communication and dialogue. However, at the political level of the college, it seems to be regarded as an unclear policy field in which no short term political gain can be achieved. As a result, the lack of a strategy and co-ordination in the field has only given further impetus to individual DG information policies.

Communciation by the DGs: bureaucratic politics in action

This section explores how the interests and internal and external limitations of the Commission's role in EMU have influenced the activities of the various DGs. The services that are discussed are those that were responsible for general information activities on the euro to the general public in former DG X, the DG for economic and financial affairs (ECFIN; former DG II), the DG for enterprise (ENTR; former DG XXIII for small and medium enterprises and tourism) and finally the DG for health and consumer protection (SANCO; former DG XXIV). Emphasis will be placed upon the activities of the former DG X. More precisely, the interests, limitations and possibilities of this administration will be used as a point of comparison with those of the other services relevant to this research.

Directorate General for audio-visual, information, communication and cultural policy

In 1996, three 'Priority Information Actions' were launched of which 'The euro, a currency for Europe' was to run until the end of 2001. From early 1997 onwards, a separate unit, which would be responsible for the co-ordination of all these actions, was created within DG X. As one of the services involved in 'horizontal' activities, those units in DG X that were responsible for general information to the wider public were expected to have an interest more in line with the so-called European interest than the more sector-oriented services. Consequently, it could be argued that DG X would have liked to execute information and communication activities on such a salient and visible subject as the euro in order to step up its competences, influence and status. Moreover, dissemination of information on the introduction of the euro would be a unique opportunity to communicate with every single citizen in the EU; not only on EMU but on the larger perspective of European integration. However, the fact that it became involved in large-scale information activities on the single European currency does not seem to have been such a conscious and calculated effort. Rather than initiated from within the Commission, the information activities on the EMU and the euro seem to have been enforced by the European Parliament, the German government and the Bundesbank. The latter two actors urged the Commission to undertake a large-scale publicity campaign out of concern for public opinion on the euro in Germany, whereas the EP is believed to have pressed the Priority Information Actions out of concern for lack of public support for European integration in general (Kirchner 1996).

Nevertheless, within DG X an awareness developed that the reasons behind EMU should be explained, partly in order to reduce misgivings about the Commission in general:

> One should continue explaining the reasons for EMU since many people don't understand the rationale behind it and they make the mistake of thinking that it is a Commission initiative which is only meant to centralize. However, there are very good reasons for EMU.
>
> (Interview, DG X official, July 1999)

Most officials in this DG agreed that the Commission should point out the 'political' reasoning behind the euro. After all, 'the euro was a political project from the first moment onwards' (Interview, DG X official, July 1999). Nevertheless, it has been pointed out that the Commission and governments alike have presented the euro mainly in terms of economic benefits (Verdun and Christiansen 2000). To what extent can this apparent contradiction be explained?

In reality, the Commission's ability to act efficiently was limited by both internal and external factors. Internally, responsibilities on the Priority Information Actions have been dispersed. Most of the officials interviewed in former DG X were quite frustrated about the internal limits of the Commission on their work:

> There is no Information Strategy ... We have tried everything to improve the information strategy but one really needs the political will at the level of the college and the President's cabinet. One needs a '*pilote dans l'avion*'; a competent college.
>
> (Interview, DG X official, July 1999)

> In DG X we just muddle through (*on fait du bricolage*).
>
> (Interview, DG X official, July 1999)

Externally, restraints arose from the fact that autonomous information and communication activities of DG X on the euro were received with unequal enthusiasm in the member states. Moreover, in general, activities became more decentralized over the years under pressure from the widespread conviction in both the EP and the Council that dissemination of information should be executed at a level that was as close as possible to citizens (Schlesinger and Kevin 2000). As a result, the activities of DG X shifted from development of actual information material, to co-ordination and administration of activities executed by national governments and interested organizations. It can be speculated to what extent the lack of sectoral coalition partners has determined the limits and opportunities of DG X. It has put the Directorate in a rather weak position both within the Commission and vis-à-vis national governments. As a result, it seems understandable that the chosen option was increased co-operation with national information and communication services.

Given these restrictions, DG X seems to have been relatively successful in pursuing its interests by expanding its involvement and influence both inside and outside the Commission. It became the co-ordinator for a wide range of activities within the Commission that are not strictly speaking communication activities, but rather fall under the wider umbrella of achieving public support for EMU. This tendency of DG X to get involved in the actual policy of the changeover to the euro, rather than limiting itself to dissemination of information on the matter, was not always well appreciated in the sectoral DGs (Interview, DG ECFIN officials, June 1999). The role of DG X as internal co-ordinator was strengthened by its function as interlocutor between the Commission and the national governments concerning information and communication activities on the euro. From 1997 onwards, DG X had set up partnerships with all member states, except for Britain and Denmark. By giving financial support, which was meant to stimulate action, they also safeguarded influence upon the national activities. The member states had to present communication plans, which then needed to be agreed by the Commission. Moreover, all national directors of information on the euro, national civil servants from the ministries of finance, gathered twice a year in Brussels and committed themselves to report extensively to the Commission on their activities.

According to Commission officials, these conventions had, amongst others, successfully made 'the general public aware that action taken nationally has a European dimension'. Furthermore, it was regarded as a very efficient tool for maintaining an overview of what was going on in the member states. Moreover, these meetings were believed to be very important since member states motivated each other to take action. As one interviewee put it, 'it is the dynamic of the group that counts'. Most senior officials attributed this to peer pressure rather than to stimulation from the Commission. However, others refuted this consensual picture and attributed the group dynamic to a more 'pushy' attitude from the Commission (Interviews, DG X officials, June 1999). Nevertheless, the meetings of directors of information on the euro were officially believed to have contributed to co-ordination, bench-marking and exchange of best practice (EC 1999a). Finally, the activities on EMU allowed DG X to step up contacts with its pre-existing information relays and the creation of new ones.

Notwithstanding these developments, DG X has ultimately not been successful in pursuing its institutional interests. In contradiction to this DG's preferred type of information, the content of information on the euro became more technical over the years, the political aspect lost out and the emphasis on 'dialogue' diminished. However, more seriously for DG X is that it was abolished during the latest reform of the Commission. The services responsible for general information and communication on the euro were transferred to DG ECFIN, after having been stalled for a while in the new DG for education and culture. Both formal and informal networks thus seem to have been lost as a result of the latest reforms of the Commission, whereby contacts with information relays and the execution of actual communication activities came to be defined as 'negative priorities' (EC 2000c).

Directorate General for economic and financial affairs

DG ECFIN has a very long tradition of involvement in monetary integration. It has been argued that the DG had only 'one deep aim; the construction of an integrated EU economy' (Middlemas 1995: 247). As one official put it: 'the whole DG felt that the creation of the euro on

1 January 1999 was a big day for them' (Interview, DG ECFIN official, July 1999). Since EMU has been regarded as an important aim for the Commission as a whole, and economic and financial affairs as a crucial policy area, the DG has been very influential within the Commission and benefited from good status and high profile commissioners.

Traditionally, the way for DG ECFIN to advance policies has been to persuade national governments and national banks. Since they used to deal strictly with central bankers and national ministries of finance, a very dense network of about 100 people at the highest level had been formed. According to a senior official, this made co-operation very smooth (Interview, DG ECFIN official, June 1999). As a result, DG ECFIN seemed to be rather confident to be able to compensate for the loss of formal competences by continuing informal contacts. It has been argued that the Commission can still make a significant contribution to the single currency by means of 'soft practices', which means offering input of high quality information and initiative to the Eurogroup, in particular in the field of a single fiscal policy, and by stimulating the process of structural economic reform in the EU (Hall 2000).

The DG did not seem to grant much importance to negative public opinion on EMU and dissemination of information to the general public. DG ECFIN mainly got involved in the overall communication activities on EMU because former commissioner de Silguy was worried about the lack of initiatives emanating both from DG X and national governments. The DG started with information initiatives around mid 1997 and the main aim was to make authorities aware that EMU would actually take place and that they had to prepare themselves for the introduction of the euro. Although the idea was equally present in DG ECFIN that economic and monetary union was a political project from the first moment onwards, the dominant approach within this DG was pragmatic. Since the decisions had already been taken and the Treaty had been ratified by the member states in a democratic way, emphasis had to be laid on the practical implications of EMU, rather than the political ones. 'Dialogue' was definitely not regarded as a priority:

> The Commission has every right to explain the arguments and the political reasons behind EMU. However, if it works against you, why would you do it?
>
> (Interview, DG ECFIN official, June 1999)

> If you use political arguments, you create possibilities for opponents to attack you on this basis, which might be counter-productive.
>
> (Interview, DG ECFIN official, July 1999)

Since the latest reforms of the Commission, DG ECFIN has been responsible for the dissemination of information on the euro to the general public. Co-operation with the national directors of information in their meetings in Brussels seems to be well in line with the standard practices of the DG. It became the major focus of their activities and in the last year before the actual introduction of the euro, they planned a total of five meetings. The ultimate example of the use of peer pressure was the 'score-board' that DG ECFIN introduced to make clear to all how well the Commission thought the various member states were doing in their respective preparation for the changeover to the single European currency.

Directorate General for enterprise

Ever since its creation, the former DG XXIII has had a clear sectoral focus; maximizing the interest of small and medium enterprises (SMEs) and the tourist sector (Middlemas 1995). With regards to the introduction of the euro, its main aim was to limit the costs of the changeover to the euro for this sector and optimize any possible profits. DG XXIII, which was, on 1 January 2000, merged into DG enterprise with parts of former DG III for industry and innovation, traditionally stressed co-operation with interest groups by means of consultation, round tables, exchanges of ideas etc. It has very close relations with its sectoral organizations, with whom they meet on a weekly basis (Interview, DG ENTR official, June 1999). The same approach has been followed for the introduction of the euro. An expert working group was set up on small businesses and the euro, consisting of representatives of SMEs, the craft sector, the commercial sector and the tourist sector. Furthermore, the DG seemed to a major extent to rely on co-operation with the lobby group 'the Association for the Monetary Union of Europe'. Finally, widespread use was made of the European Information Centres for SMEs. The latter are relatively independent but there are several structures in place to safeguard co-ordination and coherence in their actions. Moreover, these centres have been used by DG ENTR to find out what is happening at the grass-roots level in the member states, since it did not seem to have much contact with the national governments regarding information on the euro. The information disseminated by DG ENTR was by definition more technical and included costs as well as benefits, since it was especially obvious for SMEs that concrete preparations needed to be made for the introduction of the euro.

Directorate General for health and consumer protection

Given its wider constituency, the former DG XXIV (now part of DG SANCO) had an outlook that was more in line with the general European interest and, in particular in the case of EMU, more in line with the preferences of DG X. As a result, officials responsible for consumer affairs were convinced that offering practical information should be combined with explaining the political rationale behind EMU. Confronting people with the euro without explaining its origins and objectives was feared as a potential source of serious repercussions on both European and national politics:

> Just giving technical information misses the point completely since EMU is a political project.
>
> (Interview, DG SANCO official, July 1999)

DG SANCO had several institutionalized co-operation structures with interest groups. In 1995 it set up a Consumer Committee consisting of representatives of consumer organizations from the member states and representatives of the European consumer associations. In 1996, the Commission set up a euro working group through this Consumer Committee. In general, the DG has consulted widely on the approach to take in information activities. This is in line with the basic attitude of the Directorate on the principle of subsidiarity. DG SANCO analyses and indicates where the problems are, gives opinions and advice, prepares reports and carries out pilot projects. It suggests what information material should be like, rather than developing it itself. Finally, the Directorate has put a lot of effort into making regional and local authorities aware of the problems of the euro for vulnerable groups. While DG SANCO was, in general, rather content with the general information and communication activities of DG X to the general public, in its opinion of March 1999, the Consumer Committee stated that it regarded the fact that most of the money for the euro campaign went to commercial and financial institutions as 'scandalous' (Comité des Consommateurs 1999).

Conclusions

The brief overview above has shown that no clear united understanding existed within the Commission with regard to information and communication activities on the euro. While all DGs more or less agreed on the general importance of public acceptance of the euro, interests that were more closely linked to their mission as a DG seemed to have prevailed. In this respect, the following two examples of internal conflict are worth mentioning since they clearly illustrate the clash of interests within the Commission on the issue.

The first refers to the final determination of what information projects would be sponsored under a call for proposals. Officials from DG X were rather reluctant to grant subsidies to organizations that were regarded as protégés of sectoral DGs. Within the inter-service selection committee, the question was posed as to whether subsidies should be given to organizations which already seemed dependent on the Commission for most of their funding because this raised issues of legitimacy and independence.

Unsurprisingly, the issue-specific DGs seemed less concerned about this than DG X. Moreover, this DG regarded it as a lost opportunity to stimulate new organizations to participate in EU policy-making.

The second example concerns disagreement between DG ECFIN and DG SANCO. The latter had paid a lot of attention to the 'human dimension' of the introduction of the euro and, in particular, had defended the interests of vulnerable groups in society. In criticizing the Commission's overall information campaign, a senior official argued that while the introduction of the euro could have been a political opportunity to enhance social integration, instead it had turned into a project of social exclusion (Interview, DG SANCO official, July 1999). Within DG ECFIN at the same time, an official expressed the opinion that the special attention to vulnerable groups was exaggerated. He regarded the special care for this section of society merely as a tool for image building with which to show that the euro is not only the story of bankers but also of ordinary people (Interview, DG ECFIN official, July 1999). Furthermore, regarding the anticipated decrease in bank charges after the introduction of the euro, the official from DG SANCO remarked that it was important to get the message across to the general public that 'before banks were robbing you off, and now they are no longer' (Interview, DG SANCO official, July 1999). Needless to say, the official from DG ECFIN did not quite agree with his colleague.

Apart from internal fragmentation at the level of the services, there has been a clear lack of coherence in the college. Whereas DG X was responsible for the budget of the Priority Information Actions and installed a separate unit for these activities, a task force euro was set up under the political leadership of former commissioner for economic and monetary affairs, Yves de Silguy. The latter got heavily and personally involved in the dissemination of information on EMU because, in his opinion, DG X did not handle the project very professionally. Therefore, he delegated the political supervision of the project to his cabinet (Interview, ECFIN official, June 1999). This hardly encountered any opposition from commissioner Oreja, officially responsible for information and communication policy, as he was more interested in institutional reform, the other part of his portfolio (Interview, DG X official, July 1999). Consequently, the cabinets of commissioner de Silguy and his successor Solbes have over the years been particularly influential in this policy area. However, both have increasingly relied upon bench-marking and best practices and regarded their own role in this perspective to be that of a 'catalyst' (Interview, member of Pedro Solbes's cabinet, October 2000). Finally, the former commissioner for consumer affairs, Emma Bonino, has been involved. She has taken a clear political stand on the issue. According to her:

> For the consumer, the single currency will be the physical and concrete embodiment of their belonging to the European Union. This

currency, which is a way of expressing what he (*sic.*) has earned from his work, must be a sign of confidence in the future and a symbol of his pride ... Europeans joined forces in the Middle Ages to build cathedrals, and this gave them a very strong feeling of coming together to build something new. The euro will, in a way, be the first cathedral of modern Europe.

(EC 1996: 11)

In sum, the above examination of the Commission's communication activities on the euro leads to the following conclusions as regards the argument made in the introduction to this chapter. First, public support for the euro was not regarded as equally salient in all DGs. A clear discrepancy was found in the importance granted to public opinion by sectoral DGs and public-oriented services, mainly in DG X. Rather than reaching out directly to the general public in their information and communication activities, most Commission services turned to traditional Community methods which involve co-operation with both national governments and interest groups. Second, instead of executing large scale communication activities, aimed at disseminating political information with an identity-related dimension, the Commission has mainly undertaken technical information activities on the single currency. The activities of the different DGs have thus only made limited use of political messages and the strategic building of networks for reaching out to the general public. At least for a short period, DG X successfully managed to get involved in the field of EMU by means of its communication efforts, thereby acting like a political entrepreneur. Yet this has not ultimately resulted in success for the DG given that it was abolished altogether during the latest reforms of the Commission. Why has the Commission as a whole failed to mobilize and unite itself at a moment and in a policy area which many actors saw as crucial for its very survival?

The ultimate failure to come up with a coherent and purposeful information strategy seems to be due to a combination of internal and external limitations. The former include bureaucratic competition and a lack of political will and leadership, whereas the latter consist particularly of a lack of support from the national governments. Nevertheless, this does not seem sufficient explanation for the absence of strategic action. There have been numerous examples in the past where separate DGs have been very successful in pursuing their goals despite such limitations. However, the weak position of DG X may be explained by the absence of national and sectoral allies for an administration limited to making reference to the general public. Moreover, the DG has not managed to reach out to this public because of the rather elitist approach to communication which has dominated within the Commission. This has been enforced by the fact that EMU has always been characterized as a highly technocratic field of decision-making and governance.

The theoretical implications of these findings are that the Commission cannot be regarded as a purposeful opportunist. Even though a superficial common understanding of the importance of information and communication seems to exist, interests and involvement diverge amongst DGs and a deliberate strategy has been lacking in this policy area. Moreover, the separate DGs discussed here have, in varying ways and to different extents, managed to use their resources in a creative way in order to optimize their influence vis-à-vis external actors such as national governments and sectoral interest groups. Consequently, it could be concluded that maximization of competences is more an interest the separate DGs have in common than a 'common' interest. Therefore, the idea of the Commission as a unitary actor does indeed need to be dismissed. The different services have shown creativity in their interest-maximizing and have moved beyond formal limits. Yet, it may be doubted to what extent these reactions have been rational and calculated rather than ad hoc behaviour. Therefore the Commission might best be defined as a pragmatic, rather than a purposeful, opportunist.

On the basis of these conclusions, three speculations on the future role and functioning of the Commission can be made. First, by maximizing their influence the DGs all contribute to wider fragmentation of the Commission. External limitations have been circumvented by strengthened ties with issue-specific networks and national experts which, however, only serves to amplify the diversity of interests within the Commission since it leads to coalitions along sectoral, rather than institutional, lines. This tendency is likely to continue. Second, the Commission's expansionist tendency may further undermine its credibility. It has been rightly argued that the ever larger number of tasks given to the Commission and higher expectations from the public makes it increasingly difficult for this body to fulfil its functions (Cram 1999). This is enhanced by the Commission's tendency to resist any limitation upon its competencies. Finally, it can be doubted whether formal administrative reforms will manage to improve the internal functioning and public perception of the institution. Better co-ordination structures might not be sufficient to diminish a number of highly structural sectoral disagreements within the Commission. Moreover, discouragement of informal contacts might work to the detriment of effective and acceptable policy-making. Although it may work against directly reaching out to the public, the co-operation between the Commission and national governments by means of the open method of co-ordination seems to lead to incorporation of the European interest in the national interest. As this tendency is expected to continue, it might be wiser for the Commission to opt wholeheartedly for a more supportive role, thereby relying upon indirect or technical legitimacy, as opposed to a muddled political role which would give it a more direct form of legitimacy.

Notes

1 This term is generally attributed to Klein and O'Higgins (1985) *The Future of Welfare*.
2 European Commission (1994) *Information, Communication, Openness*, SEC (93) 916/9, Communication from Mr J. de Deus Pinheiro to the Commission, adopted on 30 June 1993. The three keywords were *information*, which meant giving the facts and explaining, *communication*, which meant listening and dialogue, and *transparency*, which meant priority to total openness in pursuing the first two objectives. The keyword within the new approach became 'dialogue', thus seeing communication as interaction, rather than as just the dissemination of information.
3 These observations by Gramberger (1997), Guggenbühl (1998) and Meyer (1999) have been confirmed by interviews with senior EC officials carried out by the author in Brussels in June and July 1999.
4 On 27 June 2001, the Commission approved 'a new framework for co-operation on activities concerning the Information and Communication Policy of the European Union' (EC 2001a).

11 Where is he now?

The Delors legacy

Helen Drake

Introduction

In this chapter I explore the influence that a Commission President, in and out of office, can exert over visions and utopian dreams (or nightmares) of the EU's future. I do this by means of an empirical analysis of the Delors decade (1985–1995) and of Jacques Delors' trajectory upon leaving the Commission in January 1995. I relate this analysis specifically to the EU and nation state level debates of 2001–2004 concerning the future of Europe.

Two specific conceptual questions underpin my chapter. One, what are the platforms that the Commission, especially the presidency, provides for the production and dissemination of ideas? In this respect I explore the possibility that the Commission presidency can have a long term 'Europeanizing' effect that outlives the shelf-life of the presidential mandate per se. I take 'Europeanizing' here in a general sense (after Yorndorf 1965) to refer to the influence that European-level leaders such as Delors can, and do, have back home, as well as in Brussels, as Europeanist ambassadors and opinion-formers for domestic change. In this context I pay specific attention to Delors' functions since 1996 as founder, President and general *animateur* of the Paris-based 'think tank', *Notre Europe,* as a way of exploring the avenues that Delors has taken in his 'retirement' to exercise influence on the future of the European Union.

Second, what can we say about ideas and their transmission in the specific case of European integration, with regard to the terminology and language of 'visionary thinking' about Europe's future? Here I refer to Parsons' work (2000, 2002) regarding the vagaries, in the EU's history, of the triumph of certain ideas over others; and I draw on Olsen's (2000) vocabulary for the analysis of visionary discourse. By addressing these two questions I seek to demonstrate that Delors has converted his capital as ex-Commission President into a lingering intellectual influence on the shape of Europe's union, by means of a combination of institutional and discursive resources. In these ways I aim to offer some insight into one of the overarching themes of this volume, namely how the Commission, through

its President, can influence the politics – defined here as choices – underlying European integration.

I start by briefly examining the Commission presidency as a vehicle for
exercising a Europeanizing influence. Next, I focus on the different ways
in which Delors has sought to influence the debate on the future of
Europe; finally, I focus specifically on the role of language in the successful (or otherwise) transmission of ideas in the EU context, and demonstrate Delors' singularity in this respect. Delors himself has constantly
striven to keep his legacy alive, notably via *Notre Europe*, and this chapter
offers an evaluation of his efforts.

The Commission presidency as a vehicle for visionary influence

Declaration 23 on the future of the EU, appended to the Nice Treaty
(2001), reflects the intention of the heads of state and government that
there should be a 'deeper and wider debate about the future development
of the European Union' with a view to 'constitutional' reform. Rising to
the challenge of rethinking yet again the Monnet method of integration
for the enlarged EU of the future placed a clear demand – for the supply
of ideas, consensus and support – on all parts of the EU's political system.
In so far as the situation in which the EU found itself in the period
2001–2004 appeared to invite certain of its member states to think the
unthinkable, including the contemplation of an overtly federal arrangement for the future EU, comparisons can be drawn with other founding
moments of the EU and its predecessors (1950, 1951, 1957, 1985, 1992)
when the process of integrating Europe appeared to accelerate suddenly
towards its unknown destination, and when new organizing and ordering
concepts saw the light of day. This demand for a strategy, vision and
vocabulary of reform was, of course, more challenging for some member
states than others. France, for example, in the opening years of the twenty-
first century, was faced with the specific challenge of re-intellectualizing its
commitment to European integration as a political process, strategic goal
and element of national identity.

On each of these founding, or re-founding, occasions in the EU's
history, moreover, it could not be taken for granted that the changes
would be successfully ratified across the spectrum of the member states,
and the process relied to an important degree on the presence and influence of pro-European, and Europeanizing, forces and voices in the
debate. In this context, a primary political logic, or rationale of the Commission, and specifically of its presidency (with or without the rest of the
college) is and always has been to 'Europeanize' par excellence; that is, to
facilitate and co-ordinate intergovernmental, common political leadership
in the pursuit of political union.

The potential of a Commission President to bring to life an incipient 'supranational power elite' (Yondorf 1965: 888) within and without the Commission lies very much at the heart of the original conception. It is the founding logic, at least from a neo-functionalist-type perspective of the High Authority and the Commission; it is a question of organizing matters so as to 'provide the impulse from without',[1] by leading national represen-tatives to supranational institutions and solutions. Commission presidents, it can be argued, are first and foremost Europeanist ambassadors in their home country, and in other, broader constitutiencies within national and transnational society. They seek, through their influence, to co-ordinate and encourage the Europeanism of national decision-makers; we could go so far as to claim that their secondary role is the provision of a European-wide form of political leadership whilst in post.

This is a process which, however defined, is at one significant level a question of the transfer and adaptation of new ideas into the dominant culture; ideas which are frequently seen to challenge established political culture, practice and interests. Parsons (2000, 2002) has demonstrated, for example, how in the case of France, the ideas on European integration held by dominant politicians at the historical origins of the European communities won over sets of interests at odds with the premise of such ideas. Indeed, the history of France's leadership of the EU has often been the surprising triumph of certain ideas over viable alternatives (Parsons 2002).

Over the course of European integration since the postwar days, the role of certain individuals such as Jean Monnet have been critical, in the battle of ideas, to the Europeanization of national politics, and it is no coincidence that the first leaders of the central Community institutions (Monnet, Hallstein) were appointed by virtue of their influence back at home, over their counterparts in neighbouring member states and, in Monnet's case, with the United States; and because of their willingness to apply unique and imaginative solutions to new problems. It has, more-over, been argued (Yorndorf 1965: 901) that one of the most significant achievements of the Jean Monnet Action Committee (1955–1975), the vehicle for Monnet's influence after leaving the European institutions, was to have co-ordinated, through its networks of influence, the ratification in France and Germany of the Treaty of Rome. Parsons (2000) is doubtful of the Committee's influence on French political circles per se, and Winand (2001) confirms that the Committee was successful in campaigning for ratification, but only indirectly so, in the French case, since the Commit-tee was unable to make an impression on the French government, or on de Gaulle's vocal opposition to Monnet's European visions.

Jacques Delors: the pragmatic visionary

The Delors decade (1985–1995) and beyond is instructive in respect of these forms of influence. I have argued elsewhere (Drake 2000) that the dominant political images of Delors as 'Mr Europe', the 'Tsar of Europe' and so on were largely accidental, in that they were as much the product of a combination of historical circumstance and contingency, including a void of leadership at the heart of the EU system, as they were of a deliberate strategy on Delors' part to lead from the front or to build a glorious political career. Moreover, Delors' impact on the presidency relates to a logic contained in the treaties all along; namely that under the right circumstances the Commission can operate as a strategic actor. The combination of an intergovernmental consensus, founding text, and 'active' (Dinan 1994: 202) Commission President has indeed been central to the turning points in the EU's history (Drake 2000: 85), whereby an 'active' Commission President's influence extends into the various domestic scenarios to facilitate the emergence of an intergovernmental consensus.

The political qualities and imagery associated with a strong President such as Delors, moreover, are as much a function of the demand that is prevalent in contemporary politics for personalized power and its imagery, as of the supply, from Delors, of behaviours and logics that could be described as political in the narrow sense in which an elected national statesperson is political. The Delors phenomenon – the apparent politicization of the Commission presidency – is none other than the combination of a 'strong' personality with political acumen, political capital and credibility (Endo 1999) with a vacuum of institutionalized power at the centre of the Union.

The input of a Commission President to the Europeanization of their environment, seen from this perspective, extends along temporal and spatial dimensions beyond the immediate lifespan of a given college or presidential mandate, to encompass the impact these can exercise on constituencies beyond the Commission and beyond the EU political system itself. The interlocking of the Commission with its environment is part and parcel of the process of spillover and of the rationale of the Commission's existence. This is an approach to the Commission presidency which invites us to acknowledge what we might see as a grey area of the political logic of the Commission presidency; namely, the potential for past, present or future Commission presidents to infiltrate and shape the politics of European integration at a multiplicity of levels of action, from supranational to national, Europeanist to partisan. This interlocking of spheres of influence can also clearly be seen to apply to European-level leaders other than the Commission President; but it is these 'statesmen of interdependence' (Duchêne 1994; Dinan 1994) who carry the most potential influence. Jean Monnet's influence on the construction of 'Europe', through the transformation of the circumstances in which he found himself in the postwar period, before, during and after his time as President of the High Authority is the best-documented in this respect (Duchêne 1994; Morgan 1992).

Du Bon Usage de Delors: the various uses of 'the Delors factor'[2]

Europeanizing the Commission presidency

Hard as it may be to establish firm causal links between Delors' presidency and its effects, we can note that Delors' decade in Brussels contributed to altering the imagery of the Commission presidency, and thereby informed new thinking on the range of logics underlying and potentially driving the role. More specifically, Delors' spell in the presidency chair found its way into fresh thinking about the legitimacy of the Commission presidency within the Community's structures of power and authority. This reflection found its way indirectly, first, into subsequent reforms of the presidency within the college and the wider Commission; and, second, into the conversion of the 'Delors factor' into lasting capital, following his departure from the Commission in January 1996.

On the first point, let us note how the Commission President saw gains in their potential personal authority under the terms of both the Amsterdam (Nugent 2001: 68) and Nice treaties. Both sets of reforms worked towards enhancing the President's authority over colleagues in the Commission, to the extent of requesting them to resign if necessary (the 'Prodi' clause); being more readily called to account by the EP for the action of 'their' college; and having the power to 'reshuffle portfolios during the term of office, appoint vice-presidents and ask a commissioner to resign, albeit obtaining the collective approval of the Commission' (Article 217. Yataganas 2001: 42). These increases in the Commission President's personal powers, and the decision that the President would henceforth be appointed by a majority vote of the European Council were, moreover, largely a source of agreement between member states at Nice (Vignes 2001: 82).

From this perspective, Delors' high profile style of Commission presidency (on average over the ten years his was a high profile presidency, despite periods of enforced low visibility, such as in the 1991–1992 Maastricht aftermath) had a measurable effect on the post in that it turned the key on a logic of the European integration process, namely the provisions in the original treaties for the emergence of a leader figure at the heart of the Union. Equally, it can be argued that the experience of the Commission presidency since Delors' departure – the Santer resignation; Prodi's uncertain influence – suggests that altering the 'constitutional' balance of power in the Commission President's favour does nothing in itself to enhance the legitimacy of the incumbent. This is true: legitimacy is at one very important level a characteristic which resides in the personal qualities or skills of the incumbent of a post, and where only the coincidence of these skills with a favourable environment can bring about the charisma of recognizable leadership.

From the broad perspective of the EU's historical development, nonetheless, one of the effects of placing in the Commission presidency the character of Jacques Delors, in 1985, was to demonstrate the influence that the President can wield over 'their' institution to the extent of infusing it with its original intention of acting as a 'bureaucracy with a mission' (Cram 1999), by imparting a sense of the general interest: Europeanization at work. This influence has since been channelled by subsequent treaty reforms into the drive for greater efficiency and responsibility within the Commission. However, this influence also remains a latent resource for would-be 'strong' Commission Presidents to provide a form of leadership of the integration process.

The Commission President at large: 'Europeanizing' the ambient power elite

Alongside Delors' contribution to altering perceptions of the Commission presidency in the Community's system of political power relations, the Delors phenomenon also invites analysis of the issue of the contours of the role: where and when does a Commission President stop being President and start being something else, say, a national champion of the European cause? The Delors case suggests a number of points worthy of further attention, all relating to the potential for a Commission President to form and influence an 'incipient power elite' (Yondorf 1965) at the European level.

In pointing to the good causes to which the Delors name and experience could be put, Duhamel (1997) had in mind a specifically national purpose: encouraging Delors to act as the spokesperson for a possibly nascent, but elusive social-democratic left in French Prime Minister Lionel Jospin's government (1997–2002). From the opposite perspective, some French journalists wrote in 1995 at the time of Delors's departure from Brussels that this meant the end of Europe *à la française* (see for example *L'Expansion*, 5–18 May, 1994: 4–8). Both sets of remarks demonstrate an instinctive sense that the borders, temporal and spatial, of the post of Commission President are inherently porous, and offer opportunities for the 'strong' – authoritative, credible – President to carry their influence well beyond the post itself.

In Delors' case, he became well-known for just such an expansion of the scope of the role of Commission President. This held for his ten-year presidency itself and for the period since leaving the presidency in 1995. In fact, it has even been argued (Dyson and Featherstone 1999) that Delors wielded his greatest Europeanizing influence – on France's commitment to EMU – *before* being appointed to the Commission presidency, by using his authority as finance Minister to sensitize French President François Mitterrand, in 1982–1983, to the imperative for France to remain a full member of the EMS and the EEC. Similarly, the first presidents of the Community institution – Jean Monnet and Walter Hall-stein – were appointed in no small part thanks to their prior experience and the influential credit that this was expected to, and did, yield in the supranational institutions.

We can identify a number of ways in which Delors' incumbency and past as Commission President enhanced his opportunities and scope to wield a Europeanizing influence in and outside Brussels. These findings are intended to supplement the evidence pointing to Delors' intense net-working activities whilst at the Commission, and his creation or reinvigora-tion of key constituencies and publics, such as the European Council; targeted heads of state and government, the social partners, or the Church (see Nugent 2001: 75–76; Ross 1995; Grant 1994; Endo 1999).

'L'homme qui dit non'[3]

Delors' decision to decline the opportunity to stand – and very probably win – as the French Socialist Party candidate for the Presidency of the French Republic in the elections of 1995 was intimately dissected, in France and elsewhere. Personal reasons were generally considered to have featured as a priority in his decision, followed by considerations of a more political, tactical order; namely the suspicions that lingered within parts of the Socialist Party regarding the extent of his socialist credentials, which might have undermined his authority over the party even if he won the election on their behalf; not to mention the effects a Delors presidency might have had on his daughter Martine Aubry's political career. Delors himself probably doubted his ability to implement reform, Grémion (2001: 56) claiming that 'In 1994, Delors declined to become a candidate in the presidential elections on the grounds that French society was not ripe for change'.

What was not in doubt was the link between Delors' European status – as Commission President – and his credibility – to the French public first and foremost – as future French head of state. Opinion polls at the time consistently rated candidate Delors higher than his opponents; and this despite the fact that Delors' experience of electoral politics and elected office was virtually nil. What counted in his favour were his European cre-dentials, which was interpreted by his sponsors in the Socialist Party (who, it has to be acknowledged, were desperately short of suitable alternative candidates) as a guarantee for the post-Mitterrand Left that France could pursue its leadership in the European integration process.

Alongside his presidential non-candidacy, moreover, Jacques Delors had never neglected a particular strand of political activity in France during his ten-year absence from the French capital: during his Commis-sion presidency he continued to 'animate' political and other groups on the French political scene with the intention of ensuring a succession of Euro-aware and Euro-friendly converts. Such activity was inevitably seen in some quarters as Delors' form of preparing for a future French presidential campaign; it may well have been so. More importantly, Delors' presence in Brussels had already greatly assisted the legitimacy and acceptability of François Mitterrand's drive to change Europe and change France with it. Voluntarily removing himself from domestic political power, Delors reverted to his more familiar methods of exerting influence over the European agenda and, indirectly, French politics.

Delors after Brussels: back to the future

Delors' activity since leaving the Commission has revolved around the establishment of a research and study institute in Paris, *Notre Europe*.[4] Beginning its activities in 1996, *Notre Europe* aims 'to study, research and educate about [sic] Europe, its history, and future prospects' and to 'contribute to the creation of a European public space'. What does it mean by 'Europe'? The group's statutes stipulate that it acts in 'the spirit of a tighter union in Europe comprising a common defence and a common currency, respecting community assets [sic] and resting on common policies that support full employment, competitiveness and solidarity'.[5]

It works towards these goals in three principal ways. First, and probably the most significant of these is the 'European Steering Committee' (*Comité d'orientation européenne* – CEO), established over time by Delors to guide *Notre Europe*'s activities and, importantly, to debate specific EU policy and institutional issues, and on occasion publish recommendations. The Committee, a collection of co-opted, influential 'personalities' from the member states, sees itself in a role not dissimilar to that of Jean Monnet's Action Committee for the United States of Europe: institutionalizing existing networks of influence for specific purposes. It has been suggested (see *Le Monde*, 20 May 1998: 4) that certain of its proposals (such as the appointment of Romano Prodi as Jacques Santer's successor, or the idea that the European parties nominate a candidate) have indeed been influential on heads of state and government. It may also be the case that mobilizing and sustaining this exercise in intimate, collective, focused *réflexion* is frustrated by logistical difficulties, which are likely to be exacerbated in an enlarged Europe; Delors himself has remarked that the Action Committee format per se is probably no longer valid for our times (in his preface to Winand 2001). *Notre Europe* is also steered by its own board of directors, which also appears to issue its own recommendations, for example to the European Convention on the Future of Europe.

Second, *Notre Europe* maintains a programme of seminars, conferences and publications, generally in collaboration with outside organizations and individuals. In this function, the organization resembles closely that of the Jean Monnet Action Committee, which routinely called upon outside expertise (individuals and organizations) to supplement its own resources, and thinking (Winand 2001: 5).[6] These activities are intended to feed, support and disseminate the Steering Committee's workings; to promote European integration in the EU, including in France, (in the relative absence, in France, of think tanks or academic associations devoted to the study or promotion of the EU, apart from the European Movement); and to sustain the organization's third level of activity: to act as a platform from which Delors has given scores, if not hundreds, of speeches in his own right, to a broad spectrum of audiences in many EU member states.

Delors himself is very much the focal point and inspiration of *Notre Europe*; the organization exists because of Delors, and is Delors' primary vehicle for personal influence. In this respect alone, *Notre Europe* can be compared to the Jean Monnet Action Committee, of which it has been said both that it functioned primarily as Monnet's carte-de-visite by which he maintained and extended his networks of influence (Winand 2001: 3); and that without Monnet there would have been no such 'elite action group' at that time. As with Jean Monnet, it was to maintain the impact of Delors' capital as ex-European leader that Delors was encouraged – by Helmut Kohl, amongst others – to set up *Notre Europe* in the first place.

Notre Europe, a non-profit making *association*, receives direct EU funding (akin to the College of Europe, Bruges, or the European University Institute, Florence), although it operates under French law, and its permanent staff are not EU civil servants (except where these are on secondment to the group). Its location in Paris is, it would appear, a function of Delors' domicile rather than of some privileged connection with the French political scene, or ambition for influence in this direction. Nonetheless, *Notre Europe* holds itself available to French journalists, and Delors' personal support of the Jospin presidential campaign in 1995, for example, is a fact, as are his connections with the former French socialist government's projects for domestic reform. (François Hollande, the current leader of the French Socialist Party, is a Delorsist, and former chair of the Delors-inspired *Témoins* political club (*Le Monde*, 14 April 1995: 6). Delors has thus maintained a public profile in France, although a declining one, apparently through his own choice, and much as Monnet's star waned in France during the years when his eponymous Committee was active (1955–1975).

Through its various functions, *Notre Europe* has thus acted as a vehicle for Delors' ideas; the organization has, however, stopped short of seeing itself as a narrowly-defined lobby along the lines of the European Movement for example (and the Jean Monnet Committtee made the same distinction). The breadth of its work and contacts seems to bear out this perception. Other opportunities since 1995 for Delors to offer advice and guidance to European policy-makers may well have eluded him, such as the absence of any call on him to act in a semi-official capacity in the 1996–1997, or indeed 2001–2004 Convention-IGC process. Nevertheless, it is not far-fetched to presume that by the institutionalization and routinization of his legacies through *Notre Europe*, Delors' influence has extended well beyond his decade as Commission President. Delors' role at *Notre Europe* has been described enthusiastically (Sauron 2000) as that of the patient 'gardener' of Europe, sowing the seeds of ideas which, initially utopian, will in time structure reality! This analogy takes us into a consideration of at least two of the many questions posed by the above description of one former Commission President's attempts to maintain a voice in the debates guiding the EU's future development; namely, how, and how much, (Parsons 2002) do ideas matter as causal variables in politics?

'How then do we get there from here?' (Olsen 2000)

In what follows we look more closely at the conditions that ideas and their expression appear to need to fulfil in order to maximize their political influence, as a way of gauging the significance of Delors' contributions to envisioning the future of Europe. Defining ideas as 'subjective claims about descriptions of the world, causal relationships, or the normative legitimacy of certain actions' (Parsons 2002: 48), Parsons argues that much of the constructivist and institutionalist literature of politics fails to show how much (or how) ideas cause outcomes. Aiming to show how much ideas matter, and under what conditions, his own analysis of French ideas about European integration in the 1950s methodically demonstrates how ideas that cross-cut 'prevailing lines of organization' (Parsons 2002: 50) – partisan, ideological – were wielded successfully by individuals in a position to 'assemble coalitional support behind them' (Parsons 2002: 53), against viable alternatives. Thus in France the 'community' idea of Europe won out, in these early days, over the 'confederal' and 'traditional' views, and effectively laid down the path that subsequent French leaders (de Gaulle included) were constrained to follow.

Parsons' work is raised here to indicate ways of measuring how an individual – here, Delors – might expect to wield influence through ideas; the variables, in essence, being the juncture of the individual's authority, political circumstances, and available support. As Commission President, Delors' decade provides much evidence, much analysed, of where and how his ideas were or were not influential in informing EU policy and policy-making. The main variable in the case of his ideas as President was his autonomy and skill in cajoling majorities around his proposals. A comparison of the Commission White Papers of 1985 and 1993 provides some examples of how this autonomy varied, and under what circumstances (Drake 2000).

Upon leaving the Commission presidency, Delors' influence became dependent on his ideas being attractive to those in power, and on the longevity of his political capital as ex-Commission President. Structurally speaking, the creation of *Notre Europe* and its expanding activities provides one channel for such influence; but realistically speaking, as with other think tanks, its reach is limited to, essentially, like-minded, elite networks; preaching to the converted would be an uncharitable way of expressing the role. Nevertheless, certain ideas – or at least expressions – readily attributed to Delors, are being, and have been, converted into policy positions by French leaders, amongst others, in particular his patented formula for a 'European Federation of Nation States'.

A European Federation of Nation States, or the repackaging of federalism

In creating and disseminating a new terminological, if not cognitive, field for discussing EU institutional reform, Delors intended to facilitate consensus between supporters and opponents of a 'federal' Europe, in part by warding off notions of 'federalism' as inevitably German-style federalism (Cohen-Tanugi 2001). By the start of the twenty-first century, this new expression had indeed become established as official French policy, espoused, if not convincingly defined, by both Lionel Jospin and Jacques Chirac in the 2002 presidential election campaign. In the French context at least, this new vocabulary of federalism appeared to offer a solution to the problem of moving France and Germany closer together towards a shared vision of the future of Europe. In this respect, and, after Parsons, in enquiring how some ideas come to matter in the political process, we can make a useful distinction between the language of pragmatic vision and utopian ideals.

In Olsen's words:

> Ordinary language makes a distinction between the utopian dreamer and the visionary political leader. The utopian offers an ideal system of governance and community. Yet, he [sic] presents no clear ideas about how and under what conditions the polity can be moved towards the ideal. Or, if he does, the ideas, together with the prescribed institutional arrangement, are generally viewed as impractical or impossible fantasies. The visionary leader has a better understanding of the relationship between human action, institutions and the flow of history. The prescribed political order can be imagined to work in practice, and there is enough understanding and control of institutional dynamics to move the polity in a consistent and desired direction.
>
> (Olsen 2000: 1)

Of the lessons that Olsen draws from his analysis of the debate following German foreign Minister Joshka Fischer's May 2000 speech on Europe's future, four seem most relevant to our enquiry. First is the need, in order to avoid the 'utopian trap', for the development of a shared vocabulary around proposed change and reform:

implementation of a reform vision depends[ing] as much on leadership through reconceptualisation as through reorganization. Success will be facilitated by the development of a shared vocabulary and concepts, or at least a repertoire of such vocabulary and concepts, so that actors can *translate* between different interpretations of key concepts.

(Olsen 2000: 10)

In the case of Delors' 'Federation of European Nation States', this lesson appears to suggest Delors as an agent of vision rather than utopia. The notion has been explained at length by Delors himself (Delors 2002a) in the simplest of terms, and has, we have seen, served as a terminological if not intellectual reference point. At the level of reconceptualization and vocabulary, Delors appears then to have had deliberate and ongoing relevance, linking us here to the body of analysis on Europe which gives weight to the significance of 'speaking Europe' (Diez 1999) and winning battles over 'polity ideas' (Jachtenfuchs *et al.* 1998) in the process of building a supranational framework for common European policy. As Commission President, moreover, Delors had fathered similarly catchy slogans which managed to mobilize national leaders ('1992' for the completion of the single market being perhaps the best known of these).

Olsen points secondly to the significance, in the struggle over competing ideas, of 'shared interpretations of experience', or narratives of the past (2000 11). This point chimes with the various discussions in the literature of European integration over the role of myth in building Europe's future (Hansen and Williams 1999; Obradovic 1996). Delors certainly, through his openness whilst in Brussels and since, has contributed to the phenomenon of the telling and retelling of the history of his presidency, as a way of seeking a common ground of beliefs – possibly a mythology? – on which to build the future (Drake 2000 preface). His memoirs, published in January 2004 (Delors 2004), this narrative.

Third, the role of clarity is, in Olsen's view, an important aspect of the conversion of utopia to vision (and thereby to the possibility of action). Delors would appear to pass the clarity test with flying colours. His 'parler clair' or plain-speaking (Drake 2000: 117) whilst Commission President took him into conflict with member state leaders on more than one occasion, and notably during the Maastricht negotiations. Moreover, in his role as *Notre Europe* President in the service of his 'European Federation of Nation States' he is clear about the need for clarity; in his view the issue boils down to deciding '*qui fait quoi, et pourquoi?*' (who does what, and why?), so clarifying lines of responsibility. Whilst in strictly academic terms the formula of a 'European Federation of Nation States' raises more questions than it answers, in the political world its 'plasticity' has been a vote-winner, and has at least provided a basis for discussion. Throughout his career, moreover, and not only at the Commission, Delors was generally regarded as a clear speaker with a genuine regard for the didactic aspects

of his task – making himself understood, in other words, at all costs. In the
2002 presidential elections, the mainstream candidates (primarily, Jacques
Chirac and Lionel Jospin) were widely deemed to have failed in speaking
clearly – or, really, speaking at all – about Europe and its significance for
France; and in this vacuum the resonance of the far Right's scaremonger-
ing on Europe was all the greater.

There is of course an argument that Europe has proceeded precisely
thanks to the opposite of clarity, namely ambiguity, including what
Andréani (1999: 5) has called 'European nominalism': the 'loading [of]
the European project with the symbolic attributes of state sovereignty
without transferring to it the corresponding powers', this being his criticism of the Maastricht Treaty. Régis Debray (2001) has suggested, moreover, that 'the less we talk about Europe, the better it does' – and he may
well have a point. Similarly, the ambiguities and multiple meanings of
much of the terminology of European integration (subsidiarity, federalism, European 'citizenship' etc) has to an important degree allowed for
forward movement behind a veil of mutually assured and wilful misunder-
standing. Clarity, in other words, may not be the best policy for Europe's
next move. However, it was the leitmotiv of the work of the Convention –
at the rhetorical level at least – and for this reason alone, the EU reform
process can be expected to proceed with overt attention paid to the principle.

Olsen's fourth and final lesson is that reform needs, essentially, to start
from where we are now – in the messy reality of things (taking full account
of the 'dynamics of *living* institutions'). This also seems to work as an
operating principle of Delors' preferred options for reform, based as they
are, we assume, on an intimate, first-hand knowledge of how the institutions and not only the Commission, work in practice and in relation to
one another.

It remains to be seen whether or not ideas such as Delors' 'Federation
of Nation States' will, operating as a guiding vision, allow for the development of 'better insight into the institutional preconditions for creating
legitimacy and deserved support' (Olsen 2000: 14) in the Europe of the
mid to long term. It is certainly one that has currency in several quarters,
and which, importantly, appears to function, for successive French governments, as a strategic objective by default (possibly in lieu of their own).

Conclusions

In the all-important and all-consuming battle for ideas in the shaping of
tomorrow's Europe we have suggested that the Commission presidency
might bequeath its own intellectual legacy to the EU's future. The contribution works at several levels: principally via a Europeanizing influence
on domestic elites; and through the moulding of the practices, expectations and images of a European leadership role, by which successors are

constrained, for better or for worse. In this respect, a perspective on the Commission presidency which conceptualizes the significance of the post in terms of the entire political lifespan of its incumbents, and the shelf-life of their impact, seems fruitful. We can conclude in these terms that in so far as Jacques Delors can be considered a European leader, a 'statesman of interdependence', it is precisely due to the fact that his influence extends in time and space beyond 'his' decade in Brussels when he encouraged the Commission to 'assert itself' (Nugent 2001: 204). Grémion (2001: 56) argues in this respect that Delors successfully used his presidency to mobilize EU social and political actors towards new goals: Grémion cites as factors Delors' 'technical rigour'; his 'unswerving commitment, and inexhaustible energy'; his support from Helmut Kohl; his understanding of Germany, which 'stood in marked contrast to the superficial ideological vision of his party comrades'; and his quickly finding favour with the US administration ('No French public figure since Monnet integrated so successfully into German and American networks'). Grémion, however, sees Delors' attempt to transfer his success to France as much less successful:

> Delors, in Europe a rocket, disintegrated on re-entering the dense layers of the political atmosphere in France. Such a trajectory provided ample confirmation that one could more readily be a personalist and a social-democrat at the European level than in France itself.
>
> (Grémion 2001: 56)

We do not disagree, since we have argued only in favour of the ongoing salience and influence of Delors' ideas in the domestic and EU-wide debates, in part due to their instrinsic value, measured on Olsen's scale. By his own hand, Delors forfeited the opportunity of political power when he withdrew from French politics in December 1994. It may also prove to be the case that his ideas – couched as ready-made slogans – end up distorted out of all recognition by those in a position to do so.

Despite the confines of the present argument, studying the life-cycle of a Commission President appears to offer insight into the wider world of the Commission presidency's political logics. To an extent, the Commission came full historical circle with Delors, who was as influential in the respects highlighted above as his predecessor Walter Hallstein and before him, Jean Monnet at the High Authority. Together they presented a particular face of European integration: the borderless and possibly timeless – critics might say 'nationless' – quality of Europeanism, as exercised from Brussels. These examples lend meaning to the spirit of the original treaty provisions for the independent but multi-networked European commissioner and Commission President, designed to sustain the two-way traffic of ideas and influence between different, but sister, galaxies: Brussels and the home capital.

Notes

1 Yondorf was citing from Monnet's farewell address to the ECSC Common Assembly, and using this expression to describe the primary purpose of the Jean Monnet Action Committee (Yondorf 1965: 889).
2 The expression is from Duhamel (1997).
3 From Milési (1995): the man who said/says 'no'.
4 I thank Professor Renaud Dehousse, consultant to *Notre Europe* in its relations with universities, for according me an interview on 7 May, 2003 (Paris).
5 From *Notre Europe*'s mission statement. *Notre Europe*, 41, bd. des Capucines, 75002 Paris; http://www.notre-europe.asso.fr/. The profile of Delors in *European Voice* 10–16 July 1997: 12 reviews the significance of *Notre Europe* as a 'vehicle' for Delors' interest in Europe.
6 Winand's account of the Jean Monnet Action Committee suggests that it had considerably more tentacles than does *Notre Europe*, including a nominally separate Research Centre, Documentation Centre, and University Studies Institute (2001: 6). It also appeared to make similar efforts to reach beyond an elite audience, through the use of the press (in the case of the Action Committee, in the US as well as Europe).

Conclusion

Politics in the European Union

Andy Smith

In the introduction to this volume, I underlined that amongst the European Union's institutions, the Commission is probably the one that has given rise to the most study and publications. I then proceeded to stress, however, that the vast majority of this work has tended to skirt around, rather than deal directly with, the Commission's relationship to politics. In tackling this question directly, the contributions to this book have shed new, original and illuminating light upon power and powering in the EU. In the lines that follow, I simply want to highlight a number of research conclusions developed in previous chapters which suggest not only that one needs to look again at the Commission as an institution, but also at the way one conducts research upon the interlocking, fragmented and competitive arenas which make up the EU as a whole.

In his book *Technocracy in the European Union* (1999a), Claudio Radaelli usefully distinguishes between three criteria frequently used in order to define politics and distinguish it from technocracy: competition, publicness and the role of value judgements. Radaelli underlines that, contrary to popular misconceptions, the EU has not evolved 'beyond politics' and neither is politics in the EU simply the stuff of clashes between heads of government. Rather, the EU's present form has emerged from a multitude of interactions and decisions where politicians, civil servants and interest group leaders have acted both 'politically' and 'technocratically'.

As the three points made in this conclusion underline, the interpretations of empirical evidence presented in this volume confirm this general hypothesis. However, on the basis of more sociological research designs, they also often seek to go beyond the straitjacket of reasoning by ideal-type. The authors do so by considering, either implicitly or explicitly, that 'politics' and 'technocracy' are 'social constructions' which actors use in order to legitimize themselves or stigmatize their opponents. Politics and technocracy are therefore studied as integral parts of the incessant struggles between different protagonists seeking to increase their respective influence within the EU's decision-making arenas. From this perspective, rather than becoming some esoteric alternative theory, this basic premise of social constructivism therefore fuels rigorous studies of the institutionalization, i.e. the construction and consolidation, of the EU. The analytical pay off for this 'sociologically constructivist' approach is that legitimation can be studied as a consubstantial process of institution-alization, and not just something actors do when attacked over the EU's democratic deficit. In short, rather than muse about the consequences for the legitimacy of the EU of an unelected Commission, the research presented in this volume shows how actors within and without this organization are constantly seeking ways of presenting themselves, their priorities and their ways of working as 'normal' and 'natural'.

Politics as competition

In Western nation states, political competition is usually associated with elections and political parties. Although both clearly have roles in the EU, these are played out indirectly by being mediated through institutions. Indeed, if one considers that struggles for power in the EU are essentially of an intra- and inter-institutional nature, representatives of the Commission certainly take part in at least three dimensions of this political competition.

The first of these dimensions concerns competition within the Commission. Many other studies enumerated in the introduction to this book develop the hypothesis that the DGs of the Commission are particularly prone to a form of internal fragmentation often labelled 'bureaucratic politics'. Numerous chapters in this book confirm this general hypothesis, in particular Jeanette Mak's analysis of publicity for the euro and Cécile Robert's study of aid to Eastern Europe. However, they also show that many such 'turf wars' also contain an ideological component that is frequently marked by the suppression of references to politics in favour of the supposedly more neutral registers of law and economics. By examining the behaviour of commissioners and their cabinets, Joana and Smith not only show that the lexicon of politics is more acceptable at this level but that, paradoxically, victories in the college are often also won using arguments of an essentially legal or economic type. In both cases, the research underlines the need to look more closely not only at Commission fragmentation, but also at the mechanisms which, despite fragmentation, produce compromises or consensus.

The second type of institutional competition pits personnel from the Commission against agents of national governments and European Parliamentarians (MEPs). The most obvious arenas for struggles with national actors are situated within the different permutations of the Council of Ministers. However, as Joana and Smith also highlight, relations between national governments and the Commission often begin to intensify as soon as a draft legislative proposal reaches the college of commissioners. The cabinets of the latter are therefore crucial bodies within, and between which, attempts are made to politicize or technicize issues before they reach the negotiating tables of the Council. Other chapters show that the Commission in general, and its hierarchy in particular, are increasingly involved in dealings with representatives of the European Parliament. Didier Georgakakis, for example, shows how MEPs worked with officials in the Commission in order to bring about the downfall of the Santer Commission. Despite the increasing power of the Parliament, however, Olivier Baisnée's study of the Brussels press corps shows that the Commission still possesses the upper hand when it comes to getting media attention for its achievements and objectives.

Finally, Sebastien Guigner's chapter on the introduction of public health onto the EU's agenda highlights how Commission personnel often find themselves in competition with other international organizations (in this case the World Health Organization and the Council of Europe). Yet again, a line of questioning about the use of 'politics' and 'technical detail' provide a means of unpacking such competition and revealing that the shape of EU intervention is determined more by a struggle for legitimacy than it is by quests for efficiency and effectiveness.

In summary, 'politicization' and 'technicization' are strategies used by actors within and without the Commission in highly competitive contexts. As François Foret's chapter on Commission information policy underlines, this is not just competition to decide; it is also competition to represent and this in two senses of the word: representing the EU as its spokesperson but also influencing how the EU is presented (i.e. as a social representation of reality).

Politics as publicness

The second part of this book has tackled such struggles to represent through analyses of the way the Commission engages in public communication. Each of the authors concerned have attempted to go beyond overgeneral and abstract claims made about the absence of an EU 'public sphere'. In so doing they have generated three recurrent ideas about this second dimension of the Commission's relationship to politics.

The first of these ideas concerns how Commission personnel are simultaneously interested in achieving maximum publicity for the EU and their organization, whilst depoliticizing the content of the information they transmit. François Foret tackles this question by examining the processes of censorship and self-censorship which surround the production of brochures for the general public. Olivier Baisnée encounters similar phenomena in his longitudinal study of the relationship between the Commission's press services and Brussels-based journalists. In both cases, representatives of the Commission constantly seek to paper over conflict, often going so far as to consider journalistic accounts of clashes between commissioners as a form of 'betrayal'. More generally, as Cécile Robert underlines, this aversion to conflict can be interpreted as the incapacity of Commission officials to accept political defeats. Having spent months, if not years, piecing together delicate compromises, losing in Council or the Parliament is frequently seen as a disavowal of the Commission itself.

The second recurrent trait that emerges from these studies of the communication of the Commission is its profound awkwardness. More precisely, whereas national governments tend to have relatively clear visions of what their respective publics expect in terms of public appearances and protocol, the Commission frequently engages in a hybrid form of communication which ends up sounding foreign in every member state. As previous studies have shown (Abélès 1996; Schlesinger and Deirdre 2000), a major cause of this problem is the fragmentation of European society and culture. However, as Véronique Dimier shows in her analysis of the invention of DG VIII and Jeannette Mak underlines in the case of the euro, tensions within the Commission are also responsible for muddying its own message.

These messages are also muddied by a third and final recurrent feature of the Commission and its relationship to public communication: the difficulty of striking a balance between remaining independent of national governments and dealing with them on a daily basis. In general terms, as Jarle Trondal's analysis of the European socialization of seconded officials testifies, each representative of the Commission largely has to work this problem out for him or herself. In terms of communication, this issue becomes particularly acute in the case of commissioners and their cabinets. As Joana and Smith underline elsewhere (2002: part III), the unstable role prescriptions of these actors mean that they very often consider it necessary to invent their own method of communicating about the EU. The problem is therefore not one of not enough communication, but of commissioners being interpreted by the media as representing themselves rather than the Commission as a whole.

Despite the importance attached to communication at national and local levels of government, studies of this activity within EU institutions are still in their infancy. This question got off to a bad start because it was tackled first by philosophy-inspired academics quite content to present their vision of communication in the EU in the form of an 'aerial photograph' taken from the safety of their armchairs (Smith 1998). By conducting sociologically-grounded fieldwork into the way communication is actually carried out in the Commission, the chapters in the second part of this book offer a much more convincing and stimulating way forward.

Politics as value judgements

Claudio Radaelli's third and final criteria for distinguishing between politics and technocracy concerns the basis upon which arguments for EU legislation and decisions are founded. According to these ideal-types, when such arguments are essentially about values – whether something is judged 'good' or 'bad' – they are political; in contrast, they are technocratic when based upon expertise. The contributions to this volume clearly present cases of both forms of argumentation. In most instances, however, the most striking trait is the way 'political' and 'technocratic' discourse fuels intra- and inter-institutional struggles for power.

From this perspective, Cécile Robert's chapter provides an illuminating insight into the role of values in EU politics. In implementing the programme of development aid to the pre-accession countries (PHARE), the Commission has had considerable leeway to interpret general aims and objectives set by the Council. One of the areas over which, at least potentially, Commission officials could have developed considerable autonomy concerns the way the Eastern European countries have developed their respective social policies. Based upon value-laden argumentation, part of the Commission (DG RELEX) sought to make a high standard of social rights, particularly employment rights, part of the conditions for accession. However, concerned that this would lead to conflict in the Council, another part of the Commission (DG EMPLOI) used EU law-based arguments to stigmatize the DG RELEX approach as impracticable. Contrary to many other clashes of this type, this particular conflict apparently never gave rise to formal debate in the college of commissioners, thereby virtually ensuring the victory of the technocratic priority.

Value-based arguments are also highly visible whenever Commission representatives involve themselves in debates about the future institutional arrangements of the EU. As Helen Drake's chapter underlines, Jacques Delors developed a discourse on European integration and built himself a position within the Commission from which to engage in such forms of 'institutional engineering'. In the long run, however, it is probably Delors' inside knowledge of the Commission and its workings that have given the greatest credence to his views. In other words, even when acting as a 'visionary', Delors' legitimacy has stemmed in large part from his expertise and that of his closest advisers.

Ultimately, as Sébastien Guigner's chapter on the Commission and public health underlines, the Commission is not 'beyond politics', but intensely embroiled in it. Analyses carried out by experts can always be found and used as reasons for EU inaction. For example, in many areas of public intervention, such as the structural funds in Northern Europe, it would not be difficult for an independent expert to show that EU intervention has little added value compared to national and local policies, and can even make these less 'efficient' (Smith 1995). Nonetheless, such arguments are often defeated by actors using other sources of expertise and/or arguments about the intrinsic, even if impalpable, worth of EU intervention.

These conclusions are both original and vitally important from the point of view of research on the EU. As has been stressed throughout this book, its 'sociological' dimension stems as much from the research designs and methods adopted to generate data, as it does from more abstract meta-theoretical debates. As many of the bibliographical references testify, strongly influenced by a long tradition of theory-driven political sociology, these chapters also show the benefit of connecting reflection about the EU to previous and present analyses of the construction and evolution of the nation state. Of course, the EU 'is different', just as any state differs from any other. Nevertheless, by examining comparable processes using universally applicable research questions and methods, new light can be shed upon the causes and consequences of the Commission's, and more generally the EU's, past and current relationship to politics.

This point is also important to underline because some readers may be frustrated that this data is rarely used here in order speculate on the future of the Commission and the EU. Instead, our objective has been to demonstrate some recurrent traits of the linkage between the Commission and politics as they have been and are now. Nevertheless, we consider that this book can and should also be read as a modest contribution to the generation of a more empirically informed debate on the future of the government and politics of Europe.

Bibliography

Abélès, M. (1992) *La vie quotidienne au Parlement européen*, Paris: Hachette.

Abélès, M. (1994) 'L'Europe en trois dimensions', *Esprit* June: 99–108.

Abélès, M. (1996) *En attente d'Europe*, Paris: Hachette.

Abélès, M. (1997) 'La mise en représentation du politique', in M. Abélès and H.P. Jeudy (eds) *Anthropology du politique*, Paris: Armand Colin: 247–272.

Abélès, M. and I. Bellier (1996) 'La Commission européenne: du compromis culturel à la culture politique du compromis', *Revue française de science politique* 46 (3): 431–456.

Abélès, M., I. Bellier and M. McDonald (1993) 'Approche Anthropologique de la Commission Européenne', unpublished report to the European Commission, Brussels.

Acheson, E.D. (1988) *Public Health in England: The Report of the Committee of Enquiry into the Future Development of the Public Health Function*, London: Her Majesty's Stationery Office.

Alink, F., A. Boin and P. t'Hart (2001) 'Institutional crisis and reforms in policy sectors: the case of asylum policy in Europe', *Journal of European Public Policy* 8 (2): 286–306.

Anderson, P.J. and T. Weymouth (1999) *Insulting the Public? The British Press and the European Union*, London: Longman.

Andréani, G. (1999) 'Europe's uncertain identity', Centre for European Reform Essays (www.cer.org.uk).

Baisnée, O. (2000) 'Les journalistes, seul public de l'Union européenne?', *Critique Internationale* 9: 30–35.

Baisnée, O. (2002) 'Can political journalism exist at the EU level?', in R. Kuhn and E. Neveu (eds) *Political Journalism*, London: Routledge: 108–128.

Barkin, N. and A. Cox (eds) (1998) *EMU Explained*, 2nd edition, London: Reuters Ltd.

Barnett, M. (1993) 'Institutions, rules, and disorder: The case of the Arab states system', *International Studies Quarterly* 37: 271–296.

Bastin, G. (2002) 'Les journalistes accrédités auprès des institutions européennes à Bruxelles. Quelques signes du changement d'un monde de travail', in D. Georgakakis (ed.) *Les métiers de l'Europe politique. Acteurs et professionnalisations de l'Union européenne*, Strasbourg: Presses Universitaires de Strasbourg.

Becker, H. (1985) *Outsiders. Etudes de sociologie de la déviance*, Paris: Métailié (1st edition 1963).

Bellier, I. (1994) 'La Commission européenne: hauts fonctionnaires et "culture du management"', *Revue Française d'Administration Publique* 70.

Bellier, I. (1997) 'The Commission as an actor: An anthropologist's view', in H. Wallace and A. Young (eds) *Participation and Policy-Making in the European Union*, Oxford: Clarendon Press.

Bellier, I. (1999) 'Le lieu du politique, l'usage du technocrate. "Hybridation" à la Commission européenne', in V. Dubois and D. Dulong (eds) *La question technocratique: de l'invention d'une figure aux transformations de l'action publique*, Strasbourg: Presses Universitaires de Strasbourg, Collection Sociologie Politique Européenne: 233–253.

Berger, P. and T. Luckmann (1966) *The Social Construction of Reality. A Treatise in the Sociology of Knowledge*, New York: Penguin Books.

Berlin, D. (1987) 'Organisation et fonctionnement de la Commission des Communautés européennes' in D. Berlin, C. Bourtembourg and S. Pag under the direction of S. Cassese, *The European Administration*, IISA/IEAP: 443–496.

Berthod-Wurmser, M. (ed.) (1994) *La santé en Europe*, Paris: La Documentation Française.

Bodiguel, J.-L. (1995) 'The civil service of the European Union', *International Review of Administrative Sciences* 61: 433–453.

Bomberg, E. (1998) 'Policy networks in the EU: Explaining EU environmental policy', in D. Marsh (ed.) *Policy Networks in Comparative Perspective*, Milton Keynes: Open University Press.

Byrne, D. (2000) Speech on new public health strategy, European Parliament – Committee on the Environment, Public Health and Consumer Policy, Strasbourg, 16 May 2000.

Byrne, D. (2001) European Health Forum, Bad Gastein (Austria) 28th September 2001.

Calame, P. (1999) *Mettre la coopération européenne au service des acteurs et des processus: un processus collectif de diagnostic et de propositions*, C.L. Mayer (ed.), document de travail no. 111.

Cassan, M. (1989) *L'Europe communautaire de la santé*, Paris: Economica.

Cassese, S. (1987) 'Divided powers: European administration and national bureaucracies', in S. Cassese (ed.) *The European Administration*, Brussels and Maastricht: IIAS and EIPA.

Cassese, S. and G. della Cananea (1992) 'The Commission of the European Economic Community: the administrative ramifications of its political development (1957–1967)', *Yearbook of European Administrative History* 4: 75–94.

Cerny, P. (1988) 'The process of personal leadership: the case of de Gaulle', *International Political Science Review* 9 (2): 131–142.

Chauler, P. (1958) 'Le Marché Commun et l'Afrique, thème des 10ème journées Internationales de la Foire du Gand', *Marchés Tropicaux* 10.

Checkel, J. (2001a) 'Why comply? Social learning and European identity change', *International Organization* 55 (3): 553–588.

Checkel, J. (2001b) 'Constructing European institutions', in G. Schneider and M. Aspinwall (eds) *The Rules of Integration. Institutionalist Approaches to the Study of Europe*, Manchester: Manchester University Press.

Chirac, J. (2001) Interview to *Les Dernières Nouvelles d'Alsace*, 5 February.

Christiansen, T. (1996) 'A maturing bureaucracy? The role of the Commission in the policy process', in J.J. Richardson (ed.) *European Union, Power and Policy-Making*, London: Routledge: 77–95.

Christiansen, T. (1997) 'Tensions of European governance: politicized bureau-cracy and multiple accountability in the European Commission', *Journal of European Public Policy* 4 (1): 73–90.

Christiansen, T. (2001) 'Relations between the European Commission and the Council Secretariat: The administrative complex of European governance', *Politique Européenne* 5: 11–26.

Christiansen, T. and K.E. Jørgensen (1999) 'The Amsterdam process: a structura-tionist perspective on EU treaty reform', European Integration Online papers (EioP) 3, 1. http://eiop.or.at/eiop/texte/1999-001a.htm.

Christiansen, T., K.E. Jørgensen and A. Wiener (1999) 'The social construction of Europe', *Journal of European Public Policy* 6 (4): 528–544.

Christiansen, T., K.E. Jørgensen and A. Wiener (eds) (2001) *The Social Construction of Europe*, London: Sage.

Cini, M. (1996a) *The European Commission. Leadership, Organisation and Culture in the EU Administration*, Manchester: Manchester University Press.

Cini, M. (1996b) 'La Commission européenne, lieu d'émergence de cultures administratives. L'exemple de la DG IV et de la DG XI', *Revue Française de Science Politique* 46 (3): 457–473.

Cini, M. (1997) 'Administrative culture in the European Commission: The cases of competition and environment', in N. Nugent (ed.) *At the Heart of the Union. Studies of the European Commission,* Houndmills: Macmillan Press.

Cini, M. (2000) 'Organizational culture and reform: The case of the European Commission under Jacques Santer', *EUI Working Paper*, European Forum Series, RSC No. 2000/25, European University Institute, Florence.

CLENAD (2003) *Report of the Working Group 'Life after SNE'*, Brussels.

Cohen-Tanugi, L. (2001) 'Fédération d'Etats-nations, mode d'emploi', *Le Monde*, 7 June: 16.

Cole, A. (2001) 'National and partisan contexts of Europeanization: the case of the French Socialists', *Journal of Common Market Studies* 39 (1): 15–36.

Collowald, P. (1996) 'L'information européenne face aux rumeurs et aux humeurs', *L'Europe en formation*, 302.

Comité des Consommateurs (1999) *Avis du Comité des Consommateurs – Attentes et inquiétudes des consommateurs face à l'introduction de l'Euro*, 22 March 1999.

Commaille, J. (1994) *L'esprit sociologique des lois. Essai de sociologie politique du droit*, Paris: Presses Universitaires de France.

Commission (Société française de Santé Publique) (1999) *Priorities for Public Health Action in the European Union*, Employment and Social Affairs Directorate General.

Commission des Communautés Européennes (CEC) (1993) *Deuxième rapport annuel de la Commission au Conseil et au Parlement européen sur la mise en oeuvre de l'aide communautaire aux pays d'Europe centrale et orientale en 1991*, CE: Brussels [COM (93) 172 final].

Commission of the European Communities (CEC) (1958) *Premier rapport général sur l'activité de la Communauté*, Brussels.

Commission of the European Communities (CEC) (1963) Règlement intérieure de la Commission, JOCE, 17, 31 January: 181–185.

Commission of the European Communities (CEC) (1968) *Directory of the European Communities*, Brussels.

Commission of the European Communities (CEC) (1988) *Directory of the European Communities*, Luxembourg: Office for Official Publications of the European Communities.

Commission of the European Communities (CEC) (2000) 'Strategic objectives 2000–2005: Shaping the New Europe', COM (2000) 154 final.

Commission of the European Communities (CEC) (2002) 'A project for the European Union', COM (2002) 247 final.

Condorelli-Braun, N. (1973) 'La Commission des "Neuf"', *Revue du marché commun* 164, avril: 134–140.

Consoli, L. (1997) 'Comment la Commission européenne communique', *Limes* 4: 127–135.

Coombes, D. (1970) *Politics and Bureaucracy in the European Community*, London: George Allen & Unwin.

Council of Europe (2002) *The Council of Europe, 800 Million Europeans*, Strasbourg: Council of Europe–Communication and Online Information Division.

Cram, L. (1994) 'The European Commission as a multi-organization: social policy and IT policy in the EU', *Journal of European Public Policy* 1 (2): 195–217.

Cram, L. (1997) *Policy-Making in the European Union. Conceptual Lenses and the Integration Process*, London: Routledge.

Cram, L. (1999) 'The Commission', in L. Cram, D. Dinan and N. Nugent (eds) (1999) *Developments in the European Union*, New York: St Martin's Press: 44–62.

Cram, L. (2001) 'Whither the Commission? Reform, renewal and the issue-attention cycle', *Journal of European Public Policy* 8 (5): 770–786.

Cresson, E. (1998) *Innover ou subir?*, Paris: Flammarion.

Davis, A. (2000) 'Public relations, news production and changing patterns of source access in the British national media', *Media Culture and Society* 22: 39–59.

Davis, A. (2002) *Public Relations Democracy*, Manchester: Manchester University Press.

De Baecque, F. and J.-L. Quermonne (eds) (1982) *Administration et politique sous la Cinquième République*, Paris: Presses de la FNSP.

Debray, R. (2001) 'All passion spent', *Prospect*, April: 10–11.

De Clercq, W. (rapporteur) (1993) 'Réflexion sur la politique d'information et de communication de la Communauté européenne', The European Parliament.

de Gaulle, C. (1970) *Mémoires d'espoir, Le Renouveau, 1958–1962*, T. 1, Paris: Plon.

Deloche-Gaudez, F. and C. Lequesne (1996) 'Le programme PHARE: mérites et limites de la politique d'assistance de la Communauté Européenne aux pays d'Europe centrale et orientale', *Politiques et Management Public* 14 (1): 143–154.

Delors, J. (1996) 'A personal tribute by former European Commission President Jacques Delors', *European Voice*, 5–11 September.

Delors, J. (2000) Interview Le Grand Jury, RTL-LCI-Le Monde, 18 June.

Delors, J. (2001) 'L'avant garde en tant que moteur de l'intégration européenne', Intervention devant le forum international Bertelsmann, 'Europe without borders', Paris: Notre Europe.

Delors, J. (2002a) 'Visions d'Europe: perspectives et priorités pour l'Union européenne', speech to the French European Movement, Palais du Luxembourg, 6 July (available from Notre Europe).

Delors, J. (2002b) 'Les dirigeants français n'assument plus l'Europe', *Le Monde* 2 May 2002.

Delors, J. (2004l) *Memoires*, Paris: Plon.

Déloye, Y., C. Haroche and O. Ihl (eds) (1996) *Le protocole ou la mise en forme de l'ordre politique,* Paris: Harmattan.

Demmke, C. (1998) 'The secret life of comitology or the role of public officials in EC Environment Policy', *EIPASCOPE* 3.

Deremez, J.L., O. Ihl and G. Sabatier (eds) (1998) *Un cérémoniel politique: les voyages officiels des chefs d'Etat,* Paris: l'Harmattan.

De Sélys, G. (1996) 'La machine de propagande de la Commission', *Le Monde diplomatique,* June.

Dewost, J.-L. (1984) 'La présidence dans le cadre institutionnel des communautés européennes', *Revue du marché commun* 273, janvier: 31–34.

Diez, T. (1999) 'Speaking Europe: The politics of integration discourse', *Journal of European Public Policy* 6, 4: 598–613.

Dimier, V. (1998) 'L'idéologie des méthodes coloniales en France et en Grande-Bretagne des années 1920 aux années 1960', *Travaux et Documents du CEAN,* 58–59, I.E.P. de Bordeaux.

Dimier, V. (2001) 'Leadership et institutionnalisation de la Commission Européenne: le cas de la Direction Générale Développement, 1958–1975', *Sciences de la Société* 53: 183–200.

Dimier, V. (2002) 'De la dictature des drapeaux au sein de la commission européenne: loyautés multiples et constitution d'une identité commune au sein d'une administration multinationale', conference of the Association Française de Science Politique, Table Ronde, L'institutionnalisation de l'Europe, Septembre 2002.

Dimier, V. (2003a) 'Institutional change within a multinational organisation: life and death of DG DEV (1958–2002)', conference ECPR, Edinburgh, workshop no. 5, March.

Dimier, V. (2003b) 'Institutionnalisation et bureaucratisation de la Commission Européenne: le cas de la DG Développement', *Politique Européenne* 11.

Dimier, V. (2003c) 'Administrative reform as a means for political control: lessons from DG VIII', in D. Dimitrakopoulos (ed.) *The Changing European Commission,* Manchester: Manchester University Press.

Dinan, D. (1994) *Ever Closer Union? An Introduction to the European Community,* London: Macmillan.

Dinan, D. and S. Vanhoonacker (2000) 'IGC 2000 watch (Part I): Origin and preparation', *ECSA Review* 13, 2, Spring: 1, 20–21.

Dobry, M. (1986) *Sociologie des crises politiques,* Paris: Presses de la Fondation Nationale des Sciences politiques.

Donnelly, M. and E. Ritchie (1994) 'The college of commissionners and their cabinets', in G. Edwards and D. Spence (eds) *The European Commission,* London: Longman: 31–61.

Drake, H. (2000) *Jacques Delors, Perspectives on a European Leader,* London: Routledge.

Dubois, V. and D. Dulong (eds) (1999) *La question technocratique. De l'invention d'une figure aux transformations de l'action publique,* Strasbourg: Presses Universitaires de Strasbourg.

Duchêne, F. (1994) *Jean Monnet. The First Statesman of Interdependence,* London: Norton.

Duhamel, A. (1997) 'Du bon usage de Jacques Delors', *Libération* 17 January: 4.

Duran, P. (1999) *Penser l'action publique,* Paris: LGDJ.

Dyson, K. and K. Featherstone (1999) *The Road to Maastricht: Negotiating Economic and Monetary Union*, Oxford: Oxford University Press.

Eberhard Harribey, L. (2002) *L'Europe et la jeunesse: comprendre une politique européenne au regard de la dualité institutionnelle Conseil de l'Europe – Union européenne*, Paris: L'Harmattan.

Economist, The (1996) 'Obituary: Emile Noël', 7 September 1996: 96.

Edelman, M. (1988) *Constructing the Political Spectacle*, Chicago: University of Chicago Press.

Edwards, G. and D. Spence (eds) (1997) *The European Commission*, Harlow: Longman.

EEA (2002) *Guidelines for Secondment of EEA EFTA National Experts to the European Commission*, Standing Committee of the EFTA States, 4/00/W/031, 1 Annex, Brussels.

EFTA Secretariat (2000) *Evaluation of Arrangements with Secondments*, 4/FE/W/008, 2 Annexes, Brussels.

Egeberg, M. (1980) 'The fourth level of government: on the standardization of public policy within international regions', *Scandinavian Political Studies* 3 (3): 235–248.

Egeberg, M. (1996) 'Organization and nationality in the European Commission services', *Public Administration* 74 (4): 721–735.

Egeberg, M. (1999) 'Transcending intergovernmentalism? Identity and role perceptions of national officials in EU decision-making', *Journal of European Public Policy* 6 (3): 456–474.

Egeberg, M. and J. Trondal (1999) 'Differentiated integration in Europe: the case of the EEA country Norway', *Journal of Common Market Studies* 37 (1): 133–142.

Egeberg, M., G. Schaefer and J. Trondal (2003) 'The many faces of EU Committee governance', ARENA working paper 2, CES working paper 4.

Eichener, V. (1992) 'Social dumping or innovative regulations ? Processes and outcomes of European decision-making in the sector of health and safety at work harmonisation', Florence: European University Institute working paper SPS no. 92/98.

Endo, K. (1999) *The Presidency of the European Commission under Jacques Delors. The Politics of Shared Leadership*, London: Macmillan.

Eriksen, E.O. and J.E. Fossum (eds) (2000) *Democracy in the European Union. Integration through Deliberation?*, London: Routledge.

Ernst, A. (1998) '1997: une année charnière pour la santé publique en Europe', *Actualité et dossier en santé publique* 22: 10–12.

Esser, F., C. Reinemann and D. Fan (2000) 'Spin doctoring in British and German election campaigns', *European Journal of Communication* 17 (2): 209–239.

EUobserver (2003) 'Commission starts recruitment search in accession countries', http://www.euobserver.com/index.phtml?aid=9438.

European Commission (1963)

European Commission (1993a) *Communication . . . concernant le cadre de l'action dans le domaine de la santé publique*, COM (1993) 559 final, Brussels.

European Commission (1993b) 'Vade-Mecum de l'éditeur', Brussels: EC.

European Commission (1994) 'Information, communication, transparence', Brussels: EC.

European Commission (1995) *One Currency for Europe*, Green Paper on the Practical Arrangements for the Introduction of the Euro, 31 May 1995.

European Commission (1996) *Round Table on the Euro*, The Communications Challenge, 22–24 January 1996.

European Commission (1997) *La santé publique en Europe*, Luxembourg: Office des publications officielles des Communautés européennes.

European Commission (and Société Française de Santé Publique) (1999) *Priorities for Public Health Action in the European Union*, Employment and Social Affairs Directorate General.

European Commission (1999a) Minutes of the Meeting of Information Services from the European Union Countries, DG X, internal document, 1 July 1999, Brussels.

European Commission (1999b) *Designing Tommorow's Commission. A Review of the Commission's Organisation and Operation*, Brussels.

European Commission (1999c) *A Commission Communication on communication strategy in the last phases of the completion of EMU*, Communication from the Commission to the Council, the European Parliament, the Economic and Social Committee and the Committee of the Regions, ECFIN/99/684, Brussels.

European Commission (2000a) *The Commission's Work Programme for 2000*, Communication from the Commission, COM (2000) 155 final, Brussels, 9 February 2000.

European Commission (2000b) Speech of Romano Prodi, President of the European Commission, in General Affairs Council, IGC-Enlargement, 20 March 2000, Speech/00/93/.

European Commission (2000c) *The Role of the Commission Representations in the Member States*, A New Direction, Draft Communication from the President to the Commission, Internal Document, Press and Communication Service, 15 May 2000, Brussels.

European Commission (2000d) *Reforming the Commission*, white paper – Part II. Action Plan. COM (2000) 200 final, Brussels.

European Commission (Chantraine, A.) (2000e) *Rapport sur la situation des services de la Commission à Luxembourg*, préparé à la demande de M. le Vice-Président N. Kinnock, Luxembourg (11 Décembre 2000).

European Commission (2001a) Communication from the Commission on a new Framework for co-operation on Activities Concerning the Information and Communication Policy on the European Union, COM (2001) 354 final, 27 June 2001, Brussels.

European Commission (2001b) Commission proposes a new framework for co-operation on activities concerning the Information and Communication Policy of the European Union, IP/01/910, 27 June 2001, Brussels.

European Commission (2001c) *Ensuring a High Level of Health Protection*, MH/D (2001) Luxembourg (17th December 2001).

European Commission (2001d) *European Governance*, white paper. COM (2001) 428 final, Brussels.

European Commission (2002a) Communication from the Commission to the European Council; Review of the introduction of euro notes and coins, *Euro Papers*, Number 44, April 2002, Brussels.

European Commission (2002b) *Saying goodbye to the national currencies*, Press Release, IP/02/344, Brussels, 28 February 2002.

European Commission (2002c) *Proposal for Directive . . . on setting standards of quality and safety of human tissues and cells*, COM (2002) 319 final, 2002/0128 (COD) Brussels.

European Commission (2003) *Staff Regulations of Officials of the European Community*, Brussels.

European Parliament (1994) 'Rapport sur le contrôle de l'utilisation des crédits d'information inscrits au budget général des Communautés européennes', rapporteur E.G. Andenna, 9th December.

European Parliament (1998) 'Résolution sur la politique d'information et de communication dans l'Union européenne' du 14 May 1998, JOCE C 167 du 1 June 1998.

Fassin, D. (1996) *L'espace politique de la santé. Essai de généalogie*, Paris: Presses Universitaires de France.

Featherstone, K. (1994) 'Jean Monnet and the "democratic deficit" in the European Union', *Journal of Common Market Studies* 32 (2): 149–170.

Featherstone, K. (1999) 'The political dynamics of EMU', in L. Cram, D. Dinan and N. Nugent (eds) (1999) *Developments in the European Union*, New York: St. Martin's Press: 311–329.

Feld, W.J. and J.K. Wildgen (1975) 'National administrative elites and European Integration. Saboteurs at work?', *Journal of Common Market Studies*, XIII: 244–265.

Ferrandi, J. (1973) Speech to conference at Killarney, on 31 May 1973, on 'l'Europe des neufs, les EAMA et les pays africains du Commonwealth associables', *Marchés Tropicaux*.

Flynn, P. (1997) 'Reactions to the Treaty of Amsterdam', *Eurohealth* 3 (2): 2–3.

Foret, F. (2001) 'L'Europe en représentations. Eléments pour une analyse de la politique symbolique de l'Union européenne', Phd. Dissertation, Université Paris 1 Panthéon-Sorbonne.

Fouilleux, E. (2003) *La politique agricole commune et ses réformes. Une politique européenne à l'épreuve de la globalisation*, Paris: L'Harmattan.

Fouilleux, E., J. de Maillard and A. Smith (2002) 'Council working groups: their role in the production of European problems and policies', in G. Schaefer (ed.) *Committees in EU Governance*, Report to the European Commission (DG Research).

François, B. (2000) 'Préalables avant de prendre le droit comme objet. Notations en forme de plaidoyer pour un point de vue a-disciplinaire mais néanmoins soucieux des impensés disciplinaires' in J. Commaille, L. Dumoulin and C. Robert (eds) (2000) *La juridicisation du politique. Leçons scientifiques*, Paris: LGDJ: 115–121.

Franklin, B. (ed.) (1999) *Social Policy, the Media and Misrepresentation*, London: Routledge.

Franklin, M.N. and S.E. Scarrow (1999) 'Making Europeans? The socializing power of the European Parliament', in R.S. Katz and B. Wessels (eds) *The European Parliament, the National Parliaments, and European Integration*, Oxford: Oxford University Press.

Gans, H.J. (1979) *Deciding What's News*, London: Constable.

Garraud, P. (2000) *Le chômage et l'action publique. Le bricolage institutionnalisé*, Paris: L'Harmattan.

Garrigou, A. (1992a) 'Le président à l'épreuve du scandale. Destabilisation apparente et consolidation fonctionnelle', in B. Lacroix and J. Lagroye (eds) *Le président de la république, usages et genèses d'une institution*, Paris: Presses de la Fondation nationale des sciences politiques.

Garrigou, A. (1992b) 'Le boss, la machine et le scandale', *Politix* 17: 7–35.

Georgakakis, D. (1999) 'Les portraits de fonctionnaires dans la *Commission en direct*', paper presented to a workshop on 'Institutions européennes', Congress of the Association Française de Science Politique, Rennes, September.

Georgakakis, D. (2000) '*La démission de la Commission européenne: scandale et tournant institutionnel (oct.1998–mars 1999)*', Cultures et Conflits, 38–39: 39–72.

Georgakakis, D. (2001) 'Les instrumentalisations de la morale: lutte anti-fraude, scandales et nouvelle gouvernance européene', in J.-L. Briquet and P. Garraud (eds) *Juger la politique*, Rennes: Presses Universitaires de Rennes.

Georgakakis, D. (2002a) 'Une mobilisation formatrice: les eurofonctionnaires contre la réforme du statut (printemps 1998)', in D. Georgakakis (ed.) *Les métiers de l'Europe politique. Acteurs et professionnalisations de l'Union Européenne*, Strasbourg: Presses Universitaires de Strasbourg.

Georgakakis, D. (2002b) *Les métiers de l'Europe politique. Acteurs et professionnalisations de l'Union européenne*, Strasbourg: Presses Universitaires de Strasbourg.

Geyer, R. (2003) 'European integration, the problem of complexity and the revision of theory', *Journal of Common Market Studies* 41 (1): 15–35.

Gitlin, T. (1980) *The Whole World is Watching: Mass Media and the Making and the Unmaking of the New Left*, Los Angeles: University of California Press.

Goffman, E. (1969) *Strategic Interaction*, Philadelphia: University of Pennsylvania Press.

Gramberger, M.R. (1997) *Die Öffentlichkeitsarbeit der Europäischen Kommission 1952–1996*, PR zur Legitimation von Integration, Nomos Verlagsgesellschaft, Baden-Baden.

Grant, C. (1994) *Delors. Inside the House that Jacques Built*, London: Nicholas Brealey.

Grant, C. (1998) 'Interview: Jacques Delors', *New Statesman* 2 January: 14–16.

Grémion, C. (1979) *Profession: décideurs. Pouvoir des hauts fonctionnaires et réforme de l'Etat*, Paris: Gauthier Villars.

Grémion, P. (2001) 'State, Europe and Republic' in A. Menon and V. Wright (eds) *From the Nation State to Europe?* Oxford: Oxford University Press: 46–59.

Guigner, S. (2001) *L'européanisation de la santé ou la capacité de leadership de la Commission européenne en question. Contribution à une approche syncrétique de l'intégration européenne*, MA Dissertation, Rennes: Institut d'Études Politiques de Rennes.

Guiraudon, V. (2000) 'L'espace sociopolitique européen, un champ encore en friche', special issue of *Cultures et conflits* ('Sociologie de l'Europe') 38–39: 7–38.

Guggenbühl, A. (1998) 'A miracle formula or an old powder in a new packaging? Transparency and openness after Amsterdam', in V. Deckmyn and I. Thomson (1998) *Openness and Transparency in the European Union*, Maastricht: European Institute of Public Administration: 9–38.

Guyomard, J. (1995) *L'intégration de l'environnement dans les politiques intra-communautaires*, Publications du CEDRE, Rennes: Apogée.

Haas, E. (1958) *The Uniting of Europe*, Stanford: Stanford University Press.

Haas, P. (1992) 'Introduction: Epistemic communities and international coordination', *International Organization* 46: 1–35.

Haegel, F. (1992) 'Des journalistes pris dans leurs sources. Les accrédités de l'Hôtel de Ville de Paris', *Politix* 19: 102–119.

Hall, B. (2000) *European Governance and the Future of the Commission*, London: Centre for European Reform.

Hall, S., C. Crichter, T. Jefferson, J. Clarke and B. Roberts (1978) *Policing the Crisis. Mugging, the State, and Law and Order*, London: Macmillan.

Hallin, D.C. (1989) *The 'Uncensored War'*, Los Angeles: University of California Press.

Hammond, T.H. (1986) 'Agenda control, organizational structure, and bureaucratic politics', *American Journal of Political Science* 30 (1): 379–420.

Hansen, L. and M.C. Williams (1999) 'The myths of Europe: legitimacy, community and the crisis of the EU', *Journal of Common Market Studies* 37 (2): 233–249.

Hay, C. and B. Rosamond (2002) 'Globalization, European integration and the discursive construction of economic imperatives', *Journal of European Public Policy* 9 (2): 147–167.

Held, D., A. McGrew, D. Goldblatt and J. Perraton (1999) *Global Transformations: Politics, Economics and Culture*, Cambridge: Polity Press.

Héritier, A. (1999) *Policy-Making and Diversity in Europe, Escaping Deadlock*, Cambridge: Cambridge University Press.

Héritier, A. (2001) 'Overt and covert institutionalization in Europe', in A. Stone Sweet, W. Sandholtz and N. Fligstein (eds) *The Institutionalization of Europe*, Oxford: Oxford University Press: 56–70.

Hill, F. (1994) 'The capabilities–expectations gap, or conceptualising Europe's international role', in S. Bulmer and A. Scott (eds) *Economic and Political Integration in Europe*, Oxford: Blackwell.

Hobsbawm, E. (1983) *The Invention of Tradition*, Cambridge: Cambridge University Press.

Holland, W. and E. Mossialos (eds) (1999) *Public Health Policies in the European Union*, Aldershot: Ashgate.

Hooghe, L. (1997) *Images of Europe, Orientations to European Integration among Senior Commission Officials*, EUI working paper, RSC No. 98/48.

Hooghe, L. (1999a) 'Images of Europe: orientations to European integration among senior officials of the Commission', *British Journal of Political Science* 29 (2): 345–367.

Hooghe, L. (1999b) 'Supranational activists or intergovernmental agents? Explaining the orientations of senior Commission officials towards European integration', *Comparative Political Studies* 32 (4): 435–453.

Hooghe, L. (2001) *The European Commission and the Integration of Europe. Images of Governance*, Cambridge: Cambridge University Press.

Hopkins, M. (ed.) (1985) *European Communities Information. Its Use and Users*, London: Mansell Publishing Limited.

Hopkins, R.F. (1976) 'The international role of "domestic" bureaucracy', *International Organzation* 30 (3): 405–432.

IEP (Institut für Europäische Politik) (1989) *Comitology, Characteristics, Performance and Options*, Bonn: Selbstverlag.

Ionescu, G. (1995) 'Reading notes, Winter 1995', *Government and Opposition* 30 (1): 101–110.

Jabko, N. (1999) 'In the name of the market: how the European Commission paved the way for monetary union', *Journal of European Public Policy* 6 (3): 475–495.

Jachtenfuchs, M., T. Diez and S. Jung. (1998) 'Which Europe? Conflicting models of a legitimate European political order', *European Journal of International Relations* 4 (4): 409–445.

Janis, I.L. (1982) *Groupthink. Psychological Studies of Policy Decisions and Fiascoes*, Boston: Houghton Mifflin Company.

Jenkins, R. (1989) *European Diary*, London: HarperCollins.

Joana, J. and A. Smith (2002) *Les commissaires européens: technocrates, diplomates ou politiques?*, Paris: Presses de sciences po.

Jones, N. (1995) *Soundbites and Spindoctors*, London: Cassell.

Jørgensen, K.E. (1999) 'The social construction of the acquis communautaire: a cornerstone of the European edifice', *European Integration online Papers* 3 (5), http://eiop.or.at/eiop/texte.

Jourdain, L. (1995) *Recherche scientifique et construction européenne*, Paris: L'Harmattan.

Jourdain, L. (1996) 'La Commission européenne et la construction d'un nouveau modèle d'intervention publique. Le cas de la politique de recherche et de développement technologique', *Revue Française de Science Politique* 46 (3): 496–520.

Jupille, J. and J.A. Caporaso (1999) 'Institutionalism and the European Union: Beyond international relations and comparative politics, *Annual Review of Political Science* 2 (1): 429–444.

Kaïpoulos, K.D. (1992) 'De l'information à la communication: la Communauté européenne à la recherche d'une image médiatique', in 'Epistimoniki epetirida', Tmina Xenon glosson, metafrassis kai diermineias, Corfu: Ionio Panepistimio.

Kassim, H. (2004) 'A historic achievement: Administrative reform and the Prodi Commission', forthcoming in D. Dimitrakopoulos (ed.) *The Prodi Commission*, Manchester: Manchester University Press.

Kauppi, N. (1996) 'European Union institution and French political careers', *Scandinavian Political Studies* 19 (1).

Kavanagh, D. (2000) 'Les politiciens face aux médias', *Pouvoirs* 93: 161–175.

Kerr, H.H. Jr. (1973) 'Changing attitudes through international participation: European parliamentarians and integration', *International Organization* 27 (1): 45–83.

Kingdon, J. (1984) *Agendas, Alternatives, and Public Policies*, Washington: HarperCollins Publishers.

Kirchner, E.J. (1996) 'Germany and the European Union: From junior to senior role', in G. Smith, W.E. Paterson and S. Padgett (eds) *Developments in German Politics 2*, London: Macmillan.

Knill, C. (2001) *The Europeanisation of National Administrations. Patterns of Institutional Change and Persistence*, Cambridge: Cambridge University Press.

Koivusalo, M. (1998) 'Les organisations internationales et les politiques de santé', *Revue Française des Affaires Sociales* 3–4: 57–75.

Lagroye, J. (1985) 'La légitimation', in M. Grawitz and J. Leca (eds) *Traité de science politique*, tome 1, Paris: PUF.

Lagroye, J. (1997) 'On ne subit pas son rôle', *Politix* 38: 7–17.

Lamy, P. (1991) 'Choses vues de l'Europe', *Esprit* Octobre: 67–81.

Lascoumes, P. (1997) *Elites irrégulières. Essais sur la délinquance d'affaires*, Paris: Gallimard.

Lefèbvre, A. (1999) 'L'Europe, la santé et les crises sanitaires', *Actualité et dossier en santé publique* 29: 16–18.

Legavre, J.B. (1992) 'Off the record. Mode d'emploi d'un instrument de coordination', *Politix* 19: 135–157.

Legavre, J.B. (1993) *Conseiller en communication politique: l'institutionnalisation d'un rôle*, PhD. thesis, Université de Paris I.

Lemaignen, R. (1964) *L'Europe au berceau. Souvenirs d'un technocrate*, Paris: Plon.

Le Naëlou, A. (1995) *Politiques européennes de développement avec les pays du Sud*, Paris: L'Harmattan.

Lequesne, C. (1996) 'La Commission européenne entre autonomie et indépendance', *Revue Française de Science Politique* 46 (3): 389–408.

Lequesne, C. and A. Smith (1997) 'Interpréter l'Europe: éléments pour une relance théorique', *Cultures et conflits* 28: 175.

Lewis, J. (2000) 'The methods of community in EU decision-making and administrative rivalry in the Council's infrastructure', *Journal of European Public Policy* 7 (2): 261–289.

Lindberg, L. (1963) *The Political Dynamics of European Integration*, Stanford: Princeton University Press.

Lord, C. (2000) 'Legitimacy, democracy and the EU: when abstract questions become practical policy problems', One Europe or Several? Policy Paper 03/00, University of Sussex.

Lord, C. and D. Beetham (2001) 'Legitimizing the EU', *Journal of Common Market Studies*, 39 (3): 443–62.

Louis, J.-V. (2000) 'La réforme des institutions de l'Union européenne. Schéma pour une réflexion', *Revue du marché commun et de l'Union européenne* 443, décembre: 681–689.

Ludlow, P. (1991) 'The European Commission', in R.O. Keohane and S. Hoffman (eds) *The New European Community*, Boulder: Westview Press: 85–132.

Ludlow, P. (1998) 'Frustrated ambitions: The European Commission and the formation of a European identity', in R. Poidevin, W. Loth and M.-T. Bitsch (eds) *Institutions européennes et identitées européennes*, Brussels: Bruylant.

McDonald, M. (1997) 'Identities in the European Commission', in N. Nugent (ed.) *At the Heart of the Union. Studies of the European Commission*, Houndmills: Macmillan Press.

Macmullen, A. (1999) 'Political responsibility for the administration of Europe: The Commission's resignation March 1999', *Parliamentary Affairs* 52 (4): 703–718.

Majone, G. (1996) *Regulating Europe*, London: Routledge.

Mak, J. (2002) *Selling Europe: Communicating Symbols or Symbolic Communication*, PhD thesis, Florence: European University Institute.

March, J. (1999) 'A learning perspective on the network dynamics of institutional integration', in M. Egeberg and P. Lægreid (eds) *Organizing Political Institutions. Essays for Johan P. Olsen,* Oslo: Scandinavian University Press.

March, J. and J. Olsen (1989) *Rediscovering Institutions. The Organizational Basis of Politics*, New York: The Free Press.

March, J. and J. Olsen (1998) 'The institutional dynamics of International political orders', *International Organization* 52 (4): 943–969.

March, J.G. (1994) *A Primer on Decision Making. How Decisions Happen*, New York: The Free Press.

March, J.G. and J.P. Olsen (1984) 'The new institutionalism: organizational factors in political life', *American Political Science Review* 78 (3): 734–749.

March, J.G. and J.P. Olsen (1986) 'Garbage can models of decision making in organizations', in K.G. March and R. Weissinger-Baylon (eds) *Ambiguity and Command*, Marshfield: Pitman: 11–35.

Marjolin, R. (1986) *Le travail d'une vie*, Paris: Editions Plon.

Marks, G., L. Hooghe and K. Blank (1996) 'European integration from the 1980s: state-centric *v.* multi-level governance', *Journal of Common Market Studies* 34 (2): 341–378.

Matlary, J.H. (1997) *Democratic Legitimacy and the Role of the Commission*, working paper no. 3/97, Oslo: ARENA.

Maurer, A. (2003) 'Les rôles des Parlements nationaux dans l'Union européenne: Options, Contyraintes et obstacles', submission to the Convention on the Future of Europe.

Mazey, S. (1995) 'The development of EU equality policies: bureaucratic expansion on behalf of women?', *Public Administration* 73 (4): 591–609.

Mazey, S. and J. Richardson (1996) 'La Communauté européenne: une bourse pour les idées et les intérêts', *Revue Française de Science Politique*, 46 (3): 309–430.

Mazey, S. and J. Richardson (1997) 'The Commission and the lobby', in G. Edwards and D. Spence (eds) (1997) *The European Commission*, 2nd edition, London: Cartermill International Ltd.

Méchet, P. and R. Pache (2000) 'L'autre Europe que veulent les Européens', in B. Cautrès and D. Reynié (eds) *L'opinion européenne*, Paris: Presses de Sciences Po.

Merkel, H. and M. Huëbel (1999) 'Public health policy in the European Community', in W. Holland and E. Mossialos (eds), *Public Health Policies in the European Union*, Aldershot: Ashgate: 48–69.

Meyer, C. (1999) 'Political legitimacy and the invisibility of politics: Exploring the European Union's communication deficit', in *Journal of Common Market Studies* 37 (4): 617–639.

Meyer, J.W. and B. Rowan (1991) 'Institutionalised organizations: Formal structure as myth and ceremony', in W.W. Powell and P.J. DiMaggio (eds) *The New Institutionalism in Organizational Analysis*, Chicago: The University of Chicago Press.

Meyer, K. (1994) 'Appendix A Emile Noël's contribution to Europe', in S. Martin (ed.) *The Construction of Europe*, Dordrecht: Kluwer.

Middlemas, K. (1995) *Orchestrating Europe, The Informal Politics of the European Union 1973–95*, London: Fontana Press.

Milési, G. (1995) *Jacques Delors. L'homme qui dit non*, Paris: Edition 1.

Miller, D. (1993) 'Official sources and "primary definition": the case of Northern Ireland', *Media Culture and Society* 15 (3): 385–406.

Moravscik, A. (1998) *The Choice for Europe*, Ithaca: Cornell University Press.

Morgan, D. (1995) 'British media and European Union news. The Brussels news beat and its problems', *European Journal of Communication* 10 (3): 321–343.

Morgan, R. (1992) 'Jean Monnet and the ECSC administration: Challenges, functions and the inheritance of ideas', in Die Anfänge der Verwaltung der Europäischen Gemeinschaft', Jahrbüch für europäische Verwaltungsgeschichte, 4.

Moscovici, P. (2001) Speech, Ludwigsburg, 1 February.

Mossialos, E. and G. Permanand (2000) *Public Health in the European Union: Making it Relevant*, Discussion paper no. 17, London: LSE Health.

Mountford, L. (1998) *European Union Health Policy on the Eve of the Millennium– Background Study for the Public Hearing on Health Policy*, Public Health and Consumer series SACO 102 EN, Luxembourg: European Parliament – Directorate General for Research.

Muntean, A.M. (2000) 'The European Parliament's political legitimacy and the Commission's "misleading management": Towards a "parliamentarian" European Union?', European Integration Online Papers (EioP) vol. 4, no. 5, http://eiop.or.at/eiop/texte/2000–005a.htm.

Narjes, K.-H. (1998) 'Walter Hallstein and the early phase of the EEC', in W. Loth, W. Wallace and W. Wessels (eds) *Walter Hallstein. The Forgotten European?*, London: Macmillan: 109–130.

Nathe, H. (1998) 'Brussels needs its muck-rakers', *La lettre de l'API*, no. 2.

Nicolas, J. (1999) *L'Europe des fraudes*, Luxembourg: Editions PNA.

Niemann, A. (1998) 'The PHARE programme and the concept of spill-over: neofunctionalism in the making', *Journal of European Public Policy* 5 (3): 428–446.

Noël, E. (1992) 'Témoignage: l'administration de la Communauté européenne dans la rétrospective d'un ancien haut fonctionnaire', *Yearbook of European Administrative History* 4: 145–158.

Noël, E. (1998) 'Walter Hallstein: a personal testimony', in W. Loth, W. Wallace and W. Wessels (eds) *Walter Hallstein. The Forgotten European?*, London: Macmillan: 131–134.

Nugent, N. (1994) *The Government and Politics of the European Union*, London: Macmillan.

Nugent, N. (1995) 'The leadership capacity of the European Commission', *Journal of European Public Policy* 2 (4): 603–623.

Nugent, N. (ed.) (1997) *At the Heart of the Union. Studies of the European Commission*, Houndmills: Macmillan Press.

Nugent, N. (2001) *The European Commission*, Houndmills: Palgrave.

Nugent, N. and S. Saurugger (2002) 'Organizational structuring: the case of the European Commission and its external policy responsibilities', *Journal of European Public Policy* 9 (3): 345–364.

Obradovic, D. (1996) 'Policy legitimacy and the European Union', *Journal of Common Market Studies* 34 (2): 191–221.

Olsen, J. (1998) 'The new European experiment in political organization', paper presented at the conference *Samples of the Future*, SCANCOR, Stanford University, September.

Olsen, J. (2001) 'Organising European institutions of governance. A prelude to an institutional account of political integration', in H. Wallace (ed.) *Interlocking Dimensions of European Integration*, London: Palgrave.

Olsen, J. (2003) 'Reforming European Institutions of Governance', in J.H.H. Weiler, I. Begg and J. Peterson (eds) *Integration in an Expanding European Union. Reassessing the Fundamentals*, Oxford: Blackwell.

Olsen, J. (2000) 'How, then, does one get there? An institutionalist response to Herr Fischer's vision of a European Federation', Arena working papers WP 00/22, http://www.arena.uio.no/publications/wp00_22.htm.

Page, E. (1997) *People Who Run Europe*, Oxford: Clarendon.

Page, E. and L. Wouters (1994) 'Bureaucratic politics and political leadership in Brussels', *Public Administration*, vol. 72, Autumn: 445–459.

Parsons, C. (2000) 'Domestic interests, ideas and integration: Lessons from the French case', *Journal of Common Market Studies* 38 (1): 45–70.

Parsons, C. (2002) 'Showing ideas as causes: the origins of the European Union', *International Organization* 56 (1): 47–84.

Pendergast, W.R. (1976) 'Roles and attitudes of French and Italian delegates to the European Community', *International Organization* 30 (4): 669–677.

Peters, G. (1992) 'Bureaucratic politics and the institutions of the European Community', in A.M. Sbragia (ed.) *Euro-Politics, Institutions and Policymaking in the 'New' European Community*, Washington: The Brookings Institute: 75–127.

Peterson, J. (1993) *High Technology and the Competition State: An Analysis of the Eureka Initiative*, London: Routledge.

Peterson, J. (1995) 'Decision-making in the European Union: Towards a framework for analysis', *Journal of European Public Policy* 2 (1): 69–93.

Peterson, J. (1999) 'The Santer era: The European Commission in normative, historical and theoretical perspective', *Journal of European Public Policy* 6 (1): 46–65.

Peterson, J. (2000) 'Romano Prodi: Another Delors?', *ECSA Review* 13 (1).

Pierson, P. (1996) 'The path to European integration. A historical institutionalist analysis', *Comparative Political Studies* 29 (2): 123–166.

Pierson, P. and S. Leibfried (eds) (1998) *Politiques sociales européennes. Entre intégration et fragmentation*, Paris: L'Harmattan.

Pollack, M. (1996) 'The new institutionalism and EC governance: The promise and limits of institutional analysis', *Governance* 9 (4): 429–458.

Pollack, M. (1997) 'Delegation, agency and agenda setting in the European Community', *International Organization* 51 (1): 99–134.

Pollack, M. (1998) 'The engines of integration? Supranational autonomy and influence in the European Union', in W. Sandholtz and A. Stone Sweet (eds) *European Integration and Supranational Governance*, Oxford: Oxford University Press: 217–249.

Poullet, E. and G. Deprez, (1977) 'The place of the Commission within the institutional system', in C. Sasse, E. Poullet, D. Coombes and G. Deprez, *Decision Making in the European Community,* New York: Praeger: 129–224.

Pourvoyeur, R. (1981) 'La politique de l'information de la Communauté européenne', *Revue du Marché Commun* 243.

Pressman, J.L. and A.B. Wildavsky (1973) *Implementation*, Berkeley: University of California Press.

Prodi, R. (2001) 'The state of the Union in 2001', Speech to the European Parliament, 13 February.

Quermonne, J.-L. (2000) 'Observations sur la réforme des institutions', *Revue du marché commun et de l'Union européenne* 443, décembre: 686–689.

Radaelli, C. (1999a) *Technocracy in the European Union. Political Dynamics of the European Union*, London: Longman.

Radaelli, C. (1999b) 'The public policy of the European Union: Whither politics of expertise?', *Journal of European Public Policy* 6 (5): 757–774.

Randall, E. (2000) 'European health policy with and without design: serendipity, tragedy and the future of EU health policy', *Policy Studies* 21 (2): 133–164.

Randall, E. (2001) *The European Union and Health Policy*, New York: Palgrave.

Risse, T. and K. Sikkink (1999) 'The power of principles: The socialization of human rights norms into domestic practices', in T. Risse, S. Ropp and K. Sikkink (eds) *The Power of Principles: International Human Rights Norms and Domestic Change*, Cambridge: Cambridge University Press.

Robert, C. (2000) 'Ressources juridiques et stratégies politiques. Analyse d'une controverse à la Commission européenne sur la dimension sociale de l'élargissement de l'Union', *Sociologie du Travail* 42 (2): 203–224.

Robert, C. (2001a) 'L'Union européenne face à son élargissement à l'Est: incertitudes politiques et construction d'un leadership administratif', *Politique Européenne*, no. 3: 38–60.

Robert, C. (2001b) *La fabrique de l'action publique communautaire. Le programme PHARE 1989–1998, enjeux et usages d'une politique européenne incertaine*, Université Grenoble II: PhD in Political Science.

Rometsch, D. and W. Wessels (1997) 'The Commission and the Council of the Union', in G. Edwards and D. Spence (eds) *The European Commission*, 2nd edition, London: Cartermill: 213–238.

Rood, J.Q.T. (2000) 'Naar een Intergouvernementele Europese Unie?', in *Internationale Spectator*, Jaargang 54, nr. 6, juni 2000, Assen: Before Van Governum.

Rosamond, B. (2000) *Theories of European Integration*, Houndmills: Macmillan.

Rosenau, J. (1969) 'Towards the study of national-international linkages', in J. Rosenau (ed.) *Linkage Politics. Essays on the Convergence of National and International Systems*, New York: The Free Press.

Ross, G. (1995) *Jacques Delors and European Integration*, New York: Oxford University Press.

Roubieu, O. (1999) 'Des "managers" très politiques. Les secrétaires généraux des grandes villes', in V. Dubois and D. Dulong (eds) *La question technocratique: de l'invention d'une figure aux transformations de l'action publique*, Strasbourg: Presses Universitaires de Strasbourg: 217–231.

Rougemont, A. (1999) *La santé en Europe: Les politiques de santé*, Genève: Actes sud.

Sandholtz, W. and A. Stone Sweet (eds) (1998) *European Integration and Supranational Governance*, Oxford: Oxford University Press.

Sauron, J.-L. (2000) *L'administration française et l'Union européenne*, Paris: La Documentation française.

Schattschneider, E.E. (1960) *The Semi-Sovereign People*, New York: Holt, Rinehard & Winston.

Scheinman, L. (1966) 'Some preliminary notes on bureaucratic relationships in the European Economic Community', *International Organization* 20: 750–773.

Scheinman, L. and W. Feld (1972) 'The European Economic Community and national civil servants of the member states', *International Organization* 26: 121–135.

Schelling, T. (1960) *The Strategy of Conflict*, Cambridge: Harvard University Press.

Schlesinger, P. (1992) 'Repenser la sociologie du journalisme. Les stratégies de la source d'information et les limites du média-centrisme', *Réseaux*, no. 51, janvier-février 1992. [First published in 1990 in Fergusson, M. (1990) *Public Communication: The New Imperatives*, London: Sage].

Schlesinger, P. and K. Deirdre (2000) 'Can the European Union become a sphere of publics?', in E.O. Eriksen and J.E. Fossum (eds) (2000) *Democracy in the European Union, Integration through Deliberation?*, London: Routledge: 206–229.

Schnabel, V. (1998) 'Elites européennes en formation. Les étudiants du "Collège de Bruges" et leurs études', *Politix* 43: 33–52.

Scully, R.M. (2002) 'Going native? Institutional and partisan loyalties in the European Parliament', in B. Steunenberg, J. Thomassen and J.J. Derrida (eds) *European Parliament: Moving Towards Democracy in the EU*, Lanham: Rowan and Littlefield.

Selznick, P. (1957) *Leadership in Administration*, New York: Harper & Son.

Senghor, L. (1953) 'Nous sommes pour la Communauté Européenne, et par delà elle, pour la Communauté Eurafricaine', *Marchés Coloniaux du Monde*, no. 1.

Shore, C. (1995) 'Usurpers or pioneers?, European Commission bureaucrats and the question of 'European Consciousness', in A.P. Cohen and N. Rapport (eds) *Questions of Consciousness*, London: Routledge: 217–236.

Shore, C. (2000) *Building Europe, The Cultural Politics of European Integration*, London: Routledge.

Sigal, L.V. (1973) *Reporters and Officials: The Organization and Politics of Newsmaking*, Lexington: Sage.

Simon, H. (1957) *Administrative Behavior*, New York: Macmillan.

Smith, A. (1995) *L'Europe politique au miroir du local*, Paris: L'Harmattan.

Smith, A. (1996) 'La Commission européenne et les fonds structurels: Vers un nouveau modèle d'action?', *Revue française de science politique* 46 (3): 474–496.

Smith A. (1998) 'La Commission et "le peuple". L'exemple de l'usage politique des Eurobaromètres', in B. Cautrès and P. Bréchon (eds) *Les enquêtes Eurobaromètres*, Paris: L'Harmattan.

Smith, A. (1999) 'L' "espace public européen": une vue trop aérienne', *Critique Internationale* 2: 169–180.

Smith, A. (2002) 'Commissaire européen, un homme politique sans métier?', in D. Georgakakis (ed.) *Les métiers de l'Europe politique. Acteurs et professionnalisations de l'Union européenne*, Strasbourg: Presses Universitaires de Strasbourg: 35–54.

Smith, A. (2003) 'Why European commissioners matter', *Journal of Common Market Studies* 41 (1): 137–155.

Smith A. (2003) 'Who governs in Brussels? Une comparaison des configurations de leadership de Delors, Santer et Prodi', in A. Smith and C. Sorbets (eds) *Le leadership politique et le territoire*, Rennes: Presses Universitaires de Rennes.

Smith, J. (2001) 'Cultural aspects of Europeanization: The case of the Scottish Office', *Public Administration* 79 (1): 147–165.

Smith, K.A. (1973) 'The European Economic Community and national civil servants of the member states – a comment', *International Organization* 27: 563–568.

Spence, D. (1992) 'The European Community and German Unification', *German Politics* 1 (3).

Spence, D. (1997) 'Structure, function and procedures in the Commission', in G. Edwards and D. Spence (eds) *The European Commission*, London: Cartermill Publishing.

Spierenburg, D. and R. Poidevin (1994) *The History of the High Authority of the European Coal and Steel Community. Supranationality in Operation?*, London: Weidenfeld and Nicolson.

Spinelli, A. (1966) *The Eurocrats. Conflict and Crisis in the European Community*, Baltimore: The Johns Hopkins Press.

Statskontoret (2001) *Svenska nationalla experter i EU-tjänst*, Stockholm.

Stephens, P. (2000) 'Chirac's way with words', *Financial Times* 30 June.

Stevens, A. and H. Stevens (2001) *Brussels Bureaucrats? The Administration of the European Union*, Houndmills: Palgrave.

Stone Sweet, A. and W. Sandholtz (1998) 'Integration, supranational governance, and the institutionalization of the European polity', in W. Sandholtz and A. Stone Sweet (eds) *European Integration and Supranational Governance*, New York: Oxford University Press.

Stone Sweet, A., W. Sandholtz and N. Fligstein (eds) (2001) *The Institutionalization of Europe*, Oxford: Oxford University Press.

Suchman, M.C. (1995) 'Managing legitimacy: strategic and institutional approaches', *Academy of Management Review* 20/3.

Suleiman, E. (1974) *Politics, Power and Bureaucracy in France*, Princeton: Princeton University Press.

Sutherland, P.D. (1996) 'Appreciation. Emile Noël', *Irish Times* 28 August 1996.

Tambou, O. (2003) 'La France et le débat sur l'avenir de l'UE', paper presented to the 8th EUSA Biennial International Conference, March 27–29, Nashville, USA.

Taylor, S. (2000a) 'Jury is still out on Prodi Commission', *European Voice* 16–22 March.

Taylor, S. (2000b) 'Prodi Commission fights back', *European Voice* 12–18 October.

Trondal, J. (1999) 'Integration through participation – Introductory notes to the study of administrative integration', *European Integration online Papers* (EIOP) 3 (4) http://www.or.at/eiop/texte/1999-004.htm.

Trondal, J. (2001) *Administrative Integration across Levels of Governance. Integration through Participation in EU Committees*. ARENA Report 7.

Trondal, J. (2002) 'Why Europeanisation happens. The socializing power of EU committees', paper presented at the IDNET workshop *International Institutions and Socialization in the New Europe*, EUI, Florence, February 2002.

Trondal, J. (2004) 'An institutionalist perspective on EU committee decision-making', in B. Reinalda and B. Verbeek (eds) *Decision Making within International Organizations*, London: Routledge.

Trondal, J. and F. Veggeland (2003) 'Access, voice and loyalty. The representation of domestic civil servants in EU Committees', *Journal of European Public Policy* 10 (1): 59–77.

Tunstall, J. (1970) *The Westminster Lobby Correspondents. A Sociological Study of National Political Journalism*, London: Routledge and Kegan Paul.

Turner, M. (1996) 'Fond memories of a "founding father"', *European Voice* 5–11 September 1996.

Van Miert, K. (2000) *Le marché et le pouvoir*, Brussels: Editions Racine.

Védrine, H. (2000) 'Future of Europe', Letter to Joschka Fischer, 8 June (Statements SAC/00/653, French Embassy in London).

Verdun, A. and T. Christiansen (2000) 'Policies, institutions, and the euro: Dilemmas of legitimacy', in C. Crouch (ed.) *After the Euro, Shaping Institutions for Governance in the Wake of European Monetary Union*, Oxford: Oxford University Press.

Vignes, D. (2001) 'Nice, une vue apaisée. Réponse à deux questions', *Revue du marché commun et de l'Union européenne* 445, février: 81–84.

von der Groeben, H. (1998) 'Walter Hallstein as President of the Commission', in W. Loth, W. Wallace and W. Wessels (eds) *Walter Hallstein. The Forgotten European?* London: Macmillan, 95–108.

Wallace, H., W. Wallace and C. Webb (eds) (1983) *Policy-Making in the European Community*, 2nd edition, Chichester: John Wiley and Sons.

Watson, R. (2000) 'Influential institutes bid to shape EU's post-Nice agenda', *European Voice* 7–13 December 2000.

Watzlawick, P. (1977) *How Real is Real? Confusion, désinformation, communication*, New York: Random House.

Weber, M. (1947) *The Theory of Economic Organization*, Oxford: Oxford University Press.

Weber, M. (1995) *Economie et Société, Tome 1: les catégories de la sociologie*, Paris: Plon (1st edition 1921).

Weil, O. and M. McKee (1998) 'Setting priorities for health in Europe: Are we speaking the same language?', *European Journal of Public Health* 8 (3): 256–258.

Weiler, J.H.H. (1997) 'Legitimacy and democracy of Union governance', in G. Edwards and A. Pijpers (eds) *The Politics of European Treaty Reform. The 1996 Intergovernmental Conference and Beyond*, London: Pinter: 249–287.

Wendon, B. (1998) 'The Commission as image-venue entrepreneur in EU social policy', *Journal of European Public Policy* 5 (2): 339–354.

Wessels, W. (1985) 'Community bureaucracy in a changing environment: Criticism, trends, questions', in J. Jamar and W. Wessels (eds) *Community Bureaucracy at the Crossroads*, Bruges: De Tempel.

Wessels, W. (1996) 'Institutions of the EU system: models of explanation', in D. Rometsch and W. Wessels (eds) *The European Union and Member States, Towards Institutional Fusion?*, Manchester: Manchester University Press.

Wessels, W. (1997) 'An ever closer fusion? A dynamic macropolitical view on integration processes', *Journal of Common Market Studies* 35 (2):267–299.

Westlake, M. (1994) *The Commission and the Parliament. Partners and Rivals in the European Policy-Making Process*, London: Butterworths.

Wilkes, G. and D. Wring (1998) 'The British press and European integration 1948–1996', in D. Baker and D. Seawright (eds) *Britain For and Against Europe: British Politics and the Question of European Integration*, London: Clarendon Press.

Wilks, S. (1992) 'Models of European administration: DG IV and the administration of competition policy', paper presented at the Conference of the European Group of Public Administration, Pisa, 2–5 September.

Winand, P. (2001) '20 ans d'action du Comité Jean Monnet (1955–1975)', *Problématiques européennes* 8, May, Paris: Notre Europe.

World Health Organization (1997), *European Health Care Reform. Analysis of Current Strategies*, Copenhagen: WHO Regional Publications.

Yataganas, X.A. (2001) 'The Treaty of Nice. The sharing of power and the institutional balance in the European Union – a Continental perspective', Harvard Jean Monnet working paper 01/01.

Yorndorf, W. (1965) 'Monnet and the Action Committee: the formative period of the European Communities', *International Organization* 19 (Autumn): 885–912.

Subject index

Author index

For Product Safety Concerns and Information please contact our EU
representative GPSR@taylorandfrancis.com
Taylor & Francis Verlag GmbH, Kaufingerstraße 24, 80331 München, Germany